P9-DCY-318

The
Supreme Court
Yearbook
1989–1990

KF
8742
.S95
1989-
1990

The
Supreme Court
Yearbook
1989-1990

Joan Biskupic

Congressional Quarterly Inc.
Washington, D.C.

KVCC WITHDRAWN
KALAMAZOO VALLEY
COMMUNITY COLLEGE
LIBRARY

APR 18 1991

Congressional Quarterly Inc.

Congressional Quarterly Inc., an editorial research service and publishing company, serves clients in the fields of news, education, business, and government. It combines specific coverage of Congress, government, and politics by Congressional Quarterly with the more general subject range of an affiliated service, Editorial Research Reports.

Congressional Quarterly publishes the *Congressional Quarterly Weekly Report* and a variety of books, including college political science textbooks under the CQ Press imprint and public affairs paperbacks on developing issues and events. CQ also publishes information directories and reference books on the federal government, national elections, and politics, including the *Guide to Congress,* the *Guide to the U.S. Supreme Court,* the *Guide to U.S. Elections,* and *Politics in America.* The *CQ Almanac,* a compendium of legislation for one session of Congress, is published each year. *Congress and the Nation,* a record of government for a presidential term, is published every four years.

CQ publishes *The Congressional Monitor,* a daily report on current and future activities of congressional committees, and several newsletters including *Congressional Insight,* a weekly analysis of congressional action, and *Campaign Practices Reports,* a semimonthly update on campaign laws.

The online delivery of CQ's Washington Alert Service provides clients with immediate access to Congressional Quarterly's institutional information and expertise.

Cover design: Julie Booth
Cover photograph: R. Michael Jenkins

Copyright © 1991 Congressional Quarterly Inc.
1414 22nd St. N.W.
Washington, D.C. 20037

All rights reserved. No part of this publication may be reproduced or transmitted in any form or by any means, electronic or mechanical, including photocopy, recording, or any information storage and retrieval system, without permission in writing from the publisher.

Printed in the United States of America

ISBN 0-87187-590-X
ISBN 0-87187-591-8 (pbk.)
ISSN 1054-2701

Contents

Preface

With publication of *The Supreme Court Yearbook, 1989-1990,* Congressional Quarterly begins a series of annual volumes to assist readers in following the actions of the Supreme Court of the United States. This book is written for people who are interested in the Court and the impact of the justices' decisions on public issues, but who are not experts in the law.

Although the book is intended to stand alone, with comprehensive coverage of the Court's activities during the year, it can be used most productively in conjunction with CQ's *Guide to the U.S. Supreme Court.* The *Guide* covers 200 years of Supreme Court history, while the annual *Yearbook* provides an in-depth look at a single year. The two complement each other: the *Yearbook* keeps information in the *Guide* up to date, while the *Guide*'s broad summary of Court actions provides useful background for understanding new decisions.

The *Yearbook* opens with a record of the larger events of the most recent term: the resignation of Justice William J. Brennan, Jr., and the confirmation process that led to Justice David H. Souter taking his place on the bench October 9, 1990. Chapter 2 is an overview of the ten major cases of the 1989-1990 term. It is followed in Chapter 3 by summaries of all the Court's written opinions for the term, arranged alphabetically by subject.

Chapter 4 offers a preview of the 1990-1991 term and focuses on the major cases that had been docketed through the end of 1990. Rulings in those cases and all other decisions from the 1990-1991 term will be the subject of the second volume of the *Yearbook.* Chapter 5 provides excerpts from the ten major cases of the 1989-1990 term.

The inner workings of the Court are detailed in Chapter 6. This chapter will be standard in all future yearbooks, providing users with an understanding of how legal disputes make their way to the nation's highest court and a window into how the justices work.

I am indebted to several people in this endeavor, chief among them Elder Witt, the editor of the *Guide to the U.S. Supreme Court.* Elder and the director of the CQ Book Department, David R. Tarr, developed the idea for the *Yearbook.* I am also indebted to Carolyn Goldinger, whose thoughtful and steady editing guided this inaugural edition to completion.

Joan Biskupic

1 | *A New Justice*

Less was known about David H. Souter than any other Supreme Court nominee in the past quarter-century. So said Senate Judiciary Committee chairman Joseph R. Biden, Jr., when the committee was considering Souter's nomination in the fall of 1990. The senator's remark called attention to President George Bush's caution in an era following the 1987 Senate rejection of the blunt and vocal Robert H. Bork. But the retirement of Justice William J. Brennan, Jr., placed the Court at a crossroads, and Biden's assertion also revealed senators' desire to know what direction Souter would take.

Even before Brennan's retirement, the Court was closely divided on matters involving the First Amendment, on protections for civil liberties and defendants' rights, and on whether there is a constitutional right to abortion. One-third of all the cases in the 1989-1990 term were decided by 5-4 votes, and senators predicted during Souter's confirmation hearings that he would have the power to shape the future of the Court, a power he may hold for a long time. Souter turned fifty-one during his September hearings, making him the youngest justice on the Court.

In addition, a new relationship was emerging between the legislative and judicial branches: Congress no longer could count on the Court for latitude on policy or for political cover. Souter's nomination was expected to strengthen the newly conservative Court in its rejection of a role as public policy maker; he took his seat as the sixth member to favor a narrower reading of the Constitution and federal statutes. This judicial conservatism tends to force legislatures, both federal and state, to write into law what the Supreme Court refuses to read into it.

The October 2 confirmation vote of 90 to 9 was a victory for Bush and his first nominee to the Court. Souter had eluded much of the tough questioning, and some of the senators who voted for the reticient twelve-year-veteran of New Hampshire state courts said they did so reluctantly. Democrats and Republicans alike said they still were not sure how Souter would decide some of the most controversial issues of the day, particularly abortion. But they said they believed he would be open-minded.

Overall, Souter's testimony was exceptionally polished—he had spent part of the summer being coached by White House aides—and what he said was more moderate than the conservative opinions he had written as a New Hampshire Supreme Court justice from 1983 to 1990. Souter began his testimony before the Judiciary Committee by asserting that the greatest responsibility a judge faces is "to make the promises of the Constitution a reality for our time and to preserve that Constitution for the generations that will follow after we are gone from here."

Court's Role in Social Policy

The stakes in the nomination hearings to replace Brennan were high, judicially and politically. While the Court's new conservative majority was evident in the 1988-1989 and 1989-1990 terms, Brennan, the Court's most senior justice and its leading liberal, still had been able to eke out a few significant wins. A bulwark for individual rights and liberties, Brennan had kept alive the activism of the Warren Court. With Brennan's departure, the Court was expected to become more conservative. The question remained how far it would go.

Brennan personified a liberal philosophy, which in a judicial context favors the individual interest over the state's and permits courts to decide issues that in an earlier era were the province of legislators. Judicial conservatives have the reverse priority. When Bush introduced Souter to the nation in a news conference, he described him as a conservative who would not "legislate from the bench."

Since the late 1950s, Congress had been able to sidestep some of the most politically sensitive issues because the Supreme Court weighed in. Particularly under Chief Justice Earl Warren (1953-1969), but extending into the tenure of Warren E. Burger (1969-1986), the majority broadly read the Constitution and federal statutes to support civil rights and affirmative action, the right to abortion, and defendants' rights. The liberal activist approach began eroding with the Court's turnover during Ronald Reagan's two terms.

Abortion, a divisive subject that most elected officials prefer not to confront, dominated news coverage of Souter's confirmation hearings. Members of the Judiciary Committee tried in vain to get the nominee to state his position. Never in the seventeen years since the *Roe v. Wade* decision has the right to abortion hung so precariously in the balance. Four justices, William H. Rehnquist, Byron R. White, Antonin Scalia, and Anthony M. Kennedy, have written that they do not believe abortion is a fundamental right guaranteed by the Constitution. They appear ready to overrule or significantly weaken the 1973 decision that made abortion legal nationwide. Three other justices, Thurgood Marshall, Harry A. Blackmun, and John Paul Stevens, remain opposed to undermining *Roe*. And one, Sandra Day O'Connor, has wavered.

In 1989 the Court upheld significant state restrictions on abortion in *Webster v. Reproductive Health Services,* and it could very well turn over to legislators all control of abortion. No longer would federal and state lawmakers, under increasing pressure from activists on both sides of the issue, be able to plead deference to the courts.

A Nominee Without a "Paper Trail"

Shortly after he was nominated, a reporter asked Souter how it felt to be snatched from obscurity. He responded, "I must say, I never thought of myself as that obscure." The dry-witted, former Rhodes scholar is by all accounts a solitary, conscientious man with a diligent and straightforward approach to the law.

Souter had published just one law article, a tribute to a state court justice in the *New Hampshire Bar Journal*. He had only months earlier been tapped by Bush for a federal appeals court judgeship but had not yet written a legal opinion on that bench. Still, the Harvard-educated Souter came with an impressive academic background, solid judicial experience, and the benefit of having been approved in April 1990 by the Senate for the U.S. Court of Appeals for the First Circuit.

Souter's lack of published writings—the opposite of Bork's well-documented views—fit with Bush's asserted philosophy that his nominee should have no agenda. Souter had been cautious in his state court opinions. His writing was spare and not given to broad analyses. Much was made by senators and the news media about how Souter was no Bork. Equally striking was that the man who nominated Souter was no Reagan. Souter was typical in many ways of Bush's nominees to the federal bench during 1989 and 1990: conservative but without an overt personal agenda; nonconfrontational (like the president himself); and, by and large, anonymous to the nation.

The Senate confirmed nominees to three Supreme Court vacancies during the 1980s, but the nomination that has become the touchstone for all others was Bork's. A former judge on the U.S. Court of Appeals for the District of Columbia Circuit, Bork is a prolific writer and committed conservative. He was frank about his views during confirmation hearings. Ultimately, senators accused him of being out of the mainstream, and Bork became the first Supreme Court nominee to be rejected since G. Harrold Carswell in 1970. The margin of defeat, 42-58, was the largest in the Court's history.

In the end, it took Reagan three tries to replace Justice Lewis F. Powell, Jr., who had retired. After Bork's rejection, a second nominee, Douglas H. Ginsburg, withdrew after admitting that he had used marijuana during the 1960s and 1970s. Anthony M. Kennedy eventually was confirmed.

Souter's Senate Appearance

When Souter and senators did come together, cases from the 1989-1990 term served as a starting point for broader constitutional questions. Committee members probed Souter for his views on abortion, flag burning, the separation of church and state, and the breadth of a federal judge's power. From the start, Souter displayed an intelligence and confidence that won over a majority on the Judiciary Committee. Most notably, Souter took refuge in the history of legal principles and declined to comment, even indirectly, on emotional social dilemmas that might arise in cases at the Court. He was unflappable yet took pains to conceal his personal views.

The nominee worked to dispel his image as an out-of-touch loner, at one point recalling how in college he counseled a Harvard freshman and his pregnant girlfriend who wanted an abortion. He would not reveal what he told the couple, even under persistent questions from senators. In every way, he managed to sidestep the abortion debate. He endorsed a fundamental right to privacy in the Constitution but declined to say whether that privacy right covers abortion.

The Constitution contains no language about privacy; the Supreme Court has extended the word "liberty" in the Due Process Clause of the Fourteenth Amendment to protect privacy. The Court's 1965 ruling in *Griswold v. Connecticut* relied on the term "privacy" to protect a married couple's use of contraception. The right to abortion flowed from this and other decisions. Souter said, agreeing with the *Griswold* holding, "I believe that the Due Process Clause of the Fourteenth Amendment does recognize and does protect an unenumerated right of privacy." He said marital privacy should be regarded as a fundamental right. But he would not say whether a woman has a constitutional right to choose not to become pregnant. He said the question implicated *Roe v. Wade.* He declined to be pinned down on the balance between a woman's "liberty interest" after conception and the state's interest in protecting the unborn.

On another issue, he implicitly separated himself from the Supreme Court's conservative justices in his reading of the Free Exercise Clause of the First Amendment. He said a state should be required to demonstrate a "compelling interest" to justify outlawing a practice associated with religious activity. *(See entry, p. 15; excerpts, p. 88)*

Souter took a middle-of-the-road approach to constitutional interpretation by saying he would look at the "principles" behind the words of the Framers and not merely the "original intent." In response to Sen. Charles E. Grassley, Jr., R-Iowa, Souter declined to cite any recent case in which the Court had "improperly created new rights." Souter passed up chances to criticize "judicial activism," refusing also to comment on an April 1990

Court ruling that allowed a federal judge to order a school district to raise taxes to put school desegregation into effect.

Other questions stemmed from the conservative Court majority's desire for explicit statutes and increasing refusal to search for congressional intent in committee reports, floor speeches, and other artifacts of legislative history. How a justice construes a statute can affect what power Congress carries, whether an executive branch interpretation wins out, or whether the Court fills in the blanks and effectively writes policy. For example, Scalia's views are that the Court should confine itself largely to the words of a statute and not search for congressional intent in legislative history—an approach that some members of Congress say leads to cramped interpretations. Souter said he turns to legislative history that is a "reliable" guide to what Congress meant. "What we are looking for is an intent which can be attributed to the institution itself . . . [evidence] we can genuinely point to and say, this represents not merely the statement of one committee member or committee staffer or one person on the floor, but . . . [the] institution or a sufficiently large enough number of the members of that institution."

Souter also endorsed the death penalty, putting himself in league with the Court majority. Brennan had opposed capital punishment.

Although he had lived most of his life in the small town of Weare, New Hampshire, Souter tried to assure senators that he was sensitive to the vicissitudes of all sorts of people. He stressed that his five years on a state trial court had left him with two lessons that would help him on the Court. One lesson was that "at the end of our task some human being is going to be affected, some human life is going to be changed in some way by what we do." The second was that people's behavior would be influenced by Court rulings. "We had better use every power of our minds and our hearts and our beings to get those rulings right."

After Souter's three days of testimony, the committee heard from witnesses who were divided on whether he should be appointed. He received bipartisan support from New Hampshire officials and national figures. Abortion rights and women's groups were the most strongly opposed to his confirmation. They said he should have been forced to state an opinion on the correctness of *Roe v. Wade* and asserted that it was disingenuous of Souter to say that he could not talk about that ruling when he readily spoke to the validity of other landmark decisions, such as *Brown v. Board of Education.*

In the end, Majority Leader George J. Mitchell, D-Maine, said he believed Souter had "a reasoned approach and sound understanding" of the Constitution. Of some senators' concerns that they still did not know what kind of justice Souter would make, Mitchell said that Congress also has a place on constitutional matters and can respond if it believes the Court is leaving a void.

2 | *The 1989-1990 Term*

In many of the ten most striking cases of the 1989-1990 term, the Supreme Court took the government's position over the rights of an individual. It said an accident victim who had lapsed into a "persistent vegetative state" could not be removed from artificial life supports, unless she had made it plain ahead of time that she would have chosen to end her life. The decision upheld a state law requiring clear and convincing evidence of a comatose patient's wishes. In separate rulings, the Court also said states could demand that a parent be notified if a teenage daughter seeks an abortion.

And in a pivotal case involving the sacramental use of peyote, justices upset precedent on the free exercise of religion by abandoning a balancing test for whether a church practice that violates a state law should be allowed under the First Amendment. The decision makes it easier for states to justify laws that incidentally conflict with religious practices.

These and other major rulings of the term demonstrated a steady conservative dominance of the Court, in addition to deep divisions among justices.

The Court continued a trend from the 1988-1989 term, undeniably a watershed, in which it made clear that it was ready to turn back to Congress and the states the reins of policy making. The majority's conservatism elevated the letter of the Constitution and statutes. In disputes between an individual and the state, the state's interest typically won out. The majority approach was to leave to lawmakers concerns over social ills. One constitutional scholar described it as a "take-your-problems-elsewhere" Court.

The more liberal approach, which has been losing ground on the Court since the early 1980s when President Ronald Reagan began filling vacancies, is to consider a desirable result for society, rather than being confined by the letter of the statute at the center of the dispute. It also tends to give more weight to an individual's position in a claim against the government.

The Court's conservative proclivity likely will flourish in the upcoming 1990-1991 term. The Court's most persuasive liberal justice, William J. Brennan, Jr., retired July 20, 1990. He was eighty-four and had been on the Court thirty-four years.

In the 1989-1990 term, judicial conservatism was matched by social conservatism, as, for example, the Court strengthened the hand of law enforcement against defendants. The Court ruled on thirty-five criminal law matters, more than one-fourth of all of its cases. In most of these decisions the state's interest won out over a defendant's argument. In a highly publicized ruling, the Court said police could stop drivers at sobriety checkpoints without reasonable suspicion that the individual drivers had been drinking.

Chief Justice William H. Rehnquist has been outspoken in his distress over the numerous challenges many death row inmates make to their convictions and the frustration states experience in carrying out executions. The Court continued to cut back on the ability of federal judges to review the constitutionality of state court convictions and sentences.

But overall, both the circumspect tone of the Court's rulings and a decrease in the number of cases it accepted revealed a resistance to enter the fray. In the tragic "right-to-die" case, the Court declined to forge a broad consensus on the rights of people who are being kept alive only through artificial means. It did, however, allow that the Constitution protects an individual's right to decide whether to end medical treatment.

Similarly, the opinions in the abortion cases were narrow, despite a request from the Bush administration to overrule the landmark 1973 *Roe v. Wade* decision that made abortion legal nationwide. The majority showed that it is more inclined to refine the decisions of the "activist" era of the 1960s and 1970s rather than to sharply depart from precedent.

Part of the resistance to charting a dramatic course likely stemmed from the Court's polarization along a 5-4 conservative-liberal divide. One-third of the Court's decisions were 5-4 rulings. A majority of those narrow decisions were in the criminal law area.

In what is generally referred to as the conservative camp were Chief Justice Rehnquist and Justices Byron R. White, Sandra Day O'Connor, Antonin Scalia, and Anthony M. Kennedy. The last three were appointed in the 1980s by President Reagan. Rehnquist, appointed by President Richard Nixon in 1971, was promoted to chief justice by Reagan in 1986. Conservatives tend to interpret the Constitution and federal statutes narrowly, leaving social policy matters to legislators. Conservatives also are inclined to support government authority rather than an individual's claim.

On the more liberal side were Justices Brennan, Thurgood Marshall, Harry A. Blackmun, and—most of the time—John Paul Stevens. Judicial liberals assume an active role in ameliorating societal ills and take a broader reading of the Constitution and federal law. They also tend to back an individual's claim of a right or freedom, rather than the government's argument against that claim.

Although White and O'Connor usually lined up on the conservative side, each occasionally swung to the liberal column, giving the liberals what was still a relatively rare victory. In the 5-4 decisions, the conservative side prevailed more often than not.

In one notable victory for liberals, the Court declined to further narrow civil rights law, as it had in the 1988-1989 term. What differentiated the Court's decision in *Metro Broadcasting, Inc. v. Federal Communications Commission* (allowing preferential treatment of minorities seeking broadcast licenses) from last year's controversial civil rights decisions was the role of Congress. Brennan wrote for the Court, "It is of overriding significance in these cases that the FCC's minority ownership programs have been specifically approved—indeed, mandated—by Congress."

The Court demonstrated that it was seeking explicit statutes from Congress. The Court appeared to be saying it is the letter of a statute, not inferred congressional intent or a social agenda, that will be its guide. More frequently individual justices have criticized other judges' reliance on legislative history and called on Congress to say what it means in the language of statutes. The Court under Chief Justice Earl Warren (1953-1969) and Chief Justice Warren E. Burger (1969-1986) had been willing to extend statutes to remedy the social ills they were originally written to attack. The present Court was not willing to do so, absent appropriate congressional language.

Overall, the Court chose to hear fewer cases. The Court issued 129 opinions this term, down slightly from the 133 of the 1988-1989 term and the 139 of the term before that. But the total is 22 fewer than the 151 cases decided in each of the terms ending in 1982 and 1983. During the 1970s the Court averaged 130 signed opinions a term. The number of cases accepted for the next term, which began October 1, 1990, also was sharply lower.

There were several reasons why the Court was hearing fewer cases. One was that the older justices (three were in their eighties) had a sense of historical perspective that caused them to be nonchalant about certain legal disputes. Another reason was that the four liberal justices did not want the Court to take up issues on which the conservative majority might be able to set precedent, so they voted defensively not to review certain cases. Another often noted factor was the decline in requests for lower court review by the current U.S. solicitor general. President Reagan's solicitors general had pushed for review of a record number of rulings. The current solicitor general, Kenneth W. Starr, pursued far fewer appeals during the 1989-1990 term.

Whatever the reason, the trend frustrated at least one justice. White, who with Brennan's departure became the most senior justice, dissented nearly seventy times from Court decisions not to review cases. By sitting on the sidelines in some disputes, White wrote in a dissent June 28, 1990, the Supreme Court is subjecting residents of different states to different rules.

"In some of these cases it is perhaps arguable that the alleged conflict was not 'real' or 'square.' In most of these cases, however, it is very difficult to deny the conflict, especially where ... the court of appeals expressly differs with another court." The Court's propensity to deny review of an increasing number of cases, White wrote, has led to federal law "being administered in different ways in different parts of the country; citizens in some circuits are subject to liabilities or entitlements that citizens in other circuits are not burdened with or entitled to."

□□□

Following are ten major cases of the 1989-1990 term:

Cruzan v. Director, Missouri Department of Health, decided by a 5-4 vote, June 25, 1990; Rehnquist wrote the opinion; Brennan, Marshall, Blackmun, and Stevens dissented.

For the first time, the Supreme Court confronted the question of who decides when artificial life supports can be withdrawn from a comatose patient. The question, heavily covered by the news media, was presented as whether an individual has a "right to die."

In a narrow vote that prevented life-sustaining treatment from being removed from a Missouri woman, the Court ruled that clear and convincing evidence of a patient's previously expressed wish to die is required before a state will allow family members to disconnect life-support systems.

The case involved Nancy Beth Cruzan, thirty-two, who lay helpless in a state hospital bed. Doctors said she was in a "persistent vegetative state," exhibiting motor reflexes but no cognitive function. Cruzan's arms and legs were severely contracted, and she was unable to respond to those around her. The victim of an automobile accident seven years earlier, she had suffered irreversible brain damage.

Like the difficult issue of abortion, this case involved the Constitution's implied right of privacy and, in the catchphrase of the times, a question of "Who decides?" The Court had avoided the question in 1976 by refusing to review a New Jersey Supreme Court ruling that allowed Karen Ann Quinlan to be removed from a respirator.

When it became clear that Nancy Cruzan would not regain her mental faculties, her parents, Lester L. and Joyce Cruzan, asked that artificial feedings be stopped. A tube surgically inserted into their daughter's stomach provided water and nutrition. Hospital officials refused, and the Cruzans went to a Missouri trial court to get an injunction.

The Missouri trial court ruled that a person in Cruzan's condition had a fundamental right under the state and federal constitutions to refuse "death prolonging procedures." The court found that Cruzan's statements at age twenty-five in a conversation with a friend "that if sick or injured she would not wish to continue her life unless she could live at least halfway normally" suggested that, given her condition, she would not have wished to continue with artificial feedings.

But the state appealed the decision and the Missouri Supreme Court reversed, saying Cruzan's statements were "unreliable for determining her intent" and stating that a Missouri living will statute favored the preservation of life. "Living wills" are documents in which people specify what kind of health care they would want should they lapse into a coma or otherwise become incompetent and unable to communicate. Generally, these documents state that no extraordinary means be used to extend life.

In the Supreme Court ruling, the majority accepted the Missouri requirement that evidence of the incompetent person's wishes for the withdrawal of treatment be clear and convincing. Rehnquist wrote, "The choice between life and death is a deeply personal decision of obvious and overwhelming finality. We believe Missouri may legitimately seek to safeguard the personal element of this choice through the imposition of heightened evidentiary requirements."

He was joined by White, Kennedy, O'Connor, and Scalia.

Rehnquist accepted that an individual has a constitutionally protected right to refuse lifesaving food and water. "It cannot be disputed that the Due Process Clause protects an interest in life as well as an interest in refusing life-sustaining medical treatment," he said. But the chief justice emphasized the need for a clear expression of the person's wishes on treatment and acknowledged that some persons' true desires will be frustrated because they were never put down in writing.

The majority seemed to sympathize with Cruzan's parents, but, raising the possibility of not-so-caring parents or guardians being involved, said, "There is no automatic assurance that the view of close family members will necessarily be the same as the patient's would have been had she been confronted with the prospect of her situation while competent."

Brennan, Marshall, Blackmun, and Stevens dissented. Brennan wrote that Cruzan has a fundamental right to be free of the feeding tube and said, "Nancy Cruzan is entitled to choose to die with dignity."

"Dying is personal," Brennan said. "And it is profound. For many, the thought of an ignoble end, steeped in decay, is abhorrent. Although the right to be free of unwanted medical intervention, like other constitutionally protected interests, may not be absolute, no state interests could outweigh the rights of an individual in Nancy Cruzan's position. Whatever a state's possible interests in mandating life-support treatment under other circumstances, there is no good to be obtained here by Missouri's insistence that Nancy Cruzan remain on life-support systems if it is indeed her wish not to do so."

Some of the justices suggested that the Court's ruling failed to resolve the larger issue of who decides when life supports may be withdrawn.

Scalia admonished his fellow justices for the various individual opinions (five justices wrote separately) in the case: "I am concerned, from the tenor of today's opinions, that we are poised to confuse that enterprise as successfully as we have confused the enterprise of legislating concerning abortion." Scalia said he would have preferred a clear statement from justices that federal courts have no business in this field.

O'Connor wrote, "[N]o national consensus has yet emerged on the best solution for this difficult and sensitive problem. Today, we decide only that one state's practice does not violate the Constitution; the more challenging task of crafting appropriate procedures for safeguarding incompetents' liberty interests is entrusted to the 'laboratory' of the states."

□□□

Hodgson v. Minnesota, Minnesota v. Hodgson, decided by separate 5-4 votes, June 25, 1990; Stevens wrote the opinion striking down a statute that required a teen-age girl to notify both biological parents of an abortion decision; Scalia, Kennedy, Rehnquist, and White dissented. A separate majority (O'Connor and the above dissenting justices) found the statute ultimately constitutional because it provided as an alternative a judicial hearing for pregnant girls who did not want to tell their parents of their decision.

Ohio v. Akron Center for Reproductive Health, decided by a 6-3 vote, June 25, 1990; Kennedy wrote the opinion upholding an Ohio parental-notification law; Blackmun, Brennan, and Marshall dissented.

Although this case and *Hodgson* dealt with a narrow area of abortion rights—when a teenage girl must tell her parents that she intends to have an abortion—the rulings illustrated the wrenching disunity among justices in 1990 over how to respond to the abortion dilemma. The justices issued nine separate opinions in the two cases. Although neither decision modified *Roe v. Wade,* the opinions demonstrated that there was no longer a majority on the Court willing to find a fundamental right to abortion in the Constitution.

The Court said in the Minnesota case that states may compel an unmarried woman under age eighteen to tell both parents before obtaining an abortion as long as she has the alternative of a judicial hearing. In the Ohio case the Court upheld a statute requiring unmarried women under eighteen to tell at least one parent. The Ohio law also allowed a judicial alternative, but the Court did not directly state whether the alternative was necessary for one-parent notification to pass constitutional muster. The Court rejected a request by the Bush administration to replace the framework for review of abortion regulations that was established in *Roe v. Wade* with a more relaxed standard.

The young women and doctors who had challenged the laws said they were unduly burdensome and interfered with the right to abortion. The states justified the requirements as promoting the well-being of minors and better relationships between parents and children.

While the Supreme Court in the past had ruled that women under eighteen must have access to a judicial alternative when parental consent is required for an abortion, it had never resolved the question on parental-notification laws.

The last time the Court reviewed parental notification, in the 1987 case of *Hartigan v. Zbaraz,* there was one Court vacancy, and the justices split 4-4 on an Illinois statute requiring that parents be told before a physician performs an abortion on an under-age girl. The ruling had the effect of affirming a federal appeals court decision that the parental notice statute was constitutional only if it allowed the girl to go before a judge as an alternative. But the split decision left the legal question unsettled.

The requirement of a judicial bypass, as it is called, stemmed from the Court's decision in *Bellotti v. Baird.* In that 1979 ruling, the Court struck down a Massachusetts parental-consent statute, saying that a minor must have access to a confidential, expeditious proceeding before a judge. The judicial bypass is intended to allow a teenager to show either that she is mature enough and well-informed enough to make the abortion decision herself or that the abortion would be in her best interest.

In the Minnesota case, the statute said no abortion could be performed on a minor until at least forty-eight hours after both biological parents had been notified. Part of the statute said that if the law was ever enjoined by a court, it would automatically be amended to allow a judicial hearing as an alternative to notifying both parents. Both parts of the law had been challenged by a group of women, their single-parent mothers, and doctors who perform abortions.

The Court ruled 5-4 that the two-parent requirement without a judicial bypass is unconstitutional. In the majority were Stevens, who wrote the opinion, Brennan, Marshall, Blackmun, and O'Connor. It was the first time that O'Connor had voted to find any abortion restriction unconstitutional.

O'Connor, clearly the pivotal vote on the Court in 1990, then sided with a different majority in finding the law ultimately constitutional because of the provision allowing a girl to seek a judge's consent if she does not want to tell her parents. The other justices approving the statute were Rehnquist, White, Scalia, and Kennedy.

O'Connor said state laws limiting abortion should be upheld as long as they do not impose an "undue burden" on women. This approach, expressed by O'Connor in earlier abortion decisions, departed from the principles of *Roe v. Wade,* which found an abortion right in a constitutional right to privacy and said state restrictions could be upheld only if they serve a "compelling" state purpose. Four justices—Rehnquist, White, Scalia, and Kennedy—have said outright that they believe there is no fundamental right to abortion in the Constitution.

The Supreme Court's decision in the Minnesota case affirmed the U.S. Court of Appeals for the Eighth Circuit, which had found the state statute unconstitutional without the judicial alternative and constitutional with it. Writing for a majority in part of the case, Stevens said that during the past fourteen years the Court had considered six abortion cases involving parental consent or notification statutes and that none had ever involved two parents.

"The requirement of notice to both of the pregnant minor's parents is not reasonably related to legitimate state interests," Stevens said, noting that Minnesota made no exception for a divorced parent, a parent who does not have custody, or a biological parent who never married or lived with the pregnant woman's mother.

Kennedy wrote for the dissenting justices, who had sought to uphold the constitutionality of the two-parent requirement without the alternative of going before a judge. He cited a "right of each parent to participate in the upbringing of her or his children." He said no judicial alternative to a notice requirement should be demanded because, unlike with parental-consent laws, a notice requirement does not give a third party the right to made a decision on behalf of the minor.

O'Connor's opinion, which led to the finding that the statute as a whole was constitutional, said the "interference" caused by the two-parent rule vanishes when a teen-age girl can avoid notifying one or both parents by appearing before a judge.

The Ohio statute barred a physician from performing an abortion on a teen-ager without giving twenty-four hours' notice in person or by telephone to one of the girl's parents or guardians. It allowed for forty-eight-hour notice by mail when actual notice was impossible. The law contained a judicial alternative, but the U.S. Court of Appeals for the Sixth Circuit found that its procedural requirements interfered with a minor's right to an abortion.

Among the reasons for the appeals court's rejection of the statute was that only the treating physician and not another qualified person could give the notice, and that, in a judicial bypass, a teen-ager had to prove with "clear and convincing" evidence that the abortion was in her best interest. It cited a chance for unnecessary delay and a lapse of confidentiality in the judicial bypass procedural requirements.

But Kennedy, who wrote for the majority, dismissed concerns that the statute unduly burdened a minor seeking an abortion. Of the specific requirement that the physician tell the parent, Kennedy said the physician would be able to obtain important medical information from the parent. He said the judicial bypass met *Bellotti* standards for a prompt and confidential hearing. He rejected arguments challenging the procedural conditions and found no problem with other components, including that the under-age woman face a heightened standard of proof. He said in such hearings rarely does anyone oppose the woman's testimony. Kennedy, however, did not address whether a judicial bypass is necessary in all notice statutes.

In dissent, Blackmun, who was joined by Brennan and Marshall, called the statute's procedure "a tortuous maze" intended to deter abortions. Blackmun is the author of *Roe v. Wade.*

Stevens, who had opposed abortion restraints in prior cases, said the Ohio judicial bypass was sufficient and voted with Rehnquist, White, O'Connor, Scalia, and Kennedy to uphold the law.

In a portion of the Court's opinion that O'Connor and Stevens declined to endorse, Kennedy said of the parent-notification law, "It is both rational and fair for the state to conclude that, in most instances, the family will strive to give a lonely or even terrified minor advice that is both compassionate and mature."

□□□

Employment Division, Department of Human Resources of Oregon v. Smith, decided by a 6-3 vote, April 17, 1990; Scalia wrote the opinion; Blackmun, Brennan, and Marshall dissented.

States may outlaw the sacramental use of the drug peyote without invading the First Amendment guarantee of free exercise of religion, the Court ruled in a decision that could have broad implications for religious rights in the future. The Court abandoned a test used in earlier cases that required a state to prove it had a "compelling interest" in enforcing a statute that infringed on religious freedom.

The Court said that the balancing test, from *Sherbert v. Verner* (1963), does not have to be used when the Free Exercise Clause is invoked in a challenge to a criminal law that is applied generally to all people in a jurisdiction. The test dictated that a statute that burdens religious exercise impose no greater restriction on religion than necessary.

The First Amendment states in part, "Congress shall make no law respecting an establishment of religion, or prohibiting the free exercise thereof." The prohibition extends to the states through the Fourteenth Amendment. Scalia, who wrote for the majority, said that if prohibiting the exercise of religion is "merely the incidental effect" of an otherwise valid state law, the First Amendment has not been breached.

Peyote, a cactus that contains the hallucinogen mescaline, is a traditional element of American Indian religious ceremonies. Oregon law subjected anyone who used the drug to criminal penalties and made no exception, as the federal government and a number of states did, for its sacramental use.

The case arose when two workers were fired from their jobs with a private drug rehabilitation program because they took peyote at an Indian church ceremony. They were then denied state unemployment compensation on the grounds that they had been discharged for criminal behavior.

The Oregon Court of Appeals reversed a decision by the state's employment division and held that the denial of benefits violated the workers' religious rights under the First Amendment. The Oregon Supreme Court agreed, ruling that there must be an exception to the criminal statute for a good-faith religious use of peyote. The court said the state could not deny unemployment benefits to the men for exercising their religious right. Reversing that decision, Scalia said, "We have never held that an individual's religious beliefs excuse him from compliance with an otherwise valid law prohibiting conduct that the state is free to regulate."

He said the clause does not exempt an individual from obeying "a valid and neutral law of general applicability" that happens to infringe on religious practice.

Scalia said a state cannot outlaw practices simply because they are used in religious exercises. "It would doubtless be unconstitutional, for example, to ban the casting of statutes that are to be used for worship purposes, or to prohibit bowing down before a golden calf. . . . Respondents in the present case, however, seek to carry the meaning of 'prohibiting the free exercise [of religion]' one step further. They contend that their religious motivation for using peyote places them beyond the reach of a criminal law that is not specifically directed at their religious practice, and that is concededly constitutional as applied to those who use the drug for other reasons."

Noting that other states had exempted the religious use of peyote from criminal penalties, Scalia said that while that might even be "desirable" for state lawmakers, the First Amendment does not require an exemption.

O'Connor disagreed with Scalia's reasoning and criticized his departure from the "compelling state interest" test of prior cases. In a concurrence that was joined by dissenting justices Brennan, Marshall, and Blackmun, O'Connor said, "In my view, today's holding dramatically departs from well-settled First Amendment jurisprudence, appears unnecessary to resolve the question presented, and is incompatible with our nation's fundamental commitment to individual religious liberty." O'Connor said religious beliefs and religious conduct cannot be separated. "A person who is barred from engaging in religiously motivated conduct is barred from freely exercising his religion," she wrote.

Still, O'Connor agreed with Scalia's judgment that the two men should have been denied unemployment benefits. She said the state convincingly argued that its interest in drug control was compelling and outweighed its burden on religious practice.

The dissenting justices said Oregon's interest was not compelling. Blackmun wrote, "The state's interest in enforcing its prohibition, in order to be sufficiently compelling to outweigh a free exercise claim, cannot be merely abstract or symbolic. . . . In this case, the state actually has not evinced any concrete interest in enforcing its drug laws against religious users of peyote." American Indians believe that the peyote plant represents their deity and eating it is an act of worship. "Without peyote," Blackmun said, "they could not enact the essential ritual of their religion."

"If Oregon can constitutionally prosecute them for this act of worship, they, like the Amish, may be forced to migrate to some other and more tolerant region," he said. Blackmun said the Court's rationale also undermines the 1978 American Indian Religious Freedom Act, a federal law that responded to religious persecution of Native Americans. He contended that the majority's ruling will reduce both the First Amendment and federal policy to "merely an unfulfilled and hollow promise."

□□□

Metro Broadcasting Inc. v. Federal Communications Commission, Astroline Communications Company Limited Partnership v. Shurberg Broadcasting of Hartford, Inc., decided by a 5-4 vote, June 27, 1990; Brennan wrote the opinion; O'Connor, Rehnquist, Scalia, and Kennedy dissented.

In a surprising endorsement of affirmative action, the Court ruled that Congress may order preferential treatment of blacks and other minorities to increase their ownership of broadcast licenses. The Court said "benign race-conscious measures," including those that do not compensate victims of past discrimination, are constitutional as long as they further important government objectives. That Congress had mandated the preferential treatment was central to the Court's opinion. It said federal lawmakers have more authority than state and local governments to set aside contracts for minorities. The ruling marked the first time the Court had upheld an affirmative action program that was not devised to relieve past discrimination.

At issue were two types of set-aside programs: one gave special credit to minorities applying for new licenses, and the other, involving a "distress sale" program, required some radio and television stations to be sold only to minority-controlled companies. During the Reagan administration, the FCC had tried to dismantle the race-preference programs, but Congress beginning in 1987 had blocked the commission from spending any of its appropriated money to examine or change the policies.

White-owned broadcasting companies challenged the practices as violating constitutional guarantees of equal protection. In separate rulings, the U.S. Court of Appeals for the District of Columbia Circuit upheld the policy giving extra credit to minority-owned companies and struck down the distress sale program.

The Supreme Court decision came on the last day of its 1989-1990 term and was delivered by Brennan. The Court's oldest and most consistently liberal member, Brennan had been outvoted in recent years as the Court's newly conservative majority, shaped by Reagan appointees, narrowly interpreted civil rights laws. Joining Brennan were Marshall, Blackmun, Stevens, and White. Stevens and White had banded with conservative justices in a February 1989 majority opinion rejecting a Richmond, Virginia, public works program that set aside 30 percent of construction funds for minority contractors. That case was *City of Richmond v. J. A. Croson.*

In his opinion, Brennan stressed Congress's finding that preference programs for minorities were necessary for broadcast diversity and that lawmakers had long given special protection to minorities. In distinguishing these cases from the *Croson* ruling, Brennan said the federal government has more authority than state and local governments.

"It is of overriding significance in these cases that the FCC's minority ownership programs have been specifically approved—indeed, mandated—by Congress," Brennan wrote. He based his opinion on the Court's 1980 decision in *Fullilove v. Klutznick,* which upheld a federal public works set-aside program on the grounds that the Constitution allows special deference to Congress.

The majority said federal affirmative action programs should be analyzed with a more lenient equal-protection standard than that applied to city and state plans. It said the strict scrutiny test used in *Croson* need not govern congressional mandates.

Brennan reasoned that the minority-ownership policies served an important government objective of broadcast diversity and agreed with the implication from Congress that "the American public will benefit by having access to a wider diversity of information sources." He said, "For the past two decades, Congress has consistently recognized the barriers encountered by minorities in entering the broadcast industry and has expressed emphatic support for the commission's attempts to promote programming diversity by increasing minority ownership." He also said that the policies do not place an undue burden on broadcasters who are not minorities.

Writing for the dissent, O'Connor said the Court had taken a mighty step backward with its opinion. "This departure marks a renewed toleration of racial classifications and a repudiation of our recent affirmation that the Constitution's equal protection guarantees extend equally to all citizens," she said.

O'Connor, the author of the *Croson* ruling, said that by providing benefits to blacks and other minorities, the FCC was denying benefits to whites based on their race. "Except in the narrowest of circumstances, the Constitution bars such racial classifications as a denial to particular individuals, of any race or ethnicity, of 'the equal protection of the laws,'" O'Connor wrote, quoting the Fourteenth Amendment. She speculated the majority's more lenient standard of review for the FCC policies might lead the government to resort to racial distinctions more readily.

□□□

Rutan v. Republican Party of Illinois, Frech v. Rutan, decided by a 5-4 vote, June 21, 1990; Brennan wrote the opinion; Scalia, Rehnquist, Kennedy, and O'Connor dissented.

In a blow to the longstanding tradition of political patronage, the Supreme Court ruled that it is unconstitutional to hire, promote, or transfer most public employees based on party affiliation. The Court said that patronage infringes on the First Amendment rights of public employees unless party membership is "an appropriate requirement" for the job.

Some legal experts had predicted that if the Supreme Court extended political association protection beyond cases in which an employee was fired, it would be the death knell for patronage. But the Court, anticipating that pronouncement, disagreed, saying, "Political parties have already survived the substantial decline in patronage employment practices in this century."

The case arose after Illinois governor James R. Thompson, a Republican, froze hiring and promotions in state agencies. The only exceptions were those granted by the governor's personnel office, according to Thompson's executive order. The workers who brought the lawsuit alleged that the personnel office kept them out of jobs because they did not support the state's Republican party. The Thompson administration asserted that political party affiliation should be a legitimate measure along with other criteria when assessing applicants.

The Court's ruling, which reversed the U.S. Court of Appeals for the Seventh Circuit, expanded two earlier decisions that had barred the dismissal of public workers based on party affiliation: *Elrod v. Burns* (1976) and *Branti v. Finkel* (1980). In these cases the Court held that patronage violates a First Amendment right of free association when government workers who are not in policy or confidential positions are fired because of their party membership. The cases did not deal with hiring, rehiring, promotions, or transfers as *Rutan* did.

Writing for the majority, Brennan opened his opinion with: "To the victor belong only those spoils that may be constitutionally obtained." He said the government cannot deny a benefit to a person on a basis that violates First Amendment belief and association rights. He said the Illinois

GOP system penalized individuals who did not affiliate with the Republican party by excluding them from positions and—for workers already on the rolls—by denying them pay increases, better hours, and, in cases of temporary layoffs, recalls. "These are significant penalties and are imposed for the exercise of rights guaranteed by the First Amendment," Brennan wrote.

He said the government's interest in party loyalty can be achieved through less restrictive means and that unless patronage practices are "narrowly tailored" to advance government interests, courts must conclude that they breach the First Amendment.

Scalia was joined in a strong dissent by Rehnquist, Kennedy, and, in part, O'Connor. He said reserving jobs in government for the party in power is an important tradition that fosters the government's interest in stable political parties. "There is little doubt that our decisions in *Elrod* and *Branti,* by contributing to the decline of party strength, have also contributed to the growth of interest-group politics in the last decade. Our decision today will greatly accelerate the trend. It is not only campaigns that are affected, of course, but the subsequent behavior of politicians once they are in power."

□□□

Missouri v. Jenkins, decided by a 5-4 vote, April 18, 1990; White wrote the opinion; Kennedy, Rehnquist, O'Connor, and Scalia dissented.

Federal courts may order local governments to raise taxes to correct constitutional violations like school segregation. The Court's narrow decision was out of step with its general proclivity against judicial activism and immediately drew criticism from the more conservative members of Congress. At the same time, the ruling gratified civil rights activists who had urged more power for federal judges who are involved in managing public institutions like schools and prisons.

While the Court said that a federal judge may not raise the property tax himself, as the judge in this Missouri case had, it ruled that the judge may order local authorities to exercise their own taxing power.

"A court order directing a local government to levy its own taxes is plainly a judicial act within the power of a federal court," White wrote, joined by Brennan, Marshall, Blackmun, and Stevens. The part of the decision that said a judge could not raise taxes himself was unanimous.

The Missouri case arose from a court-ordered plan to improve and desegregate Kansas City schools, stemming from a 1977 lawsuit filed by a group of students. The federal district judge who had ordered the desegregation plan imposed a tax increase on school district residents saying it was needed to pay the local share of the multi-million-dollar desegregation effort. Property tax rates nearly doubled. State officials objected and contended that, under the Tenth Amendment, the taxing power is reserved to the states. They said taxing authority is a legislative power not to be taken up by other branches.

The U.S. Court of Appeals for the Eighth Circuit upheld the district judge's taxing order. And the Supreme Court decision, with the qualification that the judge could only order the tax and not impose it himself, effectively affirmed that ruling.

Writing for the Court, White said, state policy must acquiesce when it interferes with vindication of federal constitutional guarantees: in this case, desegregated schools. "[A] local government with taxing authority may be ordered to levy taxes in excess of the limit set by state statute where there is reason based in the Constitution for not observing the statutory limitation." he said. "To hold otherwise would fail to take account of the obligations of local governments, under the Supremacy Clause, to fulfill the requirements that the Constitution imposes on them."

White said the Tenth Amendment was not implicated because the judge's order enforced the Fourteenth Amendment allowing judges to remedy unlawful discrimination in the states. White said the Fourteenth Amendment "permits a federal court to disestablish local government institutions that interfere with its commands."

Writing for the dissenting justices, Kennedy said, "Today's casual embrace of taxation imposed by the unelected, life-tenured federal judiciary disregards fundamental precepts for the democratic control of public institutions." Kennedy, joined by Rehnquist, O'Connor, and Scalia, asserted that the federal judiciary simply does not have the power to tax. "Few ends are more important than enforcing the guarantee of equal educational opportunity for our Nation's children. But rules of taxation that override state political structures not themselves subject to any constitutional infirmity raise serious questions of federal authority," he said.

□□□

Spallone v. United States, Chema v. United States, Longo v. United States, decided by a 5-4 vote, January 10, 1990; Rehnquist wrote the opinion; Brennan, Marshall, Blackmun, and Stevens dissented.

Called into a tense, longstanding battle between Yonkers and the federal government over segregated housing, the Supreme Court ruled that a federal judge abused his power when he imposed contempt fines against city officials who failed to put in place a court-ordered desegregation plan. The Court said the district court judge's levy of fines was not a proper exercise of judicial power under the circumstances.

A federal district court had found that Yonkers had concentrated its subsidized housing in one area of the city to segregate blacks and other minorities from whites. One of the remedies the judge ordered in a consent decree was construction of 1,000 units of low-income housing in mostly white neighborhoods. The city council rejected legislation to put the plan in place, leading the judge to hold in contempt the city and four council members who voted against the plan. The judge fined both the city and the individual members. The U.S. Court of Appeals for the Second Circuit affirmed the contempt order, which cost the city $820,000 in fines, and the council members $3,500 each.

In their appeal, the Yonkers council members asserted that the court's order infringed their free speech rights and that they should be protected from contempt charges by constitutional legislative immunity. Immunity shields members of Congress from liability in civil suits for damages.

The Court, in a ruling that did not rely on legislative immunity or the First Amendment, said the judge abused his discretion in fining the council members. The majority said traditional equitable principles dictate that federal judges use the least amount of power necessary to win compliance with an order. The Court upheld the fines against the city but said the judge should have waited to see if those fines provided enough leverage before also sanctioning the council members. The Court said a "reasonable time" should have been allowed for compliance with the consent decree.

Writing for the majority, Rehnquist said that it was likely that the city would have complied with the court order. He was joined by White, O'Connor, Scalia and Kennedy. Rehnquist wrote that judges must have the power to enforce their orders, but he said fining legislators "is designed to cause them to vote, not with a view to the interest of their constituents or of the city, but with a view solely to their own personal interests. . . . This sort of individual sanction effects a much greater perversion of the normal legislative process than does the imposition of sanctions on the city."

Dissenting, Brennan said the fines were "essential" to coerce compliance with the court order. He said that given the city's "consistent defiance" in desegregating public housing, the district judge had no reason to believe that fines only against the city would bring about compliance. He said not only would the fines have helped ensure observance of the consent decree but that they would have accelerated it. Joined by Marshall, Blackmun, and Stevens, Brennan said, "I worry that the Court's message will have the unintended effect of emboldening recalcitrant officials continually to test the ultimate reach of the remedial authority of the federal courts."

□□□

United States v. Eichman, United States v. Haggerty, decided by a 5-4 vote, June 11, 1990. Brennan wrote the opinion; Rehnquist, White, Stevens, and O'Connor dissented.

Flag burning in the course of political protest is a right guaranteed by the First Amendment, the Court said for the second year in a row. The Supreme Court ruled that a 1989 federal law making it a crime to burn, mutilate, or otherwise destroy a U.S. flag infringed on free speech rights. A five-justice majority said such a constraint on political protest is not justified by the government's asserted interest in protecting the physical integrity of the flag.

The Flag Protection Act would have subjected to arrest anyone who "knowingly mutilates, defaces, physically defiles, burns, maintains on the floor or ground, or tramples upon any flag." The law had been enacted by Congress in response to another flag-burning ruling. In June 1989 the Court in *Texas v. Johnson* had invalidated a Texas statute that made it illegal to burn a flag.

Voting to strike down the new federal statute were Brennan, Marshall, Blackmun, Scalia, and Kennedy—the five who had begun the whole controversy with the ruling in *Johnson*. Again in the minority were Rehnquist, White, Stevens, and O'Connor.

The current case arose when demonstrators in Seattle and Washington, D.C., burned flags shortly after the new law took effect, specifically to challenge its constitutionality. Separate federal district courts found the statute unconstitutional. Normally, a case would not have returned so quickly to the Supreme Court, but Congress had written into the flag act an expedited procedure allowing any challenge to go directly from district court to the Supreme Court for review. The High Court heard arguments May 14 and in a brisk four weeks issued the ruling.

Brennan, writing for the majority as he had in *Johnson*, said, "Although Congress cast the Flag Protection Act in somewhat broader terms than the Texas statute at issue in *Johnson*, the Act still suffers from the same fundamental flaw: it suppresses expression out of concern for its likely communicative impact." He rejected the idea that the language of the statute was "content-neutral," as its congressional authors had intended. "Each of the specified terms—with the possible exception of 'burns'—unmistakably connotes disrespectful treatment of the flag and suggests a focus on those acts likely to damage the flag's symbolic value," he said. Brennan noted that the statute applied only when the flag was burned in public and as such was aimed at the protester's message.

Brennan said the federal law could not be distinguished from the Texas statute. In *Texas v. Johnson*, Brennan had written, "If there is a bedrock principle underlying the First Amendment, it is that the government may not prohibit the expression of an idea simply because society finds the idea itself offensive or disagreeable."

Stevens again wrote for the minority, asserting that the flag could be protected as a national symbol. He agreed with the majority that the government may not prohibit speech simply because it is considered offensive or disagreeable. But, Stevens said, certain acts of expression may be banned if there is a legitimate societal interest unrelated to speech content—such as to protect the flag as a national symbol—and if the speaker has another way to express ideas.

□□□

Board of Education of the Westside Community Schools (Dist. 66) v. Mergens, decided by a 8-1 vote, June 4, 1990. O'Connor wrote the opinion; Stevens dissented.

Student religious groups may meet in public high schools on the same basis as other extracurricular clubs, the Court ruled. Justices said that a 1984 federal "equal access" statute does not breach the Constitution's required separation of church and state, and that an Omaha high school student who wanted to start a Bible study group should have been given permission.

The Equal Access Act cleared Congress after extensive debate over religion in the public schools. (Supreme Court decisions in 1962 and 1963 had banned Bible readings and prayers in the schools.) The act prohibits secondary schools that receive federal funds and that allow extracurricular groups to meet on school grounds from discriminating against any group because of the subject it wants to discuss.

The case before the Court began in 1985 when a student tried to gain formal status for a Christian Bible club at Westside High School in Omaha. The principal and the school board turned her down, saying that official sponsorship would violate the Establishment Clause of the First Amendment.

The student asserted that under the terms of the Equal Access Act, the high school could not exclude any groups based on what they would discuss. She claimed her club was being denied recognition solely because it was centered on the Bible. The act says that if a school permits one or more noncurriculum-related student groups to meet on campus before or after classes, it maintains a "limited open forum" and may not exclude any other noncurriculum-related group. A federal district court ruled that Westside did not have a limited open forum (requiring access) because all of the student clubs were curriculum-related. It said the act did not apply in this case and that school officials acted properly in turning down the Bible club.

The U.S. Court of Appeals for the Eighth Circuit reversed. It ruled that the equal access statute did not violate the Constitution and that under its terms many of the clubs at Westside were indeed noncurriculum-related. The Supreme Court agreed. In her opinion O'Connor pointed to a chess club and a club set up for students interested in scuba diving.

Although a Court majority said the statute does not conflict with the Establishment Clause, justices differed in their reasoning. O'Connor wrote for herself and Rehnquist, White, and Blackmun. She said, "Congress' avowed purpose—to prevent discrimination against religious and other types of speech—is undeniably secular." She said the statute does not advance religion or produce conflicts between government and religion.

Passage of the act had been championed by President Reagan, whose 1984 reelection campaign emphasized support for religious and traditional values. Acknowledging the tenor of those times, O'Connor said, "Even if some legislators were motivated by a conviction that religious speech in particular was valuable and worthy of protection, that alone would not invalidate the act, because what is relevant is the legislative *purpose* of the statute, not the possibly religious *motives* of the legislators who enacted the law.

"Because the act on its face grants equal access to both secular and religious speech," O'Connor wrote, "we think it clear that the act's purpose was not to endorse or disapprove of religion." She said a school does not have to sponsor any student organization not related to the curriculum, but once it does, it may not discriminate against other student groups based on their religious, philosophical or political viewpoint.

The ruling in effect extended the Court's 1981 decision in *Widmar v. Vincent,* which let religious groups meet on college campuses. That case involved the University of Missouri's refusal to allow a student religious group to meet in school buildings on the same terms as other groups. O'Connor said high school students are mature enough to understand that a school is not endorsing religion by permitting a Bible club to meet on a nondiscriminatory basis.

Kennedy, joined by Scalia, wrote separately and took a more relaxed view of allowing religion in the public schools. He said religious clubs are constitutional as long as no students are coerced to participate in the religious activity.

In another concurrence, Marshall, joined by Brennan, leaned the opposite way. Marshall wrote that schools with Bible study clubs must take steps to fully dissociate themselves from the club's religious message and to make sure students do not view school sponsorship of the club as an endorsement of its goals.

Stevens dissented, declaring the act should be more narrowly interpreted so that the school would not be required to open its doors "to every religious, political, or social organization, no matter how controversial or distasteful its views may be." He contended the Court's opinion would pave the way for more federal government interference in the public schools.

3 Case Summaries

The Supreme Court issued 129 signed opinions during the 1989-1990 term. The total was down slightly from the 133 opinions of the 1988-1989 term and the 139 of the term before that. In recent years, the Court has been choosing to hear fewer cases; the 1989-1990 total was 22 less than the 151 cases decided in each of the terms ending in 1982 and 1983. During the 1970s, the Court averaged 130 signed opinions a term.

Following are the case summaries for all signed opinions from the 1989-1990 term:

Business Law

Antitrust

Atlantic Richfield Co. v. USA Petroleum Co., decided by a 7-2 vote, May 14, 1990; Brennan wrote the opinion; Stevens and White dissented.

A company that alleges only that it lost sales to a competitor's nonpredatory prices under a vertical price-fixing scheme has not established an antitrust injury sufficient for standing. A company must be able to show predatory pricing, the Court said. This case involved an independent gas retailer's allegations that a competing oil company conspired with its dealers to fix prices at below-market levels. Brennan wrote for the Court that a manufacturer does not necessarily violate antitrust law when it tells its retailers to set prices at levels meeting those offered by competitors. He said that as long as prices are not set for competition at below-cost levels, a vertical, maximum-price-fixing scheme is not illegal.

California v. American Stores Co., decided by a 9-0 vote, April 30, 1990; Stevens wrote the opinion.

States and individuals, not only the federal government, may sue under the Clayton Act to try to prevent completed mergers that they claim will hurt competition and pricing. The ruling strengthened the hand of state officials seeking to use federal antitrust law to challenge corporate mergers already approved by the Federal Trade Commission.

Before the Court's ruling, it had been widely assumed that states and individuals could sue to prevent anticompetitive mergers but could not interfere once the deals were completed. But the Court said private plaintiffs may sue for divestiture and that, in this case, the California

27

attorney general's office could continue to challenge a merger of the Lucky and Alpha Beta supermarket chains.

Federal Trade Commission v. Superior Court Trial Lawyers Association, Superior Court Trial Lawyers Association v. Federal Trade Commission, decided by a 6-3 vote, January 22, 1990; Stevens wrote the opinion; Brennan, Marshall and Blackmun dissented.

A group of court-appointed criminal lawyers who agreed not to represent indigent clients and went on strike for two weeks to pressure the District of Columbia government to increase their fees engaged in an illegal price-fixing conspiracy. The Court ruled that a 1983 strike by the Superior Court Trial Lawyers Association was a violation of antitrust laws even though it was protesting rates that could be considered unreasonably low. The fees had not been raised for thirteen years.

The lawyers contended they had a First Amendment right to engage in a boycott as a political statement and to protect their indigent clients' constitutional rights to effective counsel. Writing for the majority, Stevens said the social justification offered for the strike does not make it any less unlawful. He stated, "Every concerted refusal to do business with a potential customer or supplier has an expressive component." He said that the strike constituted a per se, or automatic, violation of the Sherman Act prohibiting joint efforts in restraint of trade.

Kansas v. Utilicorp United Inc., decided by a 5-4 vote, June 21; Kennedy wrote the opinion; White, Brennan, Marshall, and Blackmun dissented.

When suppliers violate antitrust laws by overcharging a public utility for natural gas, and the utility passes the overcharge on to its customers, only the utility has a cause of action because it alone has suffered antitrust injuries.

The states of Kansas and Missouri had sued fuel suppliers and producers, alleging that they had conspired to inflate the price of their gas in violation of the antitrust laws. They asserted claims as representatives of state agencies, municipalities, and other political subdivisions. They said they should be able to sue because utilities lack incentive to go to court against suppliers when the utilities can pass on overcharges. But Kennedy, in writing for the Court, said utilities have "an established record of diligent antitrust enforcement" and the responsibility need not be shared.

Dissenting justices argued that giving states standing would lead to greater prosecution of antitrust claims and make sure injured parties were compensated.

Michigan Citizens for an Independent Press v. Dick Thornburgh, Attorney General of the United States, decided 4-4, November 13, 1989; White took no part in the case.

The Court issued a per curiam opinion that said only that the judgment of the Court of Appeals for the District of Columbia Circuit is affirmed by an equally divided Supreme Court. The opinion let stand a ruling that allowed an antitrust exemption given by the Justice Department to Detroit's two major daily newspapers. The exemption permitted a partial merger under the Newspaper Preservation Act of 1970.

Texaco Inc. v. Hasbrouck, decided by a 9-0 vote, June 14, 1990; Stevens wrote the opinion.

A gasoline supplier selling fuel to wholesalers at a price lower than the supplier charged independent retailers violated the Robinson-Patman Act prohibition against price discrimination because it could not show that the price cut was reimbursement for services. Texaco maintained that the price difference was a "functional discount," given a purchaser for performing services such as transportation and storage. The Court said such discounts are legitimate in some cases but that the wholesalers here did not qualify. The Court said there was no evidence that Texaco's lower price to wholesalers reflected a reasonable reimbursement for the value to Texaco for services.

Attorneys

Commissioner, Immigration and Naturalization Service v. Jean, decided by a unanimous vote, June 4, 1990; Stevens wrote the opinion.

Congress intended provisions of the Equal Access to Justice Act to cover the cost of all phases of successful civil litigation under the statute. At issue was a part of the act that directs courts to award fees and other expenses to private parties who prevail in litigation against the United States, if the government's position was not "substantially justified."

The Supreme Court said that once a court determines that the government's position is not justified, a second finding is not necessary for the awarding of costs in any subsequent related litigation. Stevens said the initial finding serves as a "one-time threshold" for fee eligibility.

Cooter & Gell v. Hartmarx Corp., decided by a vote of 8-1, June 11, 1990; O'Connor wrote the opinion; Stevens dissented in part.

A plaintiff who files a baseless complaint cannot escape sanctions under Rule 11 of the Federal Rules of Civil Procedure by asking to have the case dismissed at an early stage of the litigation. Rule 11 requires disciplinary sanctions against lawyers who file frivolous complaints.

The case arose from a breach-of-contract action brought by a subsidiary of Hartmarx Corp. against a discount men's clothing chain. The discounter, represented by the law firm of Cooter & Gell, counterclaimed with an antitrust suit. Soon after, Cooter & Gell filed a notice of voluntary dismissal. But a district court found that the firm still could be subjected to Rule 11 sanctions because the allegations in its antitrust complaint were completely baseless. An appeals court upheld the ruling.

The Supreme Court agreed that, despite a voluntary dismissal, a district court may still grant Rule 11 sanctions. Justice O'Connor said such jurisdiction is necessary as a means of "curbing abuses of the judicial system." However, she said that Rule 11 does not authorize a district court to award attorneys fees incurred on appeal and reversed the portion of the appeals court decision granting attorney's fees.

Keller v. State Bar of California, decided by a unanimous vote, June 4, 1990; Rehnquist wrote the opinion.

A state bar association may not use members' compulsory dues to pay for political activities with which members disagree when the spending is not related to the regulation or improvement of the legal profession. Members of the California state bar contended that using their mandatory dues—a condition of practice in the state—for political causes was a violation of their First Amendment free speech and associational rights.

The Court said that a state bar may require dues but that the scope of the permissible dues-financed activities is limited. Rehnquist said the guiding standard is whether the expenditure is for the purpose of regulating the legal profession or improving the quality of legal services available to the people of a state.

Pavelic & LeFlore v. Marvel Entertainment Group, decided by a 8-1 vote, December 5, 1989; Scalia wrote the opinion; Marshall dissented.

Only the lawyer who signs a court motion or other papers filed in federal district court can be fined under Rule 11 of the Federal Rules of Civil Procedure for violating its prohibitions against meritless filings. The signing attorney's law firm cannot be sanctioned even if the lawyer signed pleadings on behalf of the firm, the Court said. Rule 11, which was intended to deter frivolous lawsuits, requires at least one attorney of record to sign court papers to certify that he or she believes the filing to be well grounded in fact and law.

This case stemmed from a complaint in a copyright infringement action. When a district court found that the claim could not be substantiated, it awarded $100,000 in sanctions under Rule 11 and ordered the signing attorney's firm to pay half the fine. But the Supreme Court said that Rule 11 is intended to ensure that the attorney signing a pleading has fulfilled his or her individual responsibility for the required certification.

Peel v. Attorney Registration and Disciplinary Commission of Illinois, decided by a 5-4 vote, June 4, 1990; Stevens wrote the opinion; White, O'Connor, Rehnquist, and Scalia dissented.

A lawyer who included on his professional letterhead an accurate notation that he was a "certified civil trial specialist by the National Board of Trial Advocacy" should have been protected by the First Amendment against censure by the Illinois Supreme Court.

The Supreme Court said there was nothing actually or inherently misleading in the lawyer's letterhead. Stevens wrote, "The [disciplinary]

Commission's concern about the possibility of deception in hypothetical cases is not sufficient to rebut the constitutional presumption favoring disclosure over concealment." Marshall wrote separately, saying the ban was unconstitutional, but that the letterhead was "potentially" misleading.

Venegas v. Mitchell, decided by a 9-0 vote, April 18, 1990; White wrote the opinion.

Lawyers who win civil rights cases in federal court and receive fees from the losing party may still collect a portion of a client's award, pursuant to a contingent fee agreement. Federal courts had been divided over whether lawyers working on contingent fees may collect more than a court-ordered award in civil rights cases or whether the court award is the maximum, notwithstanding the client's agreement.

The Supreme Court ruled that federal civil rights law does not invalidate contingent-fee contracts that would require a winning party to pay his attorney more than the statutory award against the losing defendant. The Court said the law was intended to control what a losing defendant must pay, not what a prevailing plaintiff must pay his lawyer.

Bankruptcy

Begier, Trustee v. Internal Revenue Service, decided by a 9-0 vote, June 4, 1990; Justice Marshall wrote the opinion.

A bankruptcy trustee cannot recover withholding and excise tax payments a debtor placed in a trust fund for the Internal Revenue Service before it filed for bankruptcy. The income and FICA taxes were deposited in a special trust fund. The Court held that money from employee-wage deductions becomes the property of the IRS.

After American International Airlines became delinquent in its trust-fund tax payments, the IRS ordered it to deposit all future taxes collected into a separate bank account. Later, after the airlines had filed for bankruptcy, its trustee brought an action against the government to recover the trust-fund taxes. The Supreme Court ruled that bankruptcy trustee had no claim to the federal-tax payments.

Pennsylvania Department of Public Welfare v. Davenport, decided by a 7-2 vote, May 29, 1990; Marshall wrote the opinion; Blackmun and O'Connor dissented.

A person ordered by a court to make criminal restitution may be freed of the obligation if he then declares bankruptcy under Chapter 13 of the federal Bankruptcy Code. Restitution obligations are "debts" under that law, the Court said.

In this case, a couple pleaded guilty to welfare fraud and were ordered by a Pennsylvania state court to make restitution payments. A year later they filed for bankruptcy. The majority said congressional intent is clear that Chapter 13 of the bankruptcy code was to include, and discharge the obligation for, such debts. Dissenting justices said the code should not become "a shield to protect a criminal from punishment for his crime."

United States v. Energy Resources Co., Inc., decided by a 8-1 vote, May 29, 1990; White wrote the opinion; Blackmun dissented.

A bankruptcy judge has the authority to order the Internal Revenue Service to treat a debtor corporation's tax payments as trust fund taxes withheld from employee paychecks. The Supreme Court said a bankruptcy court may order such treatment of tax funds in cases where the bankruptcy court determines that this designation is necessary for the success of a reorganization plan. When an employer fails to make trust fund payments, the government may collect the sums due from the firm's officers.

Commercial Law

Citibank, N.A. v. Wells Fargo Asia Ltd., decided by a 8-1 vote, May 29, 1990; Kennedy wrote the opinion; Stevens dissented.

U.S. banks with branch offices overseas are not liable to depositors after foreign governments freeze and seize those accounts. The case stemmed from economic troubles in the Philippines in 1983. The Court said computerized confirmations used in international banking do not create an agreement to make U.S. banks financially responsible for deposits placed in their overseas branches.

Lewis, Comptroller of the State of Florida v. Continental Bank Corp., decided by a 9-0 vote, March 5, 1990; Scalia wrote the opinion.

The Court declared moot a case involving an Illinois bank holding company's challenge to a Florida banking law that allegedly violated the Commerce Clause. Scalia said the case was rendered moot by 1987 amendments to the federal Bank Holding Company Act, which require that a bank holding company with its principal banking operations in one state may not establish or acquire a bank in another state unless the latter state's statutes specifically authorize it to do so.

Maislin Industries, U.S. Inc. v. Primary Steel, Inc., decided by a 7-2 vote, June 21, 1990; Brennan wrote the opinion; Stevens and Rehnquist dissented.

An Interstate Commerce Commission policy that relieves a shipper of the obligation of paying the filed rate when the shipper and carrier have privately negotiated a lower rate violates the Interstate Commerce Act. The act specifically prohibits a carrier from providing services at any rate other than that filed with the commission, the Court noted. "Although the commission has both the authority and expertise generally to adopt new policies when faced with new developments in the industry . . . it does not have the power to adopt a policy that directly conflicts with its governing statute," Brennan wrote.

Reves v. Ernst & Young, decided by a 5-4 vote, February 21, 1990; Marshall wrote the opinion; Rehnquist, White, O'Connor, and Scalia dissented.

An unsecured promissory note, payable on demand by the holder, is a "security" within the meaning of the Securities Exchange Act of 1934.

The notes were issued by the Farmer's Cooperative of Arkansas and Oklahoma. After the co-op filed for bankruptcy, holders of the notes sued the accounting firm that had audited the co-op's financial statements. They alleged that the firm had intentionally failed to follow generally accepted accounting principles and had inflated the assets and net worth of the co-op. The accounting firm argued that the notes were not "securities" under the 1934 act and that the antifraud provisions did not apply to claims by the noteholders. The act excludes from coverage notes that mature in less than nine months from date issued.

The Court first ruled unanimously that the notes are presumed to be security for purposes of the federal securities laws. It then ruled 5-4 that even though the notes were payable "on demand," they did not fall under an exception to the 1934 law, because the notes can mature at a time far beyond nine months. Dissenting justices contended that a note payable on demand falls within the exception.

Intellectual Property

Eli Lilly & Co. v. Medtronic, Inc., decided by a 6-2 vote, June 18, 1990; Scalia wrote the opinion; Kennedy and White dissented; O'Connor did not participate in the case.

Activities that would otherwise constitute patent infringement are acceptable if they are undertaken to develop and submit to the Food and Drug Administration (FDA) information necessary to obtain marketing approval for medical-device substitutes. Eli Lilly contended that Medtronic infringed its patents by testing and marketing a cardiac-related medical device that included a component on which Eli Lilly held the patent. But the Court said an exemption in patent law that allows firms producing generic drugs to develop substitutes for patented drugs applies to patented medical devices as well.

Stewart v. Abend, Authors Research Co., decided by a 6-3 vote, April 24, 1990; O'Connor wrote the opinion; Stevens, Rehnquist, and Scalia dissented.

The owner of a derivative work infringes on the rights of the owner of the original work by continuing to distribute the derivative work during the copyright's renewal period. The Court said the owners of the movie *Rear Window* must share earnings from the movie's re-release with the copyright owner of the short story on which the movie was based.

The dispute arose from the re-release of Alfred Hitchcock's 1954 classic, which drew from the short story, "It Had to be Murder," written by Cornell Woolrich and first published in 1942. O'Connor said for the Court, "At heart, petitioners' true complaint is that they will have to pay more for the use of works they have employed in creating their own works. But such a result was contemplated by Congress and is consistent with the goals of the Copyright Act."

Taxation

American Trucking Associations, Inc. v. Smith, Director, Arkansas Highway and Transportation Department, decided by a 5-4 vote, June 4, 1990; O'Connor wrote the opinion; Stevens, Brennan, Marshall, and Blackmun dissented.

A state is not required to provide relief for all excessive taxes paid under a state highway-use tax invalidated for discriminating against out-of-state trucking companies. The Court ruled that a 1987 decision voiding Pennsylvania's unapportioned highway-use taxes could be applied only prospectively and that only taxes imposed by states after that decision could be refunded. At issue was an Arkansas tax similar to Pennsylvania's.

The court found that state officials could not have anticipated that the tax would be found unconstitutional. It said the 1987 decision on which this dispute rested was a sharp departure from precedent. This decision limited the scope of a 1990 companion ruling in *McKesson Corporation v. Division of Alcoholic Beverages and Tobacco, Department of Business Regulation of Florida.*

Commissioner of Internal Revenue v. Indianapolis Power & Light Co., decided by a vote of 9-0, January 9, 1990; Blackmun wrote the opinion.

The Internal Revenue Service may not tax as income the deposits utilities charge their customers to ensure payment of future bills. The Indianapolis Power & Light Co. required customers with suspect credit to make such deposits. The IRS contended that the deposits were advance payments for electricity and as such constituted taxable income to the utility on receipt. But the Supreme Court said that the deposits were not fully in the dominion of the utility when they were made, so they could not qualify as taxable income. The Court said the deposits served as security, to be returned when an account is closed, rather than as prepayments of income.

Davis v. United States, decided by a 9-0 vote, May 21, 1990; O'Connor wrote the opinion for the Court.

Parents who gave money to their two sons who were serving as missionaries for the Church of Jesus Christ of Latter-day Saints cannot deduct the funds as charitable contributions because they were not donated for the specific use of the church. The money was for the sons' personal needs. The Internal Revenue Code permits a taxpayer to claim a charitable contribution deduction only if the contribution is made "to or for the use of" a qualified organization. The Court said the church never was directly in control of the funds and the sons were able to use the money as they chose.

Franchise Tax Board of California v. Alcan Aluminium Ltd., decided by a unanimous vote, January 10, 1990; White wrote the opinion.

A foreign company, the sole shareholder of an American subsidiary, lacks standing in federal court to challenge on Foreign Commerce Clause grounds the accounting methods used by a state to determine the locally taxable income of that subsidiary.

The Court also held that a federal action for injunctive and declaratory relief is barred by the Tax Injunction Act of 1982.

Jimmy Swaggart Ministries v. Board of Equalization of California, decided by a unanimous vote, January 17, 1990; O'Connor wrote the opinion.

The constitutional separation of church and state does not bar a state from taxing religious books, tapes, and other materials sold by religious organization. This case involved the Louisiana-based Jimmy Swaggart Ministries and forced the television evangelist to pay back taxes and penalties for the years 1974-1981. The Court said the California sales and use taxes in question do not significantly burden religious practices or cause excessive entanglement with religion so as to be in conflict with the Establishment Clause of the First Amendment.

McKesson Corporation v. Division of Alcoholic Beverages and Tobacco, Department of Business Regulation of Florida, decided by a unanimous Court, June 4, 1990; Brennan wrote the opinion.

A state must provide "meaningful relief" if it collects taxes under a law later found to be unconstitutional. The Court said if a state penalizes a protesting taxpayer for failure to pay taxes on time, requiring him to pay first and obtain review of the tax's validity later, the state must give him sufficient chance to get a refund of taxes paid.

The Court reversed a state court's decision denying a refund after a taxing scheme was found unconstitutional. Brennan wrote, "The state cannot persuasively claim that 'equity' entitles it to retain tax moneys taken unlawfully from petitioner due to its pass-on of the tax where the pass-on itself furthers the very competitive disadvantage constituting the Commerce Clause violation that rendered the deprivation unlawful in the first place." The lawsuit stemmed from a state statute that provided special tax rate reductions for products commonly grown in the state and used in alcoholic beverages produced there.

Portland Golf Club v. Commissioner of Internal Revenue, decided by a 9-0 vote, June 21, 1990; Blackmun wrote the opinion.

A social club, in calculating its liability for federal income taxes, may not offset losses incurred by selling food and drink to nonmembers against income realized from investments unless it had tried to sell the food and drink for profit.

By 6-3, the Court then held that in ascertaining whether social clubs' nonmember activities are for profit, tax authorities must determine whether clubs have apportioned fixed costs between member and non-member sales according to the same method used to compute profits. Dissenting from that part of the opinion were Kennedy, joined by O'Connor and Scalia, stating that a "taxpayer's profit motive . . . cannot turn upon the particular accounting method" chosen.

United States v. Dalm, decided by a 6-3 vote, March 20, 1990; Kennedy wrote the opinion; Stevens, Brennan, and Marshall dissented.

The doctrine of equitable recoupment does not apply to a taxpayer who waits too long before filing for a refund of a gift tax paid, in addition to income taxes assessed, on the same transfer of money. In this case, the taxpayer treated money received from her deceased employer's estate as a gift and paid gift tax on the transfer. Some years later the government contended that the money she had received was for her services as administratix of the estate and should have been reported as income.

The taxpayer eventually agreed to a settlement, then filed an administrative claim for refund of money paid in gift tax, interest and penalties. Her claim was filed after the statute of limitations had run. When she litigated the original dispute within the statutory period she had not raised a recoupment claim.

United States v. Goodyear Tire & Rubber Co., decided unanimously, December 11, 1989; Marshall wrote the opinion.

"Accumulated profits," defined in the indirect tax credit provision of the Internal Revenue Code of 1954, are to be measured according to United States tax principles, not foreign tax principles, when claimed by a multinational corporation's foreign subsidiary. Marshall wrote for the Court: "[T]ax provisions should generally be read to incorporate domestic tax concepts absent a clear congressional expression that foreign concepts control. This canon has particularly strong application here where a contrary interpretation would leave an important statutory goal regarding equal tax treatment of foreign subsidiaries and foreign branches to the varying tax policies of foreign tax authorities."

Civil Procedure

Carden v. Arkoma Associates, decided by a 5-4 vote, February 27, 1990; Scalia wrote the opinion; O'Connor, Brennan, Marshall, and Blackmun dissented.

The state citizenship of each limited partner must be considered in determining diversity of citizenship among the parties in federal court disputes. The Court rejected arguments that only the citizenship of a limited partnership's general partners need be considered to preserve diversity. Dissenting justices maintained that limited partners are not real parties to a controversy and should not be considered for purposes of diversity jurisdiction.

Ferens v. John Deere Co., decided by a 5-4 vote, March 5, 1990; Kennedy wrote the opinion; Scalia, Brennan, Marshall, and Blackmun dissented.

In diversity jurisdiction cases, when a plaintiff seeks to transfer a case from one state to another, the new court must follow the rules of law that prevailed where the case began. Diversity cases involve parties who, because they are from different states, are allowed to litigate state-law claims in federal court. This dispute arose after a farmer who lost his arm in a combine filed two separate lawsuits against a manufacturer: a contract and warranty claim in federal district court in Pennsylvania, a tort claim in district court in Mississippi, based on advantageous law in each state. He then sought to transfer the Mississippi lawsuit to Pennsylvania but to retain Mississippi law.

A 1964 Supreme Court ruling had established that when a defendant initiates the transfer, the rules of law from the transferor jurisdiction apply. In this case, the Court said that no matter who initiates the transfer, the law of the state where the lawsuit began should prevail.

Kaiser Aluminum & Chemical Corp. v. Bonjorno, Bonjorno v. Kaiser Aluminum & Chemical Corp., decided by a 5-4 vote, April 17, 1990; O'Connor wrote the opinion; White, Brennan, Marshall, and Blackmun dissented.

Postjudgment interest runs from the date of entry of the court's judgment, not the date of the jury verdict. The dispute arose from an antitrust case in which the stockholders of an aluminum pipe fabrication company sued Kaiser in district court alleging that Kaiser had monopolized the market for such pipe in violation of the Sherman Act. Judgment for the pipe company on a jury verdict and damages was initially entered in 1979. The Court, however, held a limited retrial on the issue of damages, and a final judgment on damages was entered in 1981. The 1981 date applied.

W. S. Kirkpatrick & Co., Inc. v. Environmental Tectonics Corp., International, decided by a 9-0 vote, January 17, 1990; Scalia wrote the opinion.

U.S. courts have jurisdiction over lawsuits involving charges that foreign officials acted unlawfully in carrying out their official duties. The Court said the "act of state doctrine" did not apply in this bribery case because nothing in the dispute required a judge to declare invalid the official act of a foreign sovereign. Writing for the unanimous Court, Scalia said the act of state doctrine concerns the validity of foreign sovereign acts and does not establish an exception for cases that may simply embarrass foreign governments because of the wrongdoing of their representatives.

Northbrook National Insurance Co. v. Brewer, decided by an 8-1 vote, November 7, 1989; Marshall wrote the opinion; Stevens dissented.

The "direct action" proviso of federal law that says in a case against a liability insurer, the insurer shall be considered a citizen of the same state as the insured for purposes of diversity jurisdiction, does not apply to a workers compensation lawsuits brought in federal court by insurance companies.

The ruling allowed an Illinois insurance firm to proceed in federal court to challenge a worker compensation award granted to a Texas man. Marshall said the language of the proviso is unambiguously limited to actions brought against insurers and does not apply when the insurance companies are bringing the lawsuit.

Tafflin v. Levitt, decided unanimously, January 22, 1990; O'Connor wrote the opinion.

State courts have concurrent jurisdiction over civil actions brought under the federal Racketeer Influenced and Corrupt Organizations Act (RICO). Appeals courts had been split on whether federal courts have exclusive jurisdiction over RICO actions. O'Connor said nothing in the language of RICO or its legislative history suggests that Congress had intended to divest state courts of jurisdiction to hear civil RICO claims.

United States v. Munoz-Flores, decided unanimously, May 21, 1990; Marshall wrote the opinion.

The 1984 Victims of Crime Act, which requires a "special assessment" penalty on any person convicted of a federal misdemeanor, was not enacted in violation of the Origination Clause of the Constitution because it is not a "bill for raising revenue," the Court said. The Origination Clause says "[a]ll bills for raising revenue shall originate in the House of Representatives." The law in question here began in the Senate.

The defendant was found guilty of two counts of aiding the entry of illegal aliens to the United States and fined $25 on each count. He contended the fine was unconstitutional because it arose from a bill for raising revenue that had originated in the Senate. In reversing an appeals court ruling that the law was invalid, Marshall wrote that the act was not a revenue measure within the meaning of the clause because it supported a special program and not general government operations. The Court also rejected an argument by the Bush administration that the case presented a political question that exempted it from judicial scrutiny.

Criminal Law

Capital Punishment

Blystone v. Pennsylvania, decided by a 5-4 vote, February 28, 1990; Rehnquist wrote the opinion; Brennan, Marshall, Blackmun, and Stevens dissented.

States may make capital punishment the only possible sentence for some murders without violating Supreme Court rulings against a mandatory death penalty, as long as a jury is allowed to consider all relevant mitigating evidence.

The Court upheld a Pennsylvania law that said after finding a murder suspect guilty, a jury "must" impose a death sentence if it finds at least one aggravating circumstance and no countervailing mitigating circumstance.

Rehnquist wrote that the law does not make the death penalty automatic. He said a death sentence is imposed only after a jury finds whatever aggravating circumstances exist outweigh any mitigating circumstances or that there are no mitigating circumstances.

Boyde v. California, decided by a 5-4 vote, March 5, 1990; Rehnquist wrote the opinion; Marshall, Brennan, Blackmun, and Stevens dissented.

A sentencing jury in a capital case may be told it can consider a list of specific mitigating circumstances and "any other circumstances which extenuate the gravity of the crime." The majority said that such an instruction does not stop jurors from weighing mitigating factors such as the defendant's background even if those factors do not lessen the gravity of the crime.

Rehnquist said the Constitution does not guarantee unrestricted sentencing discretion in the jury. He said states are free to structure consideration of mitigating evidence in a way that produces "a more rational and equitable administration of the death penalty."

Clemons v. Mississippi, decided by a 5-4 vote, March 28, 1990; White wrote the opinion; Brennan, Blackmun, Marshall, and Stevens dissented.

An appellate court may reweigh aggravating and mitigating evidence from a murder trial to uphold a death sentence that was based in part on an invalid aggravating circumstance.

Mississippi law allowed juries to consider as an aggravating circumstance for the death penalty acts that were "especially heinous, atrocious or cruel." The Supreme Court ruled that standard unconstitutionally vague.

But White said for the majority that an appeals court could preserve a jury's sentence of death by performing its own balancing of other aggravating and mitigating circumstances.

In a dissent, Blackmun said that a capital defendant's right to present mitigating evidence cannot be fully realized if that evidence is submitted only in a paper record. "I also believe that, if a sentence of death is to be imposed, it should be pronounced by a decision maker who will look upon the face of the defendant as he renders judgment."

McKoy v. North Carolina, decided 6-3, March 5, 1990; Marshall wrote the opinion; Scalia, Rehnquist, and O'Connor dissented. (Kennedy concurred only in the judgment.)

A state death penalty law may not require that jurors be instructed to consider only mitigating circumstances that they unanimously agree exist. Mitigating circumstances are factors that could lead jurors to impose a lesser sentence than death.

The Court held that the unanimity requirement was unconstitutional because it prevented the jury from considering all mitigating evidence.

Walton v. Arizona, decided by a 5-4 vote, June 27, 1990; White wrote the opinion; Brennan, Marshall, Blackmun, and Stevens dissented.

An Arizona death sentence law giving a trial judge, rather than the jury, discretion to find aggravating circumstances that justify the death penalty is constitutional. Under Arizona law a judge determines the existence of aggravating and mitigating circumstances. It says he "shall impose" a death sentence if he finds one or more of several enumerated aggravating circumstances and if there are no mitigating circumstances that would dictate leniency.

The Court said the Constitution does not require that every finding of fact underlying a sentencing decision be made by a jury rather than a judge. The majority also said if a murder was committed in an "especially heinous, cruel or depraved" manner, that could be an aggravating factor warranting a death sentence.

Whitmore v. Arkansas, decided by a 7-2 vote, April 24, 1990; Rehnquist wrote the opinion; Marshall and Brennan dissented.

A third party cannot challenge the validity of a death sentence imposed on a defendant who has waived the right to appeal the sentence.

The Court ruled that a fellow death row inmate lacked standing to challenge another inmate's conviction. Rehnquist's opinion quoted from a similar 1901 case: "However friendly he may be to the doomed man and sympathetic for his situation; however concerned he may be lest unconstitutional laws be enforced, and however laudable such sentiments are, the grievance they suffer and feel is not special enough to furnish a cause of action in a case like this."

The petitioning inmate also had claimed standing as an Arkansas citizen to make sure that executions are not carried out in that state without appellate review. Rehnquist, however, said the claim was too general.

Confrontation

Idaho v. Wright, decided by a 5-4 vote, June 27, 1990; O'Connor wrote the opinion; Kennedy, Rehnquist, White, and Blackmun dissented.

Hearsay statements from a child who is unable to testify in an abuse case can be admitted at trial if the child's story is trustworthy. The Court said that the circumstances giving rise to the statements must demonstrate "particularized guarantees of trustworthiness" to be admitted under an exception to the hearsay rule.

In cases in which the defendant cannot confront an accuser, O'Connor wrote, the court must look at all the circumstances surrounding the child's account, including how well the child knew the accused and whether the child would make up the story.

Maryland v. Craig, decided by a 5-4 vote, June 27, 1990; O'Connor wrote the opinion; Scalia, Brennan, Marshall, and Stevens dissented.

States may shield victims of child abuse by allowing them to testify on closed-circuit television rather than face the person accused of abusing them. The Court said the state interest in protecting child witnesses from the trauma of testifying may justify permitting them to answer questions without a face-to-face confrontation with the defendant.

Writing for the Court, O'Connor said it was significant that the Maryland procedure at issue in the case preserved other elements of the confrontation right of the Sixth Amendment: that the child had to be competent to testify and testified under oath; that the defendant had an opportunity for contemporaneous cross-examination; and that the judge, jury, and defendant were able to view the demeanor of the witness as he or she testified.

Criminal Procedure

Collins, Director, Texas Department of Criminal Justice, Institutional Division v. Youngblood, decided by a 9-0 vote, June 21, 1990; Rehnquist wrote the opinion.

A defendant who was both imprisoned and fined for his crime is not entitled to a new trial when a new statute revises the law under which he was sentenced to remove the fine. The court said a state statute that "reforms" an improper sentence does not violate the Ex Post Facto Clause of Article 1 of the Constitution.

The defendant was convicted in Texas state court of aggravated sexual assault and sentenced to life in prison and a $10,000 fine. A subsequent Texas statute revised the law to allow an appellate court to remove the fine.

Holland v. Illinois, decided by 5-4 vote, January 22, 1990; Scalia wrote the opinion; Marshall, Brennan, Blackmun, and Stevens dissented.

A defendant's Sixth Amendment right to be "tried by a representative cross section of the community" is not violated when prosecutors exclude prospective jurors because of their race, in cases in which the defendant is a different race than those excluded.

The defendant was white. None of the jurors was black, and the defendant had objected during jury selection to the state's using peremptory challenges to exclude two black potential jurors. Scalia said the Sixth Amendment requirement of a fair cross section is a way of assuring not a representative jury but an impartial one.

Dissenting justices, joined by Kennedy who concurred in the opinion, raised the possibility that such an exclusion could violate a defendant's Fourteenth Amendment right to equal protection.

Michigan v. Harvey, decided by a 5-4 vote, March 5, 1990; Rehnquist wrote the opinion; Stevens, Brennan, Marshall, and Blackmun dissented.

Even when a criminal defendant is illegally interrogated by police, his responses may be used to contradict his testimony at trial. The Court said the Constitution does not bar the use of illegally obtained statements by prosecutors trying to rebut a defendant's testimony and impeach his credibility. A Michigan appeals court had ruled that statements taken in violation of the defendant's Sixth Amendment right to counsel could not be introduced at trial even for impeachment purposes. Reversing, Rehnquist wrote for the Court that while the prosecution cannot be allowed to build its case against a criminal defendant with illegally obtained evidence, it can use it for impeachment purposes. "If a defendant exercises his right to testify on his own behalf, he assumes a reciprocal obligation to speak truthfully and accurately," the chief justice said.

United States v. Montalvo-Murillo, decided by a 6-3 vote, May 29, 1990; Kennedy wrote the opinion; Stevens, Brennan, and Marshall dissented.

The state's failure to comply with a prompt-hearing provision of a federal bail-reform law does not require that the prisoner then be released. The Court said that a dangerous defendant who would likely be ordered jailed before his trial need not be freed on bail if, in violation of the Bail Reform Act of 1964, he had not been given a pretrial detention hearing at his first judicial appearance.

Kennedy said for the Court that the safety of society should not be forfeited by accidental noncompliance with the statute's time limits.

United States v. Ojeda Rios, decided by a 6-3 vote, April 30, 1990; White wrote the opinion; Stevens, Brennan, and Marshall dissented.

A good-faith misunderstanding of the federal law requiring that recordings obtained through court-authorized wiretaps be sealed as soon as the surveillance ends can be a "satisfactory explanation" for delay in sealing. The Court said that prosecutors in this case believed wrongly, but in good faith, that they were not required to seal the tapes until there was a lull in the whole investigation.

Justice White, writing for the majority, said that excuse cannot meet the legally required "satisfactory explanation" requirement unless it was made at the suppression hearing. The case was remanded to determine whether it was.

The tapes offered as evidence in this case bore seals, but the seals had not been immediately attached as is required by federal law. The seal ensures that the government has no opportunity to tamper with the conversations that have been recorded. The law states that if the tapes do not bear a seal the government must provide a "satisfactory explanation" for its absence.

Washington v. Harper, decided by a 6-3 vote, February 27, 1990; Kennedy wrote the opinion; Stevens, Brennan, and Marshall dissented.

State prison officials may force a mentally ill inmate to take antipsychotic drugs if the inmate is a danger to himself or others and the treatment is in the inmate's medical interest. The Court ruled that mentally ill prisoners are not entitled to a judicial-style hearing before the drugs are given.

Kennedy, writing for the Court, said that under the Constitution's guarantee of due process of law, prisoners have a "significant liberty interest" in being free of unwanted medication. But he said that a state rule allowing for a hearing before a panel composed of prison staff was sufficient. The rule did not provide inmates with lawyers or adhere to evidentiary rules.

Dissenting justices called the prison panel hearing "a mock trial before an institutionally biased tribunal."

Double Jeopardy

Dowling v. United States, decided by a 6-3 vote, January 10, 1990; White wrote the opinion; Brennan, Marshall, and Stevens dissented.

Neither double jeopardy nor Due Process Clause protections bar the use at trial of testimony that relates to a previous alleged crime for which the defendant was acquitted.

The Court said a jury may be told about a defendant's alleged prior criminal conduct even if a previous trial on those charges ended in an acquittal. The Court said the jury is free to assess the truthfulness and significance of the testimony.

Grady, District Attorney of Dutchess County v. Corbin, decided by a 5-4 vote, May 29, 1990; Brennan wrote the opinion; O'Connor, Scalia, Rehnquist, and Kennedy dissented.

The Double Jeopardy Clause of the Fifth Amendment bars a second prosecution for an offense based on conduct for which a defendant already has been prosecuted. Writing for the Court, Brennan said the test is whether the alleged offense is based on the same conduct as was the basis of the earlier charge. He said a defendant should be protected from repeated attempts by prosecutors to convict him for a single action.

In this case a driver was ticketed and fined for the misdemeanors of driving while intoxicated and failing to keep right of the road median. Later, prosecutors who were unaware court action had been underway on the misdemeanors wanted to bring the driver to trial for the death of a driver he allegedly hit in the oncoming lane.

Scalia in a dissent said the Double Jeopardy Clause protects an individual against a second prosecution for the same offense, not the same conduct.

Evidence

James v. Illinois, decided by a 5-4 vote, January 10, 1990; Brennan wrote the opinion; Kennedy, Rehnquist, O'Connor, and Scalia dissented.

Illegally obtained evidence cannot be used to impeach the credibility of defense witnesses. The Court's ruling barred prosecutors from using a murder defendant's own statement—gained illegally—to impeach the credibility of a defense witness who gave an account at odds with the defendant's story.

As a rule prosecutors are not allowed to use illegally seized evidence at trial. An exception to the so-called exclusionary rule allows such evidence to be used to contradict testimony in court by the defendant.

But the Court said the exception does not extend to the testimony of other defense witnesses. Acknowledging that truth is the fundamental goal of the legal system, Brennan added for the majority, "But various constitutional rules limit the means by which government may conduct this search for truth in order to promote other values embraced by the Framers and cherished throughout our nation's history."

New York v. Harris, decided by a 5-4 vote, April 18, 1990; White wrote the opinion; Marshall, Brennan, Blackmun, and Stevens dissented.

A prosecutor is not barred from using a confession made by a defendant after a warrantless arrest in his home, when the statement is taken outside of the home.

The Court said the rule against warrantless arrests in a residence was designed to protect the physical integrity of the home, not to protect criminal suspects from statements made outside their premises. The incriminating statement was uttered at a station house. The Court said that because police officers had probable cause to arrest the murder defendant, he was lawfully in custody when he made the statement.

Habeas Corpus

Butler v. McKellar, decided by a 5-4 vote, March 5, 1990; Rehnquist wrote the opinion; Brennan, Marshall, Blackmun, and Stevens dissented.

A defendant may not challenge his conviction by filing a habeas corpus petition in federal court based on a new constitutional decision that a state appellate court could not reasonably have predicted at the time of the defendant's direct appeal.

Rehnquist wrote that federal courts should not second-guess "reasonable, good faith interpretations of existing precedents made by state courts even though they are shown to be contrary to later decisions." Dissenting justices criticized the opinion, saying that inmates will languish in jail or die "because state courts were reasonable, even though wrong."

The defendant had tried to get his conviction overturned based on a new federal court ruling that said if a suspect had asked for a lawyer in the context of one investigation he may not be interrogated by police, without counsel, in another.

The High Court's decision in this case refined its 1989 ruling in *Teague v. Lane,* which made it harder for a death-row inmate to establish an appeal based on a favorable court ruling issued in another case after his own conviction became final.

Lewis, Director, Arizona Department of Corrections v. Jeffers, decided by a 5-4 decision, June 27, 1990; O'Connor wrote the decision; Blackmun, Brennan, Marshall, and Stevens dissented.

When a state court applies an aggravating factor that has been found constitutionally valid, a federal appeals court—considering the case on collateral review—should not conduct a de novo comparison of the facts of the case with other cases to see whether the aggravating factor should have been applied. The Supreme Court said an appeals court wrongly overturned a state supreme court's finding that a crime was committed in an "especially heinous, cruel or depraved manner."

Saffle, Warden v. Parks, decided by a 5-4 vote, March 5, 1990; Kennedy wrote the opinion; Brennan, Marshall, Blackmun, and Stevens dissented.

A defendant is not entitled to federal habeas corpus review of his sentence when the grounds he asserts involve a "new rule" of law, unless it comes within the narrow—and here inapplicable—exceptions of the Court's ruling in *Teague v. Lane.* The 1989 decision generally bars inmates from basing their petitions for habeas corpus on federal court rulings that have been issued since their convictions became final.

In this case, an inmate whose conviction and death sentence became final in 1983 claimed that an instruction in the penalty phase of his trial, telling the jury to avoid any influence of sympathy, violated the Eighth

Amendment. His argument was based on a 1987 court decision finding the anti-sympathy instruction unconstitutional.

The Supreme Court said good faith interpretations of legal principles at the time of a conviction should be allowed to stand even when later rulings contradict them.

Sawyer v. Smith, Interim Warden, decided by a 5-4 vote, June 21, 1990; Kennedy wrote the opinion; Marshall, Brennan, Blackmun, and Stevens dissented.

A defendant is not entitled to federal habeas corpus relief based on a new, favorable court ruling in another case unless the principle of the new case is "fundamental to the integrity of the criminal proceeding."

The Court said that a 1985 ruling that prohibited the death sentences when jurors are misled about their great responsibility in a capital punishment decision, and which the defendant in this case used as the basis for his petition, should not be applied retroactively.

The Court's opinion further clarified its 1989 decision in *Teague v. Lane,* which restricts defendants' challenges to their convictions based on new court rulings. Dissenting justices in this case said, "This raw preference for finality is unjustified."

Interrogation

Illinois v. Perkins, decided by an 8-1 vote, June 4, 1990; Kennedy wrote the opinion; Marshall dissented.

An undercover police officer posing as an inmate need not give *Miranda* warnings to an incarcerated suspect before asking questions that may elicit an incriminating answer. The Court said the *Miranda* doctrine must be enforced only when there is a coercive atmosphere, for example, when a defendant might feel compelled to speak by the fear of reprisal for remaining silent or in the hope of more lenient treatment should he confess. It said *Miranda* warnings are not required when the suspect is unaware that he is speaking to a police officer and volunteers a statement.

The case involved a defendant who implicated himself in a murder while talking to an undercover agent who was placed in his cell as part of the murder investigation. The Court said *Miranda* does not forbid authorities' taking advantage of a suspect's misplaced trust under the described circumstances.

Pennsylvania v. Muniz, decided by a vote of 8-1, June 18, 1990; Brennan wrote the opinion; Marshall dissented.

Videotaped sobriety tests can be used as evidence in a trial even when the person arrested is not given a *Miranda* warning.

By an 8-1 vote, the Court said police may videotape suspects answering routine "booking" questions, including name, address, height, weight, eye color, date of birth, and age, without first telling them they have a right to remain silent. The majority acknowledged that in this case the arrestee's slurred speech as he answered the questions was incriminating. But it said the speech was physical evidence, not evidence that it regards as "testimonial." Other examples of physical evidence are a suspect's blood or handwriting sample.

Separately, by a 5-4 vote, the Court said that a "testimonial" response to one of the videotaped questions should have been excluded from evidence. The suspect had been stumped after being asked if he knew the date of his sixth birthday. Brennan said the defendant's response should have been suppressed at trial. Unlike the other routine questions, this answer was "testimonial," Brennan wrote, because it could imply "that his mental state was confused."

Joining Brennan in this part of the opinion were Marshall, O'Connor, Scalia, and Kennedy. Dissenting from this portion were Rehnquist, White, Blackmun, and Stevens.

Restitution

Hughey v. United States, decided by a 9-0 vote, May 21, 1990; Marshall wrote the opinion.

A defendant who is ordered to make restitution under the 1982 Victim and Witness Protection Act may be ordered to make payments only for the loss stemming from his conviction.

In this case a defendant had agreed in a deal with prosecutors to plead guilty to using one unauthorized credit card. But the district court ordered the defendant to pay restitution for losses relating to his alleged theft of twenty-one credit cards.

Reversing the sentence, the Supreme Court held that Congress intended in the victim-restitution act to authorize restitution only for the loss caused by the specific conduct on which the conviction is based.

Search and Seizure

Alabama v. White, decided by a 6-3 vote, June 11, 1990; White wrote the opinion; Stevens, Brennan, and Marshall dissented.

Police officers who received and corroborated an anonymous tip had reasonable suspicion to stop a driver whom they discovered carrying illegal drugs. The decision reversed an Alabama appeals court ruling that a trial court should have suppressed evidence of marijuana and cocaine found on the defendant because the officers had no legitimate justification for stopping her car.

The Supreme Court said the tip alone would not have warranted the stop. But the majority noted that the tip was sufficiently detailed and matched particulars that the officers themselves observed. In a dissent,

Stevens wrote, "Under the court's holding, every citizen is subject to being seized and questioned by any officer who is prepared to testify that the warrantless stop was based on an anonymous tip predicting whatever conduct the officer just observed."

Florida v. Wells, decided by a unanimous vote, April 18, 1990; Rehnquist wrote the opinion.

When a state jurisdiction has no Highway Patrol policy regarding the opening of closed containers found during an inventory search, the opening of any boxes, suitcases, or other containers violates the Fourth Amendment's protection against unreasonable searches and seizures. At issue was the inventorying of containers found in impounded vehicles.

The Court said marijuana discovered in a suitcase in a car that had been seized by police was inadmissible because there was no local police policy governing which closed containers could be opened during such searches.

Horton v. California, decided by a 7-2 vote, June 4, 1990; Stevens wrote the opinion; Brennan and Marshall dissented.

Police who have entered a home without a proper search warrant may seize evidence in plain view even if the discovery of the evidence was not inadvertent. Stevens, who wrote for the Court, said that although inadvertence is a characteristic of most legitimate "plain view" seizures, it is not a necessary condition.

Stevens said two critical tests are whether the police had a right to be on the premises when the discovery was made and whether police were able to recognize immediately the incriminating nature of the object. The warrant that the officers used to gain entry was for stolen items and not for weapons used in the robbery, which were found in the search.

Illinois v. Rodriguez, decided by a 6-3 vote, June 21, 1990; Scalia wrote the opinion; Marshall, Brennan, and Stevens dissented.

Police may enter a residence without a warrant based on the consent of a third party who the police, at the time of entry, reasonably believe to possess authority over the premises but who in fact does not. In this case, the individual who allowed officers into the home had lived there but had since moved out.

Writing for the Court, Scalia said officers must act responsibly in evaluating the situation and they need not always be correct. He said a determination of consent to enter must be objectively made: "[W]ould the facts available to the officer at the moment warrant a man of reasonable caution [to believe] that the consenting party had authority over the premises?"

Maryland v. Buie, decided by a 7-2 vote, February 28, 1990; White wrote the opinion; Brennan and Marshall dissented.

A police officer without a search warrant may make a protective sweep of a house if, after making an in-home arrest, he reasonably believes he is in danger. The Court authorized a warrantless search only when justified by a "reasonable, articulable suspicion" that someone dangerous is in the house.

White said the search may extend only to a cursory inspection of places where a person may be hiding.

Michigan Department of State Police v. Sitz, decided by a 6-3 vote, June 14, 1990; Rehnquist wrote the opinion; Brennan, Marshall, and Stevens dissented.

Police may stop and examine drivers for signs of drunkenness at highway checkpoints. The Court said a state's interest in preventing drunken driving outweighs the intrusion on motorists who are briefly stopped at the sobriety checkpoints.

The majority opinion said that although Fourth Amendment protection was implicated, the checkpoints are not unreasonable "seizures" because states have a strong interest in deterring drunken driving, the checkpoints advance that interest, and the intrusion on motorists stopped is "slight."

All fifty states and the District of Columbia had tried some form of drunken-driver checkpoint. But lower courts, including in the Michigan case, had struck down the practice as infringements on the Fourth Amendment's protection against "unreasonable searches and seizures."

Rehnquist stressed for the Court that there had been no allegations of unreasonable treatment of anyone after being detained at a particular checkpoint. He said this case challenged only the use of sobriety checkpoints generally.

In a dissent, Brennan cited a Fourth Amendment protection not only to be free from police intrusion but a "right to be let alone." He said, "In the face of the 'momentary evil' of drunken driving, the Court today abdicates its role of protector of that fundamental right."

Minnesota v. Olson, decided by a 7-2 vote, April 18, 1990; White wrote the opinion; Rehnquist and Blackmun dissented.

An overnight house guest has a legitimate expectation of privacy and is entitled to Fourth Amendment protection against police intrusion on the house. The defendant in this case was a suspect in a gas station robbery-homicide. Police, who did not have a warrant for his arrest, entered the home of his acquaintance and found the defendant hiding in a closet.

Shortly after his arrest, the defendant made an incriminating statement that he argued should have been suppressed at trial because of the illegality of the arrest.

The Supreme Court ruled that the defendant had a sufficient interest in the home to challenge the legality of his warrantless arrest there. In extending the same protections of homeowners to their guests, White said, "Staying overnight in another's home is a longstanding social custom that serves functions recognized as valuable by society."

United States v. Verdugo-Urquidez, decided by a 5-4 vote, February 28, 1990; Rehnquist wrote the opinion; Brennan, Marshall, Blackmun, and Stevens dissented.

U.S. law-enforcement agents operating without warrants may search a foreigner's property in a foreign country without violating the Fourth Amendment's prohibition against unreasonable searches and seizures. In a broadly worded opinion, Rehnquist said that the Fourth Amendment's protection for "the people" extends "to a class of persons who are part of a national community or who have otherwise developed sufficient connection with this country to be considered part of that community." He said Fourth Amendment protection differs from that of the Fifth Amendment, for example, which applies to all criminal defendants.

The accused in this case was arrested in Mexico and brought back to the United States on drug charges. Before his trial, U.S. agents searched his Mexico residence and found evidence that the defendant had smuggled drugs into the United States. The Supreme Court's ruling overturned a federal appeals court that made no distinction between foreigners and American citizens and had excluded from trial evidence seized in a warrantless search in Mexico.

The vote was 5-4 in support of Rehnquist's broad opinion. Stevens concurred in the judgment but on narrower grounds. He said the foreign defendant was entitled to Fourth Amendment protection, but said that the search of his home, which occurred with the cooperation of Mexican authorities, was not "unreasonable," as defined by the amendment.

Self-Incrimination

Baltimore City Department of Social Services v. Bouknight, Maurice M. v. Bouknight, decided by a 7-2 vote, February 20, 1990; O'Connor wrote the opinion; Marshall and Brennan dissented.

A mother who has custody of her child through a court order cannot assert a Fifth Amendment privilege against self-incrimination to defend her refusal to produce the child. The Court said the mother in this case could be jailed until she revealed the whereabouts of her son, who authorities suspected was dead.

The child had been taken from the mother because of suspected child abuse. A Baltimore social services agency had returned custody to the mother but under certain conditions. When it became clear that the mother was not abiding by those conditions, the agency got a court order to take back the child. But the mother refused to reveal where her boy was and cited the Fifth Amendment.

In her opinion for the majority, O'Connor said a person whose custody derives from a court order may not claim the amendment's protection. She relied on cases that hold that the privilege does not cover orders for the production of documents—or in this case, an individual—kept "for the benefit of the public."

Miscellaneous Criminal Cases

Taylor v. United States, decided by a 9-0 vote, May 29, 1990; Blackmun wrote the opinion.

An offense constitutes a "burglary" under federal law if, regardless of its definition in state codes, it has the basic elements of a "generic" burglary: an unlawful entry into a building or other structure with intent to commit a crime.

At issue was the interpretation of a comprehensive sentencing law Congress passed in 1986. It dictated that defendants convicted of three previous felonies be given longer sentences because of their past crimes. Congress omitted a definition of burglary, causing problems for prosecutors who sought to use prior burglary convictions a basis for enhanced prison terms.

Due Process

Burnham v. Superior Court of California, County of Marin (Burnham, Real Party in Interest), decided by a 9-0 vote, May 29, 1990; Scalia wrote a plurality opinion.

The Due Process Clause of the Fourteenth Amendment does not deny state courts jurisdiction over a nonresident who was personally served with process while temporarily in the state.

In this case a New Jersey resident was served with a California court summons and his estranged wife's divorce petition during a trip to California to conduct business and visit his children. He contended that the Due Process Clause of the Fourteenth Amendment prohibited California courts from asserting jurisdiction over him because he lacked "minimum contacts" with the state. Scalia wrote that jurisdiction based on physical presence alone constitutes due process.

United States Department of Labor v. Triplett, Committee on Legal Ethics of the West Virginia State Bar v. Triplett, decided unanimously, March 27, 1990; Scalia wrote the opinion.

A federal requirement that lawyer fees paid by coal miners seeking relief under the Black Lung Benefits Act of 1972 be approved by the Labor Department does not violate the due process rights of the miners. The Court said the regulation does not deprive claimants of adequate legal assistance.

The West Virginia Supreme Court had ruled that the requirement made it too difficult for miners to get a lawyer's help.

Employment Law

Antidiscrimination Issues

Hoffmann-La Roche Inc. v. Sperling, decided by a vote of 7-2, December 11, 1989; Kennedy wrote the opinion; Scalia and Rehnquist dissented.

In an age-discrimination class action, a federal judge may authorize and help in giving notice to potential plaintiffs. The Supreme Court said such authority would help avoid multiple lawsuits. It held that a judge may issue orders allowing the discovery of names and addresses of similarly situated plaintiffs but stressed that the court must avoid appearing to endorse the merits of the claim.

Writing for the Court, Kennedy emphasized that its decision does not mean that trial courts have "unbridled discretion" in managing age-discrimination complaints. "Court intervention in the notice process for case management purposes is distinguishable in form and function from the solicitation of claims," he said. Dissenting justices contended there was no source of authority for such an exercise of federal judicial power.

Lytle v. Household Manufacturing, Inc., Schwitzer Turbochargers, decided unanimously, March 20, 1990; Marshall wrote the opinion.

A district court's resolution of issues raised by a petitioner's equitable claims does not bar relitigation of the same issues before a jury in the context of legal claims. The Court said the Seventh Amendment right to a jury trial prevents according collateral estoppel effect to a district court's ruling on issues common to both legal and equitable claims where the court resolved the equitable claims after erroneously dismissing the legal claims.

The case involved a black worker who filed a discrimination charge against his employer under Title VII of the Civil Rights Act of 1964 and under Section 1981 of Title 42 of the U.S. Code. Title VII provides equitable relief and does not allow for a jury trial; Section 1981, the basis of legal claims for money damages, entitles a claimant to a jury trial.

University of Pennsylvania v. Equal Employment Opportunity Commission, decided by a unanimous vote, January 9, 1990; Blackmun wrote the opinion.

A university does not enjoy a special privilege, grounded in either the common law or the First Amendment, against disclosure of faculty peer review materials that are relevant to charges of racial or sexual discrimination. The case arose after the University of Pennsylvania denied tenure to an associate professor, who then sued the school alleging she was the victim of discrimination based on her race, sex, and national origin.

In investigating the professor's complaint, the Equal Employment Opportunity Commission sought confidential peer review letters written by her evaluators in the tenure matter. The university contended there was a common-law privilege against disclosure of the confidential letters, and it also asserted a First Amendment right of "academic freedom" against wholesale disclosure of the contested documents.

The Supreme Court rejected both contentions. To university arguments that disclosure would have a "chilling effect" on other tenure evaluators, Blackmun said for the unanimous Court, "Although it is possible that some evaluators may become less candid as the possibility of disclosure increases, others may simply ground their evaluations in specific examples and illustrations in order to deflect potential claims of bias or unfairness. Not all academics will hesitate to stand up and be counted when they evaluate their peers."

Yellow Freight System, Inc. v. Donnelly, decided unanimously, April 17, 1990; Stevens wrote the opinion.

Federal courts do not have exclusive jurisdiction over job-discrimination claims filed under Title VII of the 1964 Civil Rights Act. The ruling allowed a Title VII sex discrimination complaint to be filed in state court.

The Court said the fact that Title VII contains no language that expressly confines jurisdiction to federal courts or deprives state courts of their jurisdiction is strong evidence that Congress did not intend to divest state courts of concurrent jurisdiction.

Ethics in Government

Crandon v. United States, Boeing Co. v. United States, decided unanimously, February 27, 1990; Stevens wrote the opinion.

A federal law that makes it a crime for a private party to supplement a government worker's salary does not cover funds paid before the individual actually begins federal work. The 1962 ethics law in question was intended to ensure the independence and loyalty of public workers. The unanimous ruling involved severance bonuses Boeing Company had paid to five high-level executives who accepted jobs at the Department of Defense.

The Court said an individual must be on the government payroll before that worker or the private firm involved can be held liable. Writing for the Court, Stevens said the law was not intended to be a disincentive to private sector workers who might join the government. He added that in construing a criminal statute, the justices were bound to resolve questions in favor of the defendants until and unless Congress plainly states that its intent has been misconstrued.

The Justice Department had maintained that Boeing made the $485,000 in severance payments solely because the employees were going to work for the government, with which the giant aircraft firm regularly contracted. Boeing had asserted that the money was for past performance and argued that the government was not entitled to penalties because none of the defendants had given Boeing preferential treatment while in government.

Labor Relations

Breininger v. Sheet Metal Workers International Association Local Union No. 6, decided by votes of 9-0 and 7-2, December 5, 1989; Brennan wrote the opinion; Stevens and Scalia dissented.

The National Labor Relations Board does not have exclusive jurisdiction over a union member's claim that his union both breached its duty of fair representation and engaged in hiring hall discrimination. The Court ruled unanimously that the member may sue the union in federal court. It said even if a breach of duty of fair representation might also be an unfair labor practice—a matter governed by the board—a federal court still has jurisdiction over the fair-representation claim.

By a 7-2 vote the Court also held that in this case the union member had not stated a claim. He had alleged that the union passed him over for job referrals because he had supported political rivals of union officials. The Court said that even if he had been discriminated against because of his political opposition, the action did not qualify as "discipline" in violation of labor law.

Chauffeurs, Teamsters and Helpers, Local No. 391 v. Terry, decided by a 6-3 vote, March 20, 1990; Marshall wrote the opinion; Kennedy, O'Connor, and Scalia dissented.

An employee who sues for back pay as a remedy for a union's alleged denial of fair representation has a right to a jury trial. The Court said that the remedy of back pay is "legal" in nature, as opposed to an equitable remedy. The Seventh Amendment entitles a plaintiff to a jury trial when a legal right is at stake.

Fair-representation complaints typically are tried without a jury because the plaintiff usually seeks equitable relief, for example, an injunction to stop a discriminatory practice. The complaint was brought by twenty-seven truck drivers who had been continually laid off and who alleged that the union failed to adequately handle their grievance.

Department of the Treasury, Internal Revenue Service v. Federal Labor Relations Authority, decided by a 6-3 vote, April 17, 1990; Scalia wrote the opinion; Brennan, Marshall, and Stevens dissented.

A federal agency, in this case the Internal Revenue Service, is not compelled by the Civil Service Reform Act of 1978 to negotiate with federal employee unions over how to resolve disputes stemming from the government policy of "contracting out," the buying of goods and services from private businesses. Scalia said the act plainly states that it is not intended to interfere with agency officials' authority to make their own decisions on contracting out.

Fort Stewart Schools v. Federal Labor Relations Authority, decided unanimously, May 29, 1990; Scalia wrote the opinion.

The Department of Defense must bargain with unions over wages and fringe benefits paid to civilian teachers at Army-run schools. The salaries of most federal workers are set by pay schedules, and those workers are prohibited from negotiating over salaries. But some workers, including school teachers, are not covered by the schedules. The Court ruled the Federal Labor Relations Authority acted properly in requiring collective bargaining for teachers at two schools at Fort Stewart in Georgia.

Golden State Transit Corp. v. City of Los Angeles, decided by a 6-3 vote, December 5, 1989; Stevens wrote the opinion; Kennedy, Rehnquist, and O'Connor dissented.

A city may be held liable for money damages in a federal court action if it illegally interferes in labor negotiations. The Court said a taxi cab company that was denied a franchise renewal permit by the City of Los Angeles because the company was in a labor dispute could sue for compensatory damages under Section 1983 of Title 42 of the U.S. Code. Section 1983 provides a federal remedy for "the deprivation of any rights, privileges, or immunities secured by the Constitution and laws."

The Court said federal labor law created "rights" in labor and management that are protected against government interference and may be the basis for a claim in federal court. The Supreme Court said that although the National Labor Relations Board has exclusive jurisdiction to hear disputes involving unfair labor practices, it has no authority to deal with claims of government interference.

National Labor Relations Board v. Curtin Matheson Scientific, Inc., decided by a 5-4 vote, April 17, 1990; Marshall wrote the opinion; Blackmun, Scalia, O'Connor, and Kennedy dissented.

The National Labor Relations Board may refuse to presume that strikebreakers oppose the union that represents the striking workers when the board evaluates an employer's claim that the union does not have majority support. Such questions arise when an employer withdraws recognition of a union after new workers are hired.

Marshall said that replacement employees may want union representation despite their willingness to cross the picket line. He said the board's refusal to presume the sentiments of replacement workers was rationally directed at protecting the bargaining process. The dissent said such workers' interests typically are inimical to unions.

United Steelworkers of America, AFL-CIO-CLC v. Rawson, decided by a vote of 6-3, May 14, 1990; White wrote the opinion, Kennedy, Rehnquist, and Scalia dissented.

A wrongful death claim brought under state law against a miners' union for negligence in mine safety is preempted by the Labor Management Relations Act. The Court said union members (or, in this case, their heirs) cannot sue a union in state court over an alleged failure to live up to its collectively bargained duties, which included inspecting the mine safety. The claim arose from a 1972 Idaho silver mine disaster that killed ninety-one people. Relatives of the dead miners alleged that the deaths were caused by union negligence in failing to point out or to correct safety problems such as corroded oxygen equipment.

Dissenting justices disagreed with the majority that the heirs' claim rested on the collective bargaining agreement.

Patronage

Rutan v. Republican Party of Illinois, Frech v. Rutan, decided by a 5-4 vote, June 21, 1990; Brennan wrote the opinion; Scalia, Rehnquist, Kennedy, and O'Connor dissented.

Hiring, promotion, and transfer policies based on political party affiliation violate the First Amendment rights of public employees unless party membership is "an appropriate requirement" for the job. *(See entry, p. 19; excerpts, p. 134)*

Pensions

Guidry v. Sheet Metal Workers National Pension Fund, decided unanimously, January 17, 1990; Blackmun wrote the opinion.

A union official found guilty of embezzlement may not be forced to repay the union with his pension benefits. The Court said that a federal law's prohibition against transfer of pension benefits prevents a district court from imposing a constructive trust on a pension fund.

After the union official pleaded guilty to embezzlement, a federal judge ordered the defendant's pension benefits placed in a special trust to repay the union. A federal appeals court upheld the decision. But the Supreme Court reversed, saying that the constructive trust violated the Employee Retirement Income Security Act of 1974 (ERISA). The justices said Congress intended to protect the income for pensioners even if it prevents others from obtaining relief from the funds for the wrongs done them.

Pension Benefit Guaranty Corporation v. LTV Corp., decided by a vote of 8-1, June 18, 1990; Blackmun wrote the opinion; Stevens dissented.

The Pension Benefit Guaranty Corporation (PBGC) does not have to follow federal bankruptcy and labor laws in deciding whether to restore a terminated pension plan under the Employee Retirement Income

Security Act (ERISA). The PBGC is a federal insurer of private pension benefits.

The Court upheld the PBGC's order to LTV Corporation to reassume liability for more than $2 billion in pension benefits that the company stopped funding when it filed for Chapter 11 bankruptcy reorganization. The Court said the pension board had a right to focus only on ERISA in making the restoration decision and affirmed the government's authority to order corporations to reinstate terminated retirement plans.

Workers' Compensation

Adams Fruit Co., Inc. v. Barrett, decided unanimously, March 21, 1990; Marshall wrote the opinion.

Migrant farm workers may sue their employer under a federal migrant protection law, even after they have recovered state workers compensation benefits. The farm workers in this case were injured in an accident while they were traveling to work in their employer's overloaded van. They sued in federal court alleging that the employer had violated the motor-vehicle safety provisions of the Migrant and Seasonal Agricultural Worker Protection Act.

The employer argued that its liability should be governed only by the state workers compensation law. But the Supreme Court said the federal act, which allows a private right of action, makes clear that a state workers compensation law is not the only system for safeguarding migrant workers.

Chesapeake & Ohio Railway Co. v. Schwalb; Norfolk & Western Railway Co. v. Goode, decided unanimously, November 28, 1989; White wrote the opinion.

Railway workers who were injured while doing work essential to the loading process are covered by the Longshoremen's and Harbor Workers' Compensation Act. The act is not limited to those who actually handle cargo, the Court said.

The rail employees who brought the lawsuits were hurt while working at coal-loading terminals in Virginia, but their injuries were sustained while they were cleaning and maintaining equipment, not handling cargo.

Justice White said that maintenance of equipment is essential to keeping the machines running. Because the injuries were covered by the Longshoremen's and Harbor Workers' Compensation Act, which provides for an exclusive remedy, the Court said the workers may not sue under the Federal Employers' Liability Act, which provides a negligence cause of action for railroad employees.

Miscellaneous Employment Law Case

English v. General Electric Co., decided unanimously, June 4, 1990; Blackmun wrote the opinion.

A laboratory technician at a nuclear plant who complained about safety violations and then was fired may sue the employer under state tort law pertaining to retaliatory discharge. The Court said the worker's complaint did not fall within a field preempted by the federal Energy Reorganization Act of 1974.

At issue was whether the technician's claim of emotional distress was so related to the radiological safety aspect involved in the operation of a nuclear facility that it must be heard under the 1974 act. That law protects nuclear industry whistleblowers from retaliation by employers but does not provide awards of punitive damages as state laws do. The Court ruled that the claim related to the technician's dismissal did not directly implicate nuclear safety issues.

Environmental Law

General Motors Corp. v. United States, decided unanimously, June 14, 1990; Blackmun wrote the opinion.

The Environmental Protection Agency (EPA) reserves the right to penalize a business for air pollution even if the agency has delayed ruling on state-authorized revisions by the companies to remedy the pollution problem. The Court said there is nothing in federal law that limits the EPA's authority to enforce antipollution rules solely in those cases in which the EPA has not unreasonably delayed action on state plan revisions for implementing the Clean Air Act. The Court said the EPA can enforce an existing state plan while a revision of it is pending before the agency.

Hallstrom v. Tillamook County, decided by a 7-2 vote, November 7, 1989; O'Connor wrote the opinion; Marshall and Brennan dissented.

A provision in the 1976 Resource Conservation and Recovery Act, which dictates that people who want to sue under the act notify the state and Environmental Protection Agency at least sixty days before filing, is mandatory and cannot be disregarded by district courts. The High Court ruled that when the sixty-day requirement is not met, a district court should dismiss the lawsuit.

The case involved a complaint by the owners of a commercial dairy farm in Oregon against a sanitary landfill near the farm. The farm owners had argued that the statute should be flexible—allowing those who miss the deadline to have the case delayed for sixty days—but the Court said that the sixty-day requirement cannot be waived for any reason. The requirement is intended to allow the agency to take steps to handle a problem and to avoid litigation.

Lujan, Secretary of the Interior v. National Wildlife Federation, decided by a 5-4 vote, June 27, 1990; Scalia wrote the opinion; Blackmun, Brennan, Marshall, and Stevens dissented.

The National Wildlife Federation lacked standing to broadly challenge the Department of Interior's reclassification of public lands. The federation sought to prevent the Bureau of Land Management from taking certain lands from the public domain and opening them up for mining. The Court said that a wholesale challenge to the agency's practices was not sufficiently supported by claims from individual federation members. It said that affidavits filed by the federation were not specific enough as to who would be hurt by the reclassification.

Federal Regulation

California v. Federal Energy Regulatory Commission, decided by a 9-0 vote, May 21, 1990; O'Connor wrote the opinion.

The standards set by the Federal Energy Regulatory Commission for water flows in streams diverted by federally licensed hydraulic projects preempt state regulations. The Court ruled that California requirements for substantially higher stream flows must yield to federal law. The case concerned the Rock Creek power plant near the South Fork American River. The Court said the federal commission set flow standards after weighing how to both protect wildlife and ensure the economic feasibility of the project.

Dole v. United Steelworkers of America, decided by a 7-2 vote, February 21, 1990; Brennan wrote the opinion; White and Rehnquist dissented.

The federal Office of Management and Budget has no authority under the Paperwork Reduction Act to block another agency's order that businesses disclose health and safety data to their employees or the public. The Court said the paperwork law empowered OMB to review requests for data intended for government use but did not extend to regulations meant to generate information for the benefit of a third party.

The Paperwork Reduction Act was passed in 1980 to minimize lengthy and redundant reporting requirements by government agencies. This case involved a regulation from the Labor Department's Occupational Safety and Health Administration (OSHA) that required employers to make certain their employees were told of potential hazards posed by chemicals at their work place.

Writing for the majority, Brennan said that Congress cleared the paperwork law out of concern for the burden imposed by a federal agency's request for information. He said the law did not cover requirements to provide information to a third party.

Office of Personnel Management v. Richmond, decided by a 7-2 vote; June 11, 1990; Kennedy wrote the opinion; Marshall and Brennan dissented.

The federal government is not prohibited from cutting benefits to a recipient who became ineligible because of a government employee's incorrect answers about eligibility. The Court said the government need not pay for its mistakes if it would require disbursement of benefits not authorized by law.

An individual who received federal disability benefits had sought information on how much he could make as a bus driver without sacrificing his disability annuity. The government then cut off his disability annuity because—contrary to the limits given—he had exceeded the ceiling.

Perpich v. Department of Defense, decided by a 9-0 vote, June 11, 1990; Stevens wrote the opinion.

The president has the power to order National Guard units to training missions outside the United States without the approval of state governors. The Court upheld the constitutionality of a federal law giving the president control.

Minnesota governor Rudy Perpich had objected to federal orders sending Minnesota National Guard troops to Honduras. He challenged the constitutionality of the so-called Montgomery Amendment. In 1986, while Congress was considering a fiscal 1987 authorization for the Department of Defense, Rep. G. V. "Sonny" Montgomery, D-Miss., had amended the bill to bar any governor from blocking the participation of his or her state's National Guard units in a Pentagon-sponsored training exercise because of the location or purpose of the exercise.

The Court said the Constitution gives to Congress the ultimate power to regulate military affairs, including ordering the National Guard to active duty over the objection of state officials.

Sullivan, Secretary of Health and Human Services v. Everhart, decided by a 5-4 vote, February 21, 1990; Scalia wrote the opinion; Stevens, Brennan, Marshall, and Kennedy dissented.

The secretary of the Department of Health and Human Services need not give Social Security or welfare recipients a method by which to appeal when the agency underpays benefits to offset overpayments from years earlier. The agency regulations, which allow overpayments and underpayments to be "netted," were intended to save the government time and money when it mistakenly overpaid beneficiaries. But the dissent said the regulations may unfairly deprive needy recipients of their full monthly benefit checks.

Sullivan, Secretary of Health and Human Services v. Finkelstein, decided by a 8-1 vote, June 18, 1990; White wrote the opinion; Blackmun dissented.

The secretary of the Department of Health and Human Services may immediately appeal a district court order that effectively invalidates a Social Security benefit eligibility requirement. The Court said such an order should be considered a "final decision" under federal statute, qualifying a party to appeal.

Sullivan, Secretary of Health and Human Services v. Stroop, decided by a 5-4 vote, June 14, 1990; Rehnquist wrote the opinion; Blackmun, Brennan, Marshall, and Stevens dissented.

Insurance benefits paid to children under Title II of the Social Security Act do not constitute "child support" payments, subject to be disregarded, when determining eligibility under Aid to Families with Dependent Children (AFDC). The Social Security Act allows states to "disregard" the first $50 of any child support payments received in calculating the monthly AFDC benefit.

The Court upheld a finding by the secretary of the Department of Health and Human Services that Social Security insurance benefits paid to children of disabled, retired, or deceased parents are not "child support" to be disregarded. The policy has the effect of lowering AFDC benefits. The Court said "child support" is a term of art referring only to payments from absent parents.

In a dissent, Blackmun said this "crabbed interpretation" of federal law "arbitrarily deprives certain families of a modest but urgently needed welfare benefit."

Sullivan, Secretary of Health and Human Services v. Zebley, decided by a 7-2 vote, February 20, 1990; Blackmun wrote the opinion; White and Rehnquist dissented.

The method used by the secretary of the Department of Health and Human Services to decide whether a child is "disabled" and therefore eligible for benefits under the Supplemental Security Income (SSI) program is too restrictive. The Court ruled that the method did not meet the statutory requirement that SSI benefits shall be provided to children with "any . . . impairment of comparable severity" to an impairment that would make an adult "unable to engage in any substantial gainful activity." The Court said the agency's test was stricter than required by law to determine whether children with disabilities were sufficiently impaired to be eligible for federal benefits.

Wilder v. Virginia Hospital Association, decided by a 5-4 vote; June 14, 1990. Brennan wrote the opinion; Rehnquist, O'Connor, Scalia, and Kennedy dissented.

Hospitals and nursing homes may use a federal civil rights law, Section 1983 of Title 42, to pursue higher Medicaid reimbursement rates from the states. Medicaid provides health care for poor persons. At issue was a 1980 amendment to the federal Medicaid act that requires states to reimburse health-care providers at rates that are "reasonable and adequate." Brennan said the amendment created a right to sue to seek better rates to meet the costs of health care. The state had contended that only health-care recipients had a right to sue. Although the amendment gave states flexibility in adopting rates, Brennan wrote, "Congress retained the underlying requirement of reasonable and adequate rates."

Individual Rights

Civil Rights

Howlett v. Rose, as Superintendent of Schools for Pinellas County, Florida, decided by a 9-0 vote, June 11, 1990; Stevens wrote the opinion.

School officials subject to a lawsuit based on a federal civil rights law cannot invoke a "sovereign immunity" defense applicable to claims raised under state law. The Court said states cannot exempt themselves from federal laws.

The case began when a high school student alleged that an assistant principal illegally searched his car while it was parked on school grounds and wrongfully suspended him from classes. He contended that the search and subsequent suspension violated his rights under the Fourth and Fourteenth Amendments and under related provisions in the Florida Constitution. He sued based on Section 1983 of Title 42 of the U.S. Code, which creates a remedy for violations of federal rights by state officials.

Justice Stevens wrote for the Court, "If we were to uphold the immunity claim in this case, every state would have the same opportunity to extend the mantle of sovereign immunity to persons who would otherwise be subject to Section 1983 liability."

Metro Broadcasting Inc. v. Federal Communications Commission, Astroline Communications Company Limited Partnership v. Shurberg Broadcasting of Hartford, Inc., decided by a 5-4 vote, June 27, 1990; Brennan wrote the opinion; O'Connor, Rehnquist, Scalia, and Kennedy dissented. Congress may order preferential treatment of blacks and other minorities to increase their ownership of broadcast licenses. *(See entry, p. 17; excerpts, p. 176)*

Missouri v. Jenkins, decided by a 5-4 vote, April 18, 1990; White wrote the opinion; Kennedy, Rehnquist, O'Connor, and Scalia dissented.

Federal courts may order local governments to raise taxes to correct constitutional violations such as segregated schools. *(See entry, p. 20; excerpts, p. 102)*

Ngiraingas v. Sanchez, decided by a 6-2 vote, April 24, 1990; Blackmun wrote the opinion; Brennan and Marshall dissented. Kennedy took no part in the case.

Neither the territory of Guam nor territory officials acting in their official capacity can be sued under a key civil rights law, Section 1983 of Title 42 of the U.S. Code. The statute allows individuals who have been wronged by persons acting as state officials to sue those states for money damages.

Writing for the Court, Blackmun said that when Congress enacted the law in 1871 it was mostly concerned with racial unrest in the southern states and specifically focused on states in the legislation to solve problems of discrimination. He said Congress did not intend to subject the territories to liability under Section 1983.

Spallone v. United States, Chema v. United States, Longo v. United States, decided by a 5-4 vote, January 10, 1990; Rehnquist wrote the opinion; Brennan, Marshall, Blackmun, and Stevens dissented.

A federal judge abused his power when he imposed contempt fines against Yonkers city officials who had refused to vote for a court-ordered housing desegregation plan. *(See entry, p. 21; excerpts, p. 77)*

Zinermon v. Burch, decided by a 5-4 vote, February 27, 1990; Blackmun wrote the opinion; O'Connor, Rehnquist, Scalia, and Kennedy dissented.

A man confined against his will at a Florida state mental hospital, without benefit of a hearing, may sue state officials in federal court for money damages, the Court ruled.

The man alleged that the state had deprived him of his liberty, without due process of law, by admitting him to the hospital as a "voluntary" mental patient when he was too mentally ill to agree to admission. Blackmun said the state has a duty to use procedural safeguards in dealing with patients incompetent to consent to voluntary admission. "We express no view on the ultimate merits of Burch's claim; we hold only that his complaint was sufficient to state a claim under Section 1983 for violation of his procedural due process rights," Blackmun said.

Freedom of Speech

Austin, Michigan Secretary of State v. Michigan State Chamber of Commerce, decided by a vote of 6-3, March 27, 1990; Marshall wrote the opinion; Kennedy, O'Connor, and Scalia dissented.

A Michigan campaign finance law barring corporations from spending money directly from their own treasuries for political campaigns does not infringe the First Amendment. The law requires corporations to make all political expenditures through a separate fund set up specifically for political purposes.

Acknowledging that expressive rights were concerned in the case, the Court said that the state had a compelling interest in "eliminating from the political process the corrosive effect of political 'war chests' amassed with the aid of the legal advantages given to corporations." Marshall noted that Michigan's law was based on a belief that corporate political spending could undermine the integrity of the political process.

Butterworth, Attorney General of Florida v. Smith, decided by a 9-0 vote, March 21, 1990; Rehnquist wrote the opinion.

States cannot prohibit grand jury witnesses from disclosing their testimony once the grand jury has completed a case. At issue was a Florida law that prohibited a witness from ever revealing testimony given to a grand jury. The Court said the law violated free speech rights.

The case involved a reporter who had testified before a state grand jury and who sought to write a story about the probe after the grand jury ended its investigation. Rehnquist said, "We have recognized that invocation of grand jury interests is not 'some talisman that dissolves all constitutional protections.' "

FW/PBS, Paris Adult Bookstore II v. City of Dallas, M. J. R. Inc. v. City of Dallas, Berry v. City of Dallas, decided 6-3, January 9, 1990; O'Connor wrote the opinion; Rehnquist, Scalia, and White dissented.

A restrictive Dallas ordinance regulating "sexually oriented businesses" is an unconstitutional constraint on free speech. The Court struck down a licensing requirement that allowed officials to block indefinitely an adult bookshop or X-rated movie house from doing business. Justices noted that the statute failed to include a deadline for a municipality's decision on a license application and did not allow for prompt judicial review of denial.

The Court was unanimous, however, in upholding a licensing requirement for motels that rent rooms for fewer than ten hours. The Court said that was a reasonable way to restrict prostitution.

John Doe Agency v. John Doe Corp., decided by a vote of 6-3, December 11, 1989; Blackmun wrote the opinion; Stevens, Scalia, and Marshall dissented.

Materials gathered for a law enforcement purpose, but not originally created for such purpose, are exempt from disclosure under the Freedom of Information Act's allowance for "records or information compiled for law enforcement purposes."

The Court said the statute does not require that compilation be done at a specific time but only dictates that, when the government invokes the exemption, the records sought have been gathered for law enforcement purposes. This case involved defense-contractor records that were part of a routine agency audit when they were originally collected but had since been used for a criminal investigation.

Milkovich v. Lorain Journal Co., decided by a unanimous vote, June 21, 1990; Rehnquist wrote the opinion.

Statements of opinion do not enjoy a special privilege under the First Amendment and are within the reach of state libel law. Writing for the Court, Rehnquist said the First Amendment's guarantee of a free airing of public issues must be balanced by social values that serve as a basis for defamation law and society's interest in preventing attacks on reputation.

The dispute arose after a newspaper columnist implied in an article that a high school wrestling coach perjured himself at a judicial hearing about a melee that erupted at a wrestling match. The Ohio Supreme Court decided the article contained "constitutionally protected opinion." Rehnquist said there is no "wholesale defamation exemption" for opinion. Labeling a column "opinion," he said, does not remove the implication that the writing is factual.

Osborne v. Ohio, decided by a 6-3 vote, April 18, 1990; White wrote the opinion; Brennan, Marshall, and Stevens dissented.

A state may ban the private possession of pornographic pictures of children. The majority said a state's interest in the physical and psychological well-being of a minor is compelling and overrides potential First Amendment concerns.

The Court said it is reasonable for the state to believe it will decrease the production of child pornography if it puts in place criminal penalties for those who have such items. The decision granted a child-pornography exception to the Court's 1969 ruling in *Stanley v. Georgia,* which said states could not make it a crime to privately possess obscene material.

United States v. Eichman, United States v. Haggerty, decided by a 5-4 vote, June 11, 1990; Brennan wrote the opinion; Rehnquist, White, Stevens, and O'Connor dissented. Flag burning in the course of political protest is a right guaranteed by the First Amendment. *(See entry, p. 22; excerpts, p. 128)*

United States v. Kokinda, decided by a 5-4 vote, June 27, 1990; O'Connor wrote the opinion; Brennan, Marshall, Stevens, and Blackmun dissented.

A U.S. Postal Service regulation that prohibits solicitation of contributions on postal premises does not violate the First Amendment when it is used to bar solicitations by a political group. This case arose after volunteers for the National Democratic Policy Committee set up a table on a post office sidewalk. A federal appeals court said the sidewalk was a traditional public forum. But O'Connor, writing for the Court in an opinion reversing the appeals court, said government ownership of property "does not automatically open that property to the public." She said the sidewalk in question was built solely to assist postal patrons.

Privacy Rights

Cruzan v. Director, Missouri Department of Health, decided by a 5-4 vote, June 25, 1990; Rehnquist wrote the opinion; Brennan, Marshall, Blackmun, and Stevens dissented.

A state may require clear and convincing evidence of a comatose patient's previously expressed wish to die before allowing family members to disconnect life-support systems. *(See entry, p. 10; excerpts, p. 144)*

Hodgson v. Minnesota, Minnesota v. Hodgson, decided by separate 5-4 votes, June 25, 1990. Stevens wrote the opinion; Scalia, Kennedy, Rehnquist, and White dissented.

The majority struck down a statute that required an unmarried woman under eighteen to notify both biological parents of an abortion decision. A separate majority (O'Connor and the above dissenting justices) found the statute constitutional because it provided the option of a judicial hearing for a pregnant teenager who did not want to tell her parents about her decision. *(See entry, p. 12; excerpts, p. 155)*

Ohio v. Akron Center for Reproductive Health, decided by a 6-3 vote, June 25, 1990; Kennedy wrote the opinion; Blackmun, Brennan, and Marshall dissented.

A state statute requiring an unmarried woman under eighteen to tell at least one parent of an abortion decision, or, in the alternative, appear before a judge, is constitutional. *(See entry, p. 12; excerpts, p. 166)*

Separation of Church and State

Board of Education of the Westside Community Schools (Dist. 66) v. Mergens, decided by a 8-1 vote, June 4, 1990; O'Connor wrote the opinion; Stevens dissented.

Student religious groups may meet in public high schools on the same basis as other extracurricular clubs. *(See entry, p. 24; excerpts, p. 102)*

Employment Division, Department of Human Resources of Oregon v. Smith, decided by a 6-3 vote, April 17, 1990; Scalia wrote the opinion; Blackmun, Brennan, and Marshall dissented.

A state may outlaw the sacramental use of the drug peyote without having to prove that it has a "compelling interest" in enforcing a statute that infringes on religious freedom. *(See entry, p. 15; excerpts, p. 88)*

Miscellaneous Cases

Admiralty

Sisson v. Ruby, decided unanimously, June 25, 1990; Marshall wrote the opinion.

Federal maritime law dictates award limits on a liability suit brought in connection with a fire on a boat docked at a marina. The fire broke out on a pleasure yacht and caused damage to other boats and to the marina on Lake Michigan in Indiana. The Court said the storage and maintenance of a vessel at a marina on navigable waters is substantially related to traditional maritime activity. Maritime law protects shipowners from having to pay large court awards in lawsuits.

Boundary Dispute

Georgia v. South Carolina, decided unanimously, June 25, 1990; Blackmun wrote the opinion.

The Barnwell Islands belong to South Carolina, not Georgia. The Court said South Carolina had established sovereignty over the islands through almost two centuries of history, including its continuing practice of taxation, policing, and patrolling of the island property. The case stemmed from a longstanding disagreement between the two states over the location of their boundary along the lower reaches of the Savannah River.

Indian Rights

Duro v. Reina, Chief of Police, Salt River Department of Public Safety, Salt River Pima-Maricopa Indian Community, decided by a 7-2 vote, May 29, 1990; Kennedy wrote the opinion; Brennan and Marshall dissented.

An Indian tribe may not assert criminal jurisdiction over a nonmember Indian. The Court said the sovereignty of a tribe to govern its own affairs does not include the authority to impose criminal sanctions against a citizen who is not a member.

In a dissenting opinion, Brennan said he does not share such a "parsimonious view" of the sovereignty retained by Indian tribes.

Property Rights/Takings

Preseault v. Interstate Commerce Commission, decided by a 9-0 vote, February 21, 1990; Brennan wrote the opinion.

Property owners who argue that the federal government's conversion of an abandoned railroad right-of-way into hiking and biking trails deprives them of their reversionary interest can file a claim for compensation under the Tucker Act. The act allows people to seek damages against the government. The Court said that the National Trails System Act Amendments of 1983, commonly known as the rails-to-trails statute, does not constitute the taking of private property because landowners may be compensated for the loss.

A Vermont couple had contended that a railway easement that crossed their land had reverted to their possession after the Vermont Railway discontinued service on the line. The Court said the rails-to-trails statute is a valid exercise of congressional power under the Commerce Clause of the Constitution and noted that the couple could apply for compensation in U.S. Claims Court under the Tucker Act.

United States v. Sperry Corp., decided by a 9-0 vote, November 28, 1989; White wrote the opinion.

The U.S. government may collect a small percentage of awards won by U.S. companies against the government of Iran in a special claims tribunal. The tribunal was set up after the 1979 seizure of the U.S. Embassy in Tehran.

Sperry, which had been contracting with the government of Iran when the embassy was seized, argued that the federal law requiring the deduction from awards shifted costs that should be borne by the nation as a whole to individual claimants. But the Supreme Court said the deduction was a reasonable "user fee" intended to reimburse the government for its costs in connection with the tribunal.

State Immunity

Port Authority Trans-Hudson Corp. v. Feeney, Port Authority Trans-Hudson Corp. v. Foster, decided unanimously, April 30, 1990; O'Connor wrote the opinion.

The Eleventh Amendment's provision for state immunity does not bar lawsuits in federal court against the Port Authority Trans-Hudson Corporation, which was created in a compact by New York and New Jersey to operate transportation facilities linking the two states. O'Connor said the states clearly agreed to waive any immunity from federal law in legislation that created the agency.

North Dakota v. United States, decided by 9-0 and 5-4 votes; May 21, 1990; Stevens wrote the opinion; Brennan, Marshall, Blackmun, and Kennedy dissented in part.

States may impose labeling and reporting requirements on distributors who sell liquor at U.S. military posts within their borders. The justices unanimously upheld North Dakota regulations requiring out-of-state shippers to file monthly reports and ruled, by a 5-4 vote, to allow a North Dakota requirement that labels be stuck to each bottle of liquor sold on the federal posts.

North Dakota law required distributors supplying the U.S. military bases in the state to make special labels and affix one to each bottle. The labels said the liquor was for consumption only on the military grounds.

4 | *Preview of the 1990-1991 Term*

After almost a decade of liberal-conservative jockeying on the Supreme Court, the question was no longer whether a conservative majority was in place, but how that majority would use its strength. The 1990-1991 term began October 1, and, as justices appointed by Presidents Ronald Reagan and George Bush consolidated their majority, the country waited to see how the conservatives would pick their targets. Would they strike out in bold new directions on politically divisive social issues or continue to peel slowly away at the legacy of the liberal activist years?

The future of legalized abortion was on most people's minds in the fall of 1990, but that was not the only potential flash point. Would the Court continue to cut back the breadth of civil rights law? Would protection for religious practices erode further? Would criminal defendants see states' interest win out more and more? And what would be Congress's role as the conservative majority ostensibly leaves policy making to lawmakers?

The greatest uncertainty was David H. Souter, a quiet New Hampshire bachelor who had written little on constitutional issues during his years on state courts and a federal appeals court. His September confirmation hearings did not reveal how he would rule on many important matters.

Yet, despite its solidifying makeup, the Court may still have the ability to surprise. Justice Byron R. White, usually found in the conservative camp, had begun to emerge as a swing vote. With the retirement of William J. Brennan, Jr., White became the Court's most senior justice; if he found himself crafting consensus, White would have new power to write and assign opinions.

□□□

Following are discussions of several important cases the Supreme Court was scheduled to hear early in the 1990-1991 term:

Pregnancy Rights

In *United Auto Workers v. Johnson Controls Inc.*, the Court was to decide whether a company may keep all women of childbearing age from jobs involving exposure to lead without violating laws against sex discrimination. A federal appeals court upheld the company's policy, 7-4, saying that it was necessary to protect unborn children. Appellate court dissenters called this "likely the most important sex discrimination case in any court since 1964" when a major anti-job-discrimination law was passed.

The case began after a Milwaukee battery manufacturer, Johnson Controls, excluded women from jobs that entail contact with lead, the primary ingredient in batteries. Studies show that lead in a pregnant woman's blood can cause physical and mental damage to the fetus. Tests indicate that the offspring of men exposed to lead also have high risks of birth defects. But the Johnson Controls policy did not cover men, and the appeals court said the danger to the unborn from a father's exposure was "speculative and unconvincing."

In its brief to the Court, the union asserts the company violated Title VII of the Civil Rights Act of 1964, which bars sex discrimination in the workplace, and the 1978 Pregnancy Discrimination Act, which forbids excluding women from jobs because of pregnancy or childbirth. The workers say such distinctions have been "the basis for many of the policies that had relegated women to inferior status in the workplace." Johnson Controls responds that Congress could not have intended to force an employer to expose the unborn to physical and mental hazards. The company says that the "health and safety of unborn children from toxic manufacturing operations" overrides "gender equality in the workplace."

The appeals court treated the company's practice as unintentional discrimination. When a practice otherwise appears fair and has a discrimination result only, a company may justify it as a "business necessity." The U.S. Court of Appeals for the Seventh Circuit held that the workers had not met their burden of proving that the practice was unnecessary. It also said that the workers had failed to offer an alternative practice for fetal protection.

A different legal test—one that the workers wanted fully explored— is used when a court decides that an employment practice intentionally discriminates. That test would require Johnson Controls to prove that the exclusionary practice was a "bona fide occupational qualification" for operating the business. This standard is more difficult to meet; a company must prove with specificity that the policy is necessary.

Dissenting Seventh Circuit judges said the court should have applied the intentional discrimination test. Among them was Judge Frank H. Easterbrook, who said Johnson Controls overtly discriminated because it used sex as a basis of employment. Easterbrook's opinion was invoked in separate briefs before the Supreme Court by the union workers and by U.S. Solicitor General Kenneth W. Starr. Both briefs argued for a tougher standard of scrutiny of the Johnson Controls policy.

Easterbrook contended that Johnson Controls's asserted concern for the health of the unborn was irrelevant to its operation. He also said the policy was too broadly cast because it applied to all women, although not all female workers become pregnant and not all would be equally exposed to dangerous lead levels.

The solicitor general's brief said the appeals court also should have weighed possible harm to male employees' offspring: "Establishing that exposure of men does not pose a similar degree of risk as exposure of women is vitally important because, in the absence of such a showing, the exclusion of fertile women cannot be a valid method for serving the employer's asserted interest in preventing direct harm to third parties."

Abortion Counseling

When members of Congress drafted Title X of the Public Health Service Act of 1970, they stipulated: "None of the funds appropriated under this title shall be used in programs where abortion is a method of family planning." The Bush administration, medical-care providers, and members of Congress differ over whether lawmakers in 1970 intended to bar federal funds for abortion counseling. The antiabortion language was part of a compromise, reached before the 1973 *Roe v. Wade* decision that made abortion legal nationwide, on legislation to expand family planning services. The legislative history of the bill offers no conclusions on how far members wanted the abortion ban to go.

At issue in the cases of *Rust v. Sullivan* and *New York v. Sullivan* is whether 1988 Reagan administration regulations barring abortion counseling violate Title X. The Bush administration says that statute's abortion ban extends to counseling. Those who have challenged the regulations—doctors, health clinics, and the city and state of New York—say the statute means only what it says explicitly: no money for the abortions. Members of Congress submitted amicus curiae briefs on both sides of the issue.

The Department of Health and Human Services (HHS) restrictions say the following: funds cannot be used for abortion counseling; grant recipients cannot lobby for abortion; recipients who use nonfederal funds to provide abortions or counseling may do so only in facilities separate from those supported by federal funds.

The challengers say the HHS rules violate the intention of Title X and infringe on the First Amendment rights of counselors. They say the rules further interfere with a woman's privacy right and ability to gain competent medical information.

The U.S. Court of Appeals for the Second Circuit upheld the funding restriction, saying the Title X ban on money for abortions extends to abortion counseling. It also said the regulations do not impermissibly burden a woman's right to an abortion because she may go to a privately funded clinic. On the First Amendment issue for health workers, the court said the government is not required to fund the exercise of any rights.

Opponents contend that the government cannot condition federal funds on the waiver of constitutional rights. "No one has a right to a subsidy for the exercise of rights to speech and privacy, but when the government chooses to provide subsidies, there are some things that it may not constitutionally do," the challengers argue. "The government cannot exact adherence to any orthodoxy through the imposition of viewpoint-based conditions on its largess."

The government's brief says the ban on abortion counseling flows from the statute's general prohibition against abortion. Countering the First Amendment argument, the solicitor general says the government has no obligation to subsidize the exercise of even fundamental rights. On the privacy question, the government adds, "While under *Roe* the government may not prohibit a woman from choosing to have a first-trimester abortion, this court has repeatedly held that the government is not obligated to provide the means to exercise any such right."

The solicitor general argues that the government may selectively fund programs in the public interest. "In this case, the government has made a decision to provide federal subsidies for pre-pregnancy family planning and infertility services, but it has decided not to fund activities that 'promote or encourage' abortion." The solicitor general maintains that HHS's interpretation is "based on a permissible construction" of an ambiguous statute.

The Reagan administration, in its justification of the regulations, and the Bush administration, in its brief, relied on comments from John D. Dingell, D-Mich., author of the abortion ban in the 1970 bill. But Dingell, now chairman of the House Energy and Commerce Committee, since has said his statements "did not suggest, either expressly or implicitly, that family-planning clinics should be prohibited from counseling pregnant women on any matter or referring them to appropriate facilities."

In an amicus brief, Rep. Patricia Schroeder, D-Colo., and 110 other members of Congress argue that Congress wanted to bar Title X funds for abortion, not abortion counseling or referral. "The very absence of any mention of 'abortion counseling' or 'abortion referral' dispels any ambiguity as to the meaning [of the law]. . . . Had Congress intended to prohibit abortion counseling, it would have done so in explicit terms." They also note that between 1981 and 1988 HHS required Title X providers to mention abortion as an option for women with unplanned pregnancies.

Sen. Gordon J. Humphrey, R-N.H., and fifty-five other members of the House and Senate take the opposing view. "Congress clearly intended to bar any Title X funds to any entity which would present abortion as a means to plan the number and spacing of one's children," Humphrey and his allies argue in their amicus brief. "Although Congress could have expressly barred 'counseling and referring for abortion' in [the law], the wisdom of doing so expressly has only been recognized more recently."

School Desegregation

The case of *Board of Education of Oklahoma City Public Schools v. Dowell* is rooted in a 1960s lawsuit challenging racial segregation and a resulting 1972 court order for desegregation. Five years later, after the school board instituted busing and integrated its schools, the board asked the federal district court to find that state-imposed racial bias had ended and to step out of the case. The court complied but did not specifically dissolve the decree.

In 1985 the school board decreased cross-town busing and re-assigned children to neighborhood schools. According to briefs, the plan caused eleven of the school district's sixty-four elementary schools to enroll 90 percent or more black students. That situation prompted a new round of litigation in the name of the black students and parents who had originated the case.

Rejecting a request to reopen the case, a federal district court judge ruled that the 1977 court order was binding, that the school district was desegregated in 1985, and that the neighborhood school plan was constitutional because it was not adopted with the intention of discriminating on the basis of race. The U.S. Court of Appeals for the Tenth Circuit reversed, saying that federal court supervision in the case "extends beyond the termination of the wrongdoing." It sent the case back to the district court to see whether the schools were racially balanced.

The school board's brief maintains that after a federal court has found that segregation has ended, a school board may adopt a neighborhood school plan, "even if it has a disproportionate racial impact, provided that the board's action is not intentionally discriminatory and, therefore, is not a new constitutional violation."

The students' brief says that court involvement should continue because the new plan perpetuates discrimination. It says that most of the virtually all-black schools reestablished by the school board's 1985 plan were the same schools that had been identified by the district court in 1972 as "substantially disproportionate in their racial composition."

In an amicus curiae brief, the solicitor general rejects the appeals court decision but also says the Oklahoma City school board policies should be thoroughly examined. A basic question, Solicitor General Starr said, is whether the schools were racially desegregated, or "unitary," at the time the neighborhood plan was adopted.

To measure unitariness, the solicitor general said, three points need to be assessed: "whether the district has continuously complied with the desegregation decree in good faith; whether the school district has abandoned any and all acts of intentional discrimination; and whether the school district has eliminated, as far as practicable, the 'vestiges' of prior discriminatory conduct." Starr said that once a district can be found "unitary" it should be relieved of a desegregation decree.

Punitive Damages

The business community repeatedly has sought relief from huge damage awards in federal court. In the Supreme Court's most recent ruling on the issue, the 1989 *Browning-Ferris Industries Inc. v. Kelco Disposal Inc.,* a majority held that the Eighth Amendment prohibition against excessive fines does not apply to punitive-damage awards in civil cases, no matter how big those awards are.

But justices suggested that huge awards disproportionate to the actual damages might violate the Fourteenth Amendment's due process guarantee. And business is hoping for relief in a new case. The dispute in *Pacific Mutual Life Insurance Co. v. Haslip* arose after members of a group health plan sued the insurer for fraud in Alabama state court. They alleged that Pacific Mutual was liable for the fraud of an agent who pocketed their premiums. The plan was canceled without notice to the members.

The jury awarded $1,040,000 to one of the plaintiffs and between $10,000 and $16,000 to three others. The Alabama Supreme Court let the award stand, saying that the trial judge did not have sufficient grounds to interfere with the jury verdict. Pacific Mutual contends that the $1 million was grossly excessive, compared with measurable damages of about $4,000, and that the Due Process Clause requires some limit to punishment a jury may deliver. It contends that Alabama law and jury guidelines are "impermissibly vague and incomprehensible."

"Punitive damages are punishment, and therefore the standard of scrutiny for vagueness should be similar to that in criminal cases," the insurance company says, arguing that the jury should have been instructed explicitly about when punishment is deserved and how stiff it should be.

The individuals who were defrauded on their premiums contend that they deserve the awards. The woman who received the $1 million award, the brief said, "suffered devastating financial and emotional harm." "After incurring hospital bills equivalent to almost half her annual take-home pay, she discovered her insurance coverage did not exist because her premiums had been stolen by Pacific Mutual's agent." The brief also alleges that Pacific Mutual did nothing after receiving complaints that the agent was engaged in fraud. It further maintains that jury discretion under Alabama law to set punitive damages conformed with historical jury procedures.

Pension Benefits

In *Ingersoll-Rand Co. v. McClendon* an employee who says he was fired because his pension was about to vest wants to sue in state court. Pension rights generally are governed by the federal Employee Retirement Income Security Act (ERISA). The Court was expected to decide whether the Texas Supreme Court improperly carved out an exception to the statute to allow the worker to sue in state court under a more lenient standard with the possibility of greater remedies.

A trial court and state appeals court ruled for the company, but the Texas Supreme Court reversed. The court said a person may bring a wrongful discharge action alleging that "the principal reason for termination was the employer's desire to avoid contributing to or paying benefits under the employee's pension fund."

In its attempt to keep such complaints out of state court, Ingersoll-Rand contends that Congress intended ERISA to be a comprehensive regulation that would preempt state laws. It says that the Texas court in its decision created an alternative set of rights and remedies. The fired worker differs, saying his complaint "has absolutely nothing to do with ERISA or the administration or regulation of a pension plan."

"The Texas Supreme Court simply held that a plaintiff can recover damages for employment termination principally motivated by an attempt to avoid pension obligations," he says. He argues that ERISA's preemption provision applies only to state laws intended to regulate the terms and conditions of employee benefit plans. He asserts that each state has the power to govern the employment relationship and that this power includes a state's ability to enact laws on firings.

Criminal Sentencing

The Court was expected to examine in *Harmelin v. Michigan* whether a mandatory life sentence without parole is cruel and unusual punishment for a first-time cocaine conviction. Although this Court has been willing to uphold strict sentences for drug dealers, a decision striking down the sentence could cast into doubt the numerous mandatory sentences that Congress and the states have passed in recent years as part of the "war on drugs."

The defendant was convicted of possession of more than 650 grams of cocaine. As required by Michigan law, he drew life in prison without parole. He contends that the sentence is disproportionate to the offense and says that there is no other crime in Michigan except first degree murder that warrants mandatory life without parole. Michigan state officials respond that state and federal courts have repeatedly upheld tough sentences for drug dealers.

In a separate sentencing case, *Burns v. United States,* the High Court was to look at an issue that has caused federal judges to chafe since 1987 when sentencing guidelines took effect: Under what conditions may judges deviate?

The guidelines were drafted by the U.S. Sentencing Commission and dictated by a sweeping 1984 anticrime law. They were designed to bring consistency to the federal sentencing process and make criminals spend more time in prison. The Supreme Court ruled in January 1989 in *Mistretta v. United States* that the guidelines were constitutional.

In this District of Columbia case, the defendant pleaded guilty to theft of government funds, making false claims against the government, and attempting to evade income tax. A federal judge sentenced him to sixty months, departing from the sentencing guideline range of thirty to thirty-seven months.

The defendant argued that because the judge did not notify him the sentence might be increased, he did not have a chance to challenge factors regarding the court's reasons for ignoring the guidelines. He observed that other federal courts have set up rules for giving such notice. Without it, the defendant maintained, due process is violated.

But, in defending the district judge's action, Solicitor General Starr argued that although the defendant might have made a stronger case if he had known the judge was going to depart from the guidelines, the guidelines do not require telling him before sentence is imposed.

5 | *Case Excerpts*

Following are excerpts from some of the most important rulings of the Supreme Court's 1989-1990 term. They appear in the order in which they were announced.

Nos. 88-854, 88-856, and 88-870

88-854: Henry G. Spallone, Petitioner v. United States et al.
88-856: Peter Chema, Petitioner v. United States et al.
88-870: Nicholas Longo and Edward Fagan, Petitioners
v. United States et al.

On writ of certiorari to the United States Court of Appeals
for the Second Circuit

[January 10, 1990]

CHIEF JUSTICE REHNQUIST delivered the opinion of the Court.

This case is the most recent episode of a lengthy lawsuit in which the city of Yonkers was held liable for intentionally enhancing racial segregation in housing in Yonkers. The issue here is whether it was a proper exercise of judicial power for the District Court to hold petitioners, four Yonkers city councilmembers, in contempt for refusing to vote in favor of legislation implementing a consent decree earlier approved by the city. We hold that in the circumstances of this case the District Court abused its discretion.

I

In 1980, the United States filed a complaint alleging, *inter alia*, that the two named defendants—the city of Yonkers and the Yonkers Community Development Agency—had intentionally engaged in a pattern and practice of housing discrimination, in violation of Title VIII of the Civil Rights Act of 1968 and the Equal Protection Clause of the Fourteenth Amendment. The Government and plaintiff-intervenor National Association for the Advancement of Colored People (NAACP) asserted that the city had, over a period of three decades, selected sites for subsidized housing in order to perpetuate residential racial segregation.

The plaintiffs' theory was that the city had equated subsidized housing for families with minority housing, and thus disproportionately restricted new family housing projects to areas of the city—particularly southwest Yonkers—already predominately populated by minorities.

The District Court found the two named defendants liable, concluding that the segregative effect of the city's actions had been "consistent and extreme," and that "the desire to preserve existing patterns of segregation ha[d] been a significant factor in the sustained community opposition to subsidized housing in East Yonkers and other overwhelmingly white areas of the City." The District Court in its remedial decree enjoined "the City of Yonkers, its officers, agents, employees, successors and all persons in active concert or participation with any of them" from, *inter alia,* intentionally promoting racial residential segregation in Yonkers, taking any action intended to deny or make unavailable housing to any person on account of race or national origin, and from blocking or limiting the availability of public or subsidized housing in east or northwest Yonkers on the basis of race or national origin. Other parts of the remedial order were directed only to the city. They required affirmative steps to disperse public housing throughout Yonkers. Part IV of the order noted that the city previously had committed itself to provide acceptable sites for 200 units of public housing as a condition for receiving 1983 Community Development Block Grant funds from the Federal Government, but had failed to do so. Consequently, it required the city to designate sites for 200 units of public housing in East Yonkers, and to submit to the Department of Housing and Urban Development an acceptable Housing Assistance Plan for 1984-1985 and other documentation. Part VI directed the city to develop by November 1986 a long-term plan "for the creation of additional subsidized family housing units . . . in existing residential areas in east or northwest Yonkers." The court did not mandate specific details of the plan such as how many subsidized units must be developed, where they should be constructed, or how the city should provide for the units.

Under the Charter of the city of Yonkers all legislative powers are vested in the city council, which consists of an elected mayor and six council members, including petitioners. The city, for all practical purposes, therefore, acts through the city council when it comes to the enactment of legislation. Pending appeal of the District Court's liability and remedial orders, however, the city did not comply with Parts IV and VI of the remedial order. The city failed to propose sites for the public housing, and in November 1986, informed the District Court that it would not present a long-term plan in compliance with Part VI. The United States and the NAACP then moved for an adjudication of civil contempt and the imposition of coercive sanctions, but the District Court declined to take that action. Instead, it secured an agreement from the city to appoint an outside housing advisor to identify sites for the 200 units of public housing and to draft a long-term plan.

In December 1987, the Court of Appeals for the Second Circuit affirmed the District Court's judgment in all respects, and we subsequently denied certiorari. Shortly after the Court of Appeals' decision, in January 1988, the parties agreed to a consent decree that set forth "certain actions which the City of Yonkers [would] take in connection with a consensual implementation of Parts IV and VI" of the housing remedy order. The decree was approved by the city council in a 5-to-2 vote (petitioners Spallone and Chema voting no), and entered by the District Court as a consent judgment on January 28, 1988. Sections 12 through 18 of the decree established the framework for the long-term plan and are the underlying bases for the contempt orders at issue in this case. Perhaps most significant was § 17, in which the city agreed to adopt, within 90 days, legislation conditioning the construction of all multifamily housing on the inclusion of at least 20 percent assisted units, granting tax abatements and density bonuses to developers, and providing for zoning changes to allow the placement of housing developments.

For several more months, however, the city continued to delay action toward implementing the long-term plan. The city was loath to enact the plan because it wished to exhaust its remedies on appeal, but it had not obtained any stay of the District Court's order. As a result of the city's intransigence, the United States and the NAACP moved the court for the entry of a Long Term Plan Order based on a draft that had been prepared by the city's lawyers during negotiations between January and April 1988. On June 13, following a hearing and changes in the draft, the District Court entered the Long Term Plan Order, which provided greater detail for the legislation prescribed by § 17 of the decree. After several weeks of further delay the court, after a hearing held on July 26, 1988, entered an order requiring the city of Yonkers to enact on or before August 1, 1988, the "legislative package" described in a section of the earlier consent decree; the second paragraph provided:

> "It is further ORDERED that, in the event the City of Yonkers fails to enact the legislative package on or before August 1, 1988, the City of Yonkers shall be required to show cause at a hearing before this Court at 10:00 a.m. on August 2, 1988, why it should not be held in contempt, and each individual City Council member shall be required to show cause at a hearing before this court at 10:00 a.m. on August 2, 1988, why he should not be held in contempt."

Further provisions of the order specified escalating daily amounts of fines in the event of contempt, and provided that if the legislation were not enacted before August 10, 1988, any councilmember who remained in contempt should be committed to the custody of the United States Marshal for imprisonment. The specified daily fines for the city were $100 for the first day, to be doubled for each consecutive day of noncompliance; the specified daily fine for members of the city council was $500 per day.

Notwithstanding the threat of substantial sanctions, on August 1 the city council defeated a resolution of intent to adopt the legislative package, known as the Affordable Housing Ordinance, by a vote of 4 to 3 (petitioners constituting the majority). On August 2, the District Court held a hearing to afford the city and the councilmembers an opportunity to show cause why they should not be adjudicated in contempt. It rejected the city's arguments, held the city in contempt, and imposed the coercive sanctions set forth in the July 26 order. After questioning the individual council members as to the reasons for their negative votes, the court also held each of the petitioners in contempt and imposed sanctions. It refused to accept the contention that the proper subject of the contempt sanctions was the city of Yonkers alone and overruled the objection that the court lacked the power to direct councilmembers how to vote, because in light of the consent judgment, it thought the city council's adoption of the Affordable Housing Ordinance would be "in the nature of a ministerial act."

On August 17, the Court of Appeals stayed the contempt sanctions pending appeal. Shortly thereafter, the court affirmed the adjudications of contempt against both the city and the councilmembers, but limited the fines against the city so that they would not exceed $1 million a day. The Court of Appeals refused to accept the councilmembers' argument that the District Court abused its discretion in selecting its method of enforcing the consent judgment. While recognizing that "a court is obliged to use the 'least possible power adequate to the end proposed,' " (quoting *Anderson v. Dunn* (1821)), it concluded that the District Court's choice of coercive contempt sanctions against the councilmembers could not be an abuse of discretion, because the city council had approved the consent judgment and thereby agreed to implement the legislation described in Section 17 of the decree. The Court of Appeals also rejected petitioners' invocation of the federal common law of legislative immunity, concluding that "[w]hatever the scope of local legislators' immunity, it does not insulate them from compliance with a consent judgment to which their city has agreed and which has been approved by their legislative body." Finally, the court held that even if "the act of voting has sufficient expressive content to be accorded some First Amendment protection as symbolic speech, the public interest in obtaining compliance with federal court judgments that remedy constitutional violations unquestionably justifies whatever burden on expression has occurred."

Both the city and the councilmembers requested this Court to stay imposition of sanctions pending filing and disposition of petitions for certiorari. We granted a stay as to petitioners, but denied the city's request. With the city's daily contempt sanction approaching $1 million per day, the city council finally enacted the Affordable Housing Ordinance on September 9, 1988, by a vote of 5 to 2, petitioners Spallone and Fagan voting no. Because the contempt orders raise important issues about the appropriate exercise of the federal judicial power against individual legislators, we granted certiorari and now reverse.

II

The issue before us is relatively narrow. There can be no question about the liability of the city of Yonkers for racial discrimination: the District Court imposed such liability on the city, its decision was affirmed in all respects by the Court of Appeals, and we denied certiorari. Nor do we have before us any question as to the District Court's remedial order; the Court of Appeals found that it was within the bounds of proper discretion, and we denied certiorari. Our focus, then, is only on the District Court's order of July 26 imposing contempt sanctions on the individual petitioners if they failed to vote in favor of the ordinance in question.

Petitioners contend that the District Court's orders violate their rights to freedom of speech under the First Amendment, and they also contend that they are entitled as legislators to absolute immunity for actions taken in discharge of their legislative responsibilities. We find it unnecessary to reach either of these questions, because we conclude that the portion of the District Court's order of July 25 imposing contempt sanctions against the petitioners if they failed to vote in favor of the court-proposed ordinance was an abuse of discretion under traditional equitable principles.

Before discussing the principles informing our conclusion, it is important to note the posture of the case before the District Court at the time it entered the order in question. Petitioners were members of the city council of the city of Yonkers, and if the city were to enact legislation it would have to be by their doing. But petitioners had never been made parties to the action, and the District Court's order imposed liability only on the named defendants in the action—the city of Yonkers and the Yonkers Community Development Agency. The remedial order had enjoined the two named defendants, and—in the traditional language of a prohibitory decree—officers, agents, and others acting in concert with them from discriminating on the basis of race in connection with the furnishing of housing, and from intentionally promoting racial residential segregation in Yonkers. The order had gone on to require extensive affirmative steps to disperse public housing throughout Yonkers, but those portions of the order were directed only against the city. There was no evidence taken at the hearing of July 26, 1988, and the court's order of that date did not make the petitioners parties to the action.

From the time of the entry of the remedial order in early 1986 until this Court denied certiorari in the case involving the merits of the litigation in June 1988, the city backed and filled in response to the court's efforts to obtain compliance with the housing portions of the decree. It agreed to a consent decree and then sought unsuccessfully to have the decree vacated. During this period of time the city had a certain amount of bargaining power simply by virtue of the length of time it took the appellate process to run its course. Although the judgment against the city was not stayed, the District Court was sensibly interested in moving as rapidly as possible toward the construction of housing which would satisfy the remedial order, rather than simply forcing the city to enact legislation. The District Court realized that for such construction to begin pursuant to the remedial decree, not only must the city comply, but potential builders and developers must be willing to put up money for the construction. To the extent that the city took action voluntarily, without threatening to rescind the action if the District Court's decision were reversed, construction could proceed before the appellate process had run its course.

All of this changed, however, in June 1988, when this Court denied certiorari and the District Court's orders on the merits of the case became final. On July 26, the court heard the comments of counsel for the parties and entered the order upon which the contempt sanctions against the individual councilmembers was based.

At this stage of the case, the court contemplated various methods by which to ensure compliance with its remedial orders. It considered proceeding under Federal Rule of Civil Procedure 70, whereby a party who is ordered to perform an act but fails to do so is nonetheless "deemed" to have performed it. It also suggested the possible transference of functions relating to housing from the city council to a court-appointed affordable housing commission; the city opposed this method. Finally, it considered proceeding by way of sanctions for contempt to procure the enactment of the ordinance.

In selecting a means to enforce the consent judgment, the District Court was entitled to rely on the axiom that "courts have inherent power to enforce compliance with their lawful orders through civil contempt." *Shillitani v. United States* (1966). When a district court's order is necessary to remedy past discrimination, the court has an additional basis for the exercise of broad equitable powers. See *Swann v. Charlotte-Mecklenburg Bd. of Ed.* (1971). But while "remedial powers of an equity court must be adequate to the task . . . they are not unlimited." *Whitcomb v. Chavis* (1971). "[T]he federal courts in devising a remedy must take into account the interests of state and local authorities in managing their own affairs, consistent with the Constitution." *Milliken v. Bradley* (1977). And the use of the contempt power places an additional limitation on a district court's discretion, for as the Court of Appeals recognized, "in selecting contempt sanctions, a court is obliged to use the 'least possible power adequate to the end proposed.' " *United States v. City of Yonkers* (quoting *Anderson v. Dunn*).

Given that the city had entered a consent judgment committing itself to enact legislation implementing the long-term plan, we certainly cannot say it was an abuse of discretion for the District Court to have chosen contempt sanctions against the city, as opposed to petitioners, as a means of ensuring compliance. The city, as we have noted, was a party to the action from the beginning, had been found liable for numerous statutory and constitutional violations, and had been subjected to various elaborate remedial decrees which had been upheld on appeal. Petitioners, the individual city councilmen, on the other hand, were not parties to the action, and they had not been found individually liable for any of the violations upon which the remedial decree was based. Although the injunctive portion of that decree was directed not only to the city but to "its officers, agents, employees, successors and all persons in active concern or participation with any of them," the remaining parts of the decree ordering affirmative steps were directed only to the city.

It was the city, in fact, which capitulated. After the Court of Appeals had briefly stayed the imposition of sanctions in August, and we granted a stay as to petitioners but denied it to the city in September, the city council on September 9, 1988, finally enacted the affordable housing ordinance by a vote of 5 to 2. While the District Court could not have been sure in late July that this would be the result, the city's arguments against imposing sanctions on it pointed out the sort of pressure that such sanctions would place on the city. After just two weeks of fines, the city's emergency financial plan required it to curtail sanitation services (resulting in uncollected garbage), eliminate part-time school crossing guards, close all public libraries and parks and lay off approximately 447 employees. In the ensuing four weeks, the city would have been forced to lay off another 1100 city employees. . . .

The nub of the matter, then, is whether in the light of the reasonable probability that sanctions against the city would accomplish the desired result, it was within the court's discretion to impose sanctions on the petitioners as well under the circumstances of this case. . . .

Sanctions directed against the city for failure to take actions such as required by the consent decree coerce the city legislators and, of course, restrict the freedom of those legislators to act in accordance with their current view of the city's best interests. But we believe there are significant differences between the two types of fines. The imposition of sanctions on individual legislators is designed to cause them to vote, not with a view to the interest of their constituents or of the city, but with a view solely to their own personal interests. Even though an individual legislator took the extreme position—or felt that his constituents took the extreme position—

that even a huge fine against the city was preferable to enacting the Affordable Housing Ordinance, monetary sanctions against him individually would motivate him to vote to enact the ordinance simply because he did not want to be out of pocket financially. Such fines thus encourage legislators, in effect, to declare that they favor an ordinance not in order to avoid bankrupting the city for which they legislate, but in order to avoid bankrupting themselves.

This sort of individual sanction effects a much greater perversion of the normal legislative process than does the imposition of sanctions on the city for the failure of these same legislators to enact an ordinance. In that case, the legislator is only encouraged to vote in favor of an ordinance that he would not otherwise favor by reason of the adverse sanctions imposed on the city. . . .

We hold that the District Court, in view of the "extraordinary" nature of the imposition of sanctions against the individual councilmen, should have proceeded with such contempt sanctions first against the city alone in order to secure compliance with the remedial orders. Only if that approach failed to produce compliance within a reasonable time should the question of imposing contempt sanctions against petitioners even have been considered. . . .

Reversed

JUSTICE BRENNAN, with whom JUSTICE MARSHALL, JUSTICE BLACKMUN, and JUSTICE STEVENS join, dissenting.

I understand and appreciate the Court's concern about the District Court's decision to impose contempt sanctions against local officials acting in a legislative capacity. We must all hope that no court will ever again face the open and sustained official defiance of established constitutional values and valid judicial orders that prompted Judge [Leonard B.] Sand's invocation of the contempt power in this manner. But I firmly believe that its availability for such use, in extreme circumstances, is essential. As the District Court was aware:

> "The issues transcend Yonkers. They go to the very foundation of the system of constitutional government. If Yonkers can defy the orders of a federal court in any case, but especially a civil rights case, because compliance is unpopular, and if that situation is tolerated, then our constitutional system of government fails. The issues before the court this morning are no less significant than that."

The Court today recognizes that it was appropriate for the District Court to hold in contempt and fine the city of Yonkers to encourage the city councilmembers to comply with their prior promise to redress the city's history of racial segregation. Yet the Court also reprimands the District Court for simultaneously fining the individual councilmembers whose continuing defiance was the true source of the impasse, holding that personal sanctions should have been considered only after the city sanctions first proved fruitless.

I cannot accept this parsimonious view of the District Court's discretion to wield the power of contempt. Judge Sand's intimate contact for many years with the recalcitrant councilmembers and his familiarity with the city's political climate gave him special insight into the best ways to coerce compliance when all cooperative efforts had failed. For our detached vantage point, we can hardly judge as well as he which coercive sanctions or combination thereof were most likely to work quickly and least disruptively. Because the Court's *ex post* rationalization of what Judge Sand should have done fails to do justice either to the facts of this case or the art of judging, I must dissent.

[I Omitted]

II

... The Court's disfavor of personal sanctions rests on two premises: (1) Judge Sand should have known when he issued the Contempt Order that there was a "reasonable probability that sanctions against the city [alone] would accomplish the desired result"; and (2) imposing personal fines "effects a much greater perversion of the normal legislative process than does the imposition of sanctions on the city." Because personal fines were both completely superfluous to and more intrusive than sanctions against the city alone, the Court reasons, the personal fines constituted an abuse of discretion. Each of these premises is mistaken.

A

While acknowledging that Judge Sand "could not have been sure in late July that this would be the result," the Court confidently concludes that Judge Sand should have been *sure enough* that fining the city would eventually coerce compliance that he should not have personally fined the councilmembers as well. In light of the information available to Judge Sand in July, the Court's confidence is chimerical. Although the escalating city fines eventually would have seriously disrupted many public services and employment, the Court's failure even to consider the possibility that the councilmembers would maintain their defiant posture despite the threat of fiscal insolvency bespeaks an ignorance of Yonkers' history of entrenched discrimination and an indifference to Yonkers' political reality.

The Court first fails to adhere today to our longstanding recognition that the "district court has firsthand experience with the parties and is best qualified to deal with the 'flinty, intractable realities of day-to-day implementation of constitutional commands.' " (quoting *Swann v. Charlotte-Mecklenburg Board of Education* (1971)). Deference to the court's exercise of discretion is particularly appropriate where, as here, the record clearly reveals that the court employed extreme caution before taking the final step of holding the councilmembers personally in contempt. Judge Sand patiently weathered a whirlwind of evasive maneuvers and misrepresentations; considered and rejected alternative means of securing compliance other than contempt sanctions; and carefully considered the ramifications of personal fines. In the end, he readily acknowledged:

> "I know of no parallel for a court to say to an elected official: 'You are in contempt of court and subject to personal fines and may eventually be subject to personal imprisonment because of a manner in which you cast a vote.' I find that extraordinary.
>
> "I find it so extraordinary that at great cost in terms of time and in terms of money and energy and implementation of court's orders, I have sought alternatives to that. But they have all been unsuccessful. . . ."

After according no weight to Judge Sand's cautious and contextual judgment despite his vastly superior vantage point, the Court compounds its error by committing two more. First, the Court turns a blind eye to most of the evidence available to Judge Sand suggesting that, because of the councilmembers' continuing intransigence, sanctions against the city alone might not coerce compliance and that personal sanctions would significantly increase the chance of success. Second, the Court fails to acknowledge that supplementing city sanctions with personal ones likely would secure compliance more promptly, minimizing the overall disruptive effect of the city sanctions on city services generally and long-term compliance with the Consent Decree in particular.

As the events leading up to the Contempt Order make clear, the recalcitrant councilmembers were extremely responsive to the strong segments of their constituencies that were vociferously opposed to racial residential integration. Councilmember Fagan, for example, explained that his vote against the Housing Ordinance required by the Consent Decree "was an act of defiance. The people clearly wanted me to say no to the judge." Councilmember Spallone declared openly that "I will be taking on the judge all the way down the line. I made a commitment to my people and that commitment remains." Moreover, once Yonkers had gained national attention over its refusal to integrate, many residents made it clear to their representatives on the council that they preferred bankrupt martyrdom to integration. . . .

Moreover, acutely aware of these political conditions, the city attorney repeatedly warned Judge Sand *not* to assume that the threat of bankruptcy would compel compliance. . . .

. . . Even if one uncharitably infers in hindsight that the city attorney was merely posturing, given the extremely high stakes I cannot agree with the Court's implicit suggestion that Judge Sand was required to call the city's bluff.

The Court's opinion ignores this political reality surrounding the events of July 1988 and instead focuses exclusively on the fact that, eight months earlier, Judge Sand had secured compliance with another remedial order through the threat of city sanctions alone. But this remedial order had required only that the city council adopt a 1987-1988 Housing Assistance Plan, a prerequisite to the city's qualification for federal housing subsidies. In essence, Judge Sand had to threaten the city with contempt fines just to convince the council to *accept* over $10 million in federal funds. Moreover, the city council capitulated by promising merely to accept the funds—any implied suggestion that it ever intended to *use* the money for housing was, of course, proven false by subsequent events. . . .

The Court . . . also inexplicably ignores the fact that imposing personal fines in addition to sanctions against the city would not only help ensure but actually *hasten* compliance. . . . [I]t seems to me entirely appropriate—indeed obligatory—for Judge Sand to have considered, not just whether city sanctions alone would *eventually* have coerced compliance, but also *how promptly* they would have done so. . . . The Court's determination to play district court-for-a-day—and to do so poorly—is indefensible.

B

. . . According to the Court, the principle of legislative independence does not preclude the District Court from attempting to coerce the city councilmembers into compliance with their promises contained in the Consent Decree. The Court acknowledges that "[s]anctions directed against the city for failure to take actions such as required by the consent decree coerce the city legislators and, of course, restrict the freedom of those legislators to act in accordance with their current view of the city's best interests." Nevertheless, the Court contends, the imposition of personal sanctions as a means of coercion "effects a much greater perversion of the normal legislative process" than city sanctions, and therefore the principle of legislative independence favors the use of personal sanctions only as a fall back position. . . .

. . . While recognizing that injunctions against such executive officials occasionally must be enforced by criminal or civil contempt sanctions of fines or imprisonment, we have never held that fining or even jailing these officials for contempt is categorically more intrusive than fining their governmental entity in order to coerce compliance indirectly. . . .

The doctrine of legislative immunity recognizes that, when acting collectively to pursue a vision of the public good through legislation, legislators must be free to represent their constituents "without fear of outside interference" that would result from private lawsuits. . . . Private lawsuits threatened to chill robust representation by encouraging legislators to avoid controversial issues or stances in order to protect themselves. . . .

But once a federal court has issued a valid order to remedy the effects of a prior, specific constitutional violation, the representatives are no longer "acting in a field where legislators traditionally have power to act." At this point, the Constitution itself imposes an overriding definition of the "public good," and a court's valid command to obey constitutional dictates is not subject to override by any countervailing preferences of the polity, no matter how widely and ardently shared. Local legislators, for example, may not frustrate valid remedial decrees merely because they or their constituents would rather allocate public funds for other uses. More to the point here, legislators certainly may not defy court-ordered remedies for racial discrimination merely because their constituents prefer to maintain segregation. . . .

III

The Court's decision today that Judge Sand abused his remedial discretion by imposing personal fines simultaneously with city fines creates no new principle of law; indeed, it invokes no principle of any sort. But it directs a message to district judges that, despite their repeated and close contact with the various parties and issues, even the most delicate remedial choices by the most conscientious and deliberate judges are subject to being second-guessed by this Court. . . .

I dissent.

□□□

No. 88-1213

Employment Division, Department of Human Resources of Oregon, et al., Petitioners v. Alfred L. Smith et al.

On writ of certiorari to the Supreme Court of Oregon

[April 17, 1990]

JUSTICE SCALIA delivered the opinion of the Court.

This case requires us to decide whether the Free Exercise Clause of the First Amendment permits the State of Oregon to include religiously inspired peyote use within the reach of its general criminal prohibition on use of that drug, and thus permits the State to deny unemployment benefits to persons dismissed from their jobs because of such religiously inspired use.

I

Oregon law prohibits the knowing or intentional possession of a "controlled substance" unless the substance has been prescribed by a medical practitioner. The law defines "controlled substance" as a drug classified in Schedules I through V of the Federal Controlled Substances Act, as modified by the State Board of Pharmacy. Persons who violate this provision by possessing a controlled substance listed on Schedule I are "guilty of a Class B felony." As compiled by the State Board of Pharmacy under its statutory authority, Schedule I contains the drug peyote, a hallucinogen derived from the plant *Lophophorawilliamsii Lemaire.*

Respondents Alfred Smith and Galen Black were fired from their jobs with a private drug rehabilitation organization because they ingested peyote for sacramental purposes at a ceremony of the Native American Church, of which both are members. When respondents applied to petitioner Employment Division for unemployment compensation, they were determined to be ineligible for benefits because they had been discharged for work-related "misconduct." The Oregon Court of Appeals reversed that determination, holding that the denial of benefits violated respondents free exercise rights under the First Amendment.

On appeal to the Oregon Supreme Court, petitioner argued that the denial of benefits was permissible because respondents' consumption of peyote was a crime under Oregon law. The Oregon Supreme Court reasoned, however, that the criminality of respondents' peyote use was irrelevant to resolution of their constitutional claim—since the purpose of the "misconduct" provision under which respondents had been disqualified was not to enforce the State's criminal laws but to preserve the financial integrity of the compensation fund, and since that purpose was inadequate to justify the burden that disqualification imposed on respondents' religious practice. . . . [T]he court concluded that respondents were entitled to payment of unemployment benefits. We granted certiorari.

Before this Court in 1987, petitioner continued to maintain that the illegality of respondents' peyote consumption was relevant to their constitutional claim. We agreed, concluding that "if a State has prohibited through its criminal laws certain kinds of religiously motivated conduct without violating the First Amendment, it certainly follows that it may impose the lesser burden of denying unemployment compensation benefits to persons who engage in that conduct." *Employment Div., Dept. of Human Resources of Oregon v. Smith* (1988) *(Smith I)*. We noted, however, that the Oregon Supreme Court had not decided whether respondents' sacramental use of peyote was in fact proscribed by Oregon's controlled substance law, and that this issue was a matter of dispute between the parties. Being "uncertain about the legality of the religious use of peyote in Oregon," we determined that it would not be "appropriate for us to decide whether the practice is protected by the Federal Constitution." Accordingly, we vacated the judgment of the Oregon Supreme Court and remanded for further proceedings.

On remand, the Oregon Supreme Court held that respondents' religiously inspired use of peyote fell within the prohibition of the Oregon statute, which "makes no exception for the sacramental use" of the drug. It then considered whether that prohibition was valid under the Free Exercise Clause, and concluded that it was not. The court therefore reaffirmed its previous ruling that the State could not deny unemployment benefits to respondents for having engaged in that practice.

We again granted certiorari.

II

... Now that the Oregon Supreme Court has confirmed that Oregon does prohibit the religious use of peyote, we proceed to consider whether that prohibition is permissible under the Free Exercise Clause.

A

The Free Exercise Clause of the First Amendment ... provides that "Congress shall make no law respecting an establishment of religion, or *prohibition the free exercise thereof....*" (emphasis added). The free exercise of religion means, first and foremost, the right to believe and profess whatever religious doctrine one desires. Thus, the First Amendment obviously excludes all "governmental regulation of religious *beliefs* as such." The government may not compel affirmation of religious belief, punish the expression of religious doctrines it believes to be false, impose special disabilities on the basis of religious views or religious status or lend its power to one of the other side in controversies over religious authority or dogma. . . .

But the "exercise of religion" often involves not only belief and profession but the performance of (or abstention from) physical acts: assembling with others for a worship service, participating in sacramental use of bread and wine, proselytizing, abstaining from certain foods or certain modes of transportation. It would be true, we think (though no case of ours has involved the point), that a state would be "prohibiting the free exercise [of religion]" if it sought to ban such acts or abstentions only when they are engaged in for religious reasons, or only because of the religious belief that they display. It would doubtless be unconstitutional, for example, to ban the casting of "statues that are to be used for worship purposes," or prohibit bowing down before a golden calf.

Respondents in the present case, however, seek to carry the meaning of "prohibiting the free exercise [of religion]" one large step further. They contend that their religious motivation for using peyote places them beyond the reach of a criminal law that is not specifically directed at their religious practice and that is concededly constitutional as applied to those who use the drug for other reasons. They assert, in other words, that "prohibiting the free exercise [of religion]" includes requiring any individual to observe a generally applicable law that requires (or forbids) the performance of an act that his religious belief forbids (or requires). As a textual matter, we do not think the words must be given that meaning. It is no more necessary to regard the collection of a general tax, for example, as "prohibiting the free exercise [of religion]" by those citizens who believe support of organized government to be sinful, than it is to regard the same tax as "abridging the freedom ... of the press" of those publishing companies that must pay the tax as a condition of staying in business. It is a permissible reading of the test, in the one case as in the other, to say that if prohibiting the exercise of religion (or burdening the activity of printing) is not the object of the tax but merely the incidental effect of a generally applicable and otherwise valid provision, the First Amendment has not been offended. . . .

Our decisions reveal that the latter reading is the correct one. We have never held that an individual's religious beliefs excuse him from compliance with an otherwise valid law prohibiting conduct that the State is free to regulate. On the contrary, the record of more than a century of our free exercise jurisprudence contradicts that proposition. . . .

. . . [Our] decisions have consistently held that the right of free exercise does not relieve an individual of the obligation to comply with a "valid and neutral law of general applicability on the ground that the law proscribes (or prescribes) conduct that his religion prescribes (or proscribes)." . . .

Our most recent decision involving a neutral, generally applicable regulatory law that compelled activity forbidden by an individual's religion was *United States v. Lee* [1982]. There, an Amish employer, on behalf of himself and his employees, sought exemption from collection and payment of Social Security taxes on the ground that the Amish faith prohibited participation in governmental support programs. We rejected the claim that an exemption was constitutionally required. There would be no way, we observed, to distinguish the Amish believer's objection to Social Security taxes from the religious objections that others might have to the collection or use of other taxes. . . .

The only decisions in which we have held that the First Amendment bars application of a neutral, generally applicable law to religiously motivated action have involved not the Free Exercise Clause alone, but the Free Exercise Clause in conjunction with other constitutional protections, such as freedom of speech and of the press, see *Cantwell v. Connecticut* [1940], (invalidating a licensing system for religious and charitable solicitations under which the administrator had discretion to deny a license to any cause he deemed nonreligious); *Murdock v. Pennsylvania* (1943) (invalidating a flat tax of solicitation as applied to the dissemination of religious ideas); or the right of parents, acknowledged in *Pierce v. Society of Sisters* (1925) to direct the education of their children, see *Wisconsin v. Yoder* (1972) (invalidating compulsory school-attendance laws as applied to Amish parents who refused on religious grounds to send their children to school). . . .

The present case does not present such a hybrid situation, but a free exercise claim unconnected with any communicative activity or parental right. Respondents urge us to hold, quite simply, that when otherwise prohibitable conduct is accompanied by religious convictions, not only the convictions but the conduct itself must be free from governmental regulation. We have never held that, and decline to do so now. . . .

B

Respondents argue that even though exemption from generally applicable criminal laws need not automatically be extended to religiously motivated actors, at least the claim for a religious exemption must be evaluated under the balancing test set for them in *Sherbert v. Verner* (1963). Under the *Sherbert* test, governmental actions that substantially burden a religious practice must be justified by a compelling governmental interest. Applying that test we have, on three occasions, invalidated state unemployment compensation rules that conditioned the availability of benefits upon an applicant's willingness to work under conditions forbidden by his religion. We have never invalidated any governmental action on the basis of the *Sherbert* test except the denial of unemployment compensation. Although we have sometimes purported to apply the *Sherbert* test in contexts other than that, we have always found the test satisfied. In recent years we have abstained from applying the *Sherbert* test (outside the unemployment compensation field) at all. . . .

Even if we were inclined to breathe into *Sherbert* some life beyond the unemployment compensation field, we would not apply it to require exemptions from a generally applicable criminal law. . . .

The "compelling government interest" requirement seems benign, because it is familiar from other fields. But using it as the standard that must be met before the government may accord different treatment on the basis of race, or before the government may regulate the content of speech, is not remotely comparable to using it for the purpose asserted here. What it produces in those other fields—equality of treatment, and an unrestricted flow of contending speech—are constitutional norms; what it would produce here—a private right to ignore generally applicable laws— is a constitutional anomaly.

Nor is it possible to limit the impact of respondents' proposal by requiring a "compelling state interest" only when the conduct prohibited is "central" to the individual's religion. It is no more appropriate for judges to determine the "centrality" of religious beliefs before applying a "compelling interest" test in the free exercise field, than it would be for them to determine the "importance" of ideas before applying the "compelling interest" text in the free speech field. What principle of law of logic can be brought to bear to contradict a believer's assertion that a particular act is "central" to his personal faith? . . .

If the "compelling interest" test is to be applied at all, then, it must be applied across the board, to all actions thought to be religiously commanded. Moreover, if "compelling interest" really means what it says (and watering it down here would subvert its rigor in the other fields where it is applied), many laws will not meet the test. Any society adopting such a system would be courting anarchy, but that danger increases in direct proportion to the society's diversity of religious beliefs, and its determination to coerce or suppress none of them. . . .

Values that are protected against government interference through enshrinement in the Bill of Rights are not thereby banished from the political process. Just as a society that believes in the negative protection accorded to the press by the First Amendment is likely to enact laws that affirmatively foster the dissemination of the printed word, so also a society that believes in the negative protection accorded to religious belief can be expected to be solicitous of that value in its legislation as well. It is therefore not surprising that a number of States have made an exception to their drug laws for sacramental peyote use. But to say that a nondiscriminatory religious-practice exemption is permitted, or even that it is desirable, is not to say that it is constitutionally required, and that the appropriate occasions for its creation can be discerned by the courts. It may fairly be said that leaving accommodation to the political process will place at a relative disadvantage those religious practices that are not widely engaged in; but that unavoidable consequence of democratic government must be preferred to a system in which each conscience is a law unto itself or in which judges weigh the social importance of all laws against the centrality of all religious beliefs.

Because respondent's ingestion of peyote was prohibited under Oregon law, and because that prohibition is constitutional, Oregon may, consistent with the Free Exercise Clause, deny respondents unemployment compensation when their dismissal results from use of the drug. The decision of the Oregon Supreme Court is accordingly reversed.

It is so ordered.

JUSTICE O'CONNOR, with whom JUSTICE BRENNAN, JUSTICE MARSHALL, and JUSTICE BLACKMUN join as to Parts I and II, concurring in the judgment.

Although I agree with the result the Court reaches in this case, I cannot join its opinion. In my view, today's holding dramatically departs from well-settled First Amendment jurisprudence, appears unnecessary to resolve the question presented, and is incompatible with our Nation's fundamental commitment to individual religious liberty.

[I Omitted]

II

The Court today extracts from our long history of free exercise precedents the single categorical rule that "if prohibiting the exercise of religion ... is ... merely the incidental effect of a generally applicable and otherwise valid provision, the First Amendment has not been offended." Indeed, the Court holds that where the law is a generally applicable criminal prohibition, our usual free exercise jurisprudence does not even apply. To reach this sweeping result, however, the Court must not only give a strained reading of the First Amendment but must also disregard our consistent application of free exercise doctrine to cases involving generally applicable regulations that burden religious conduct.

A

The Free Exercise Clause of the First Amendment commands that "Congress shall make no law ... prohibiting the free exercise [of religion]." In *Cantwell v. Connecticut* (1940) we held that this prohibition applies to the States by incorporation into the Fourteenth Amendment and that it categorically forbids government regulation of religious beliefs. As the Court recognizes, however, the "free *exercise*" of religion often, if not invariably, requires the performance of (or abstention from) certain acts.... Because the First Amendment does not distinguish between religious belief and religious conduct, conduct motivated by sincere religious belief, like the belief itself, must therefore be at least presumptively protected by the Free Exercise Clause.

The Court today, however, interprets the Clause to permit the government to prohibit, without justification, conduct mandated by an individual's religious beliefs, so long as that prohibition is generally applicable. But a law that prohibits certain conduct—conduct that happens to be an act of worship for someone—manifestly does prohibit that person's free exercise of his religion. A person who is barred from engaging in religiously motivated conduct is barred from freely exercising his religion. Moreover, that person is barred from freely exercising his religion regardless of whether the law prohibits the conduct only when engaged in for religious reasons, only by members of that religion, or by all persons. It is difficult to deny that a law that prohibits religiously motivated conduct, even if the law is generally applicable, does not at least implicate First Amendment concerns.

The Court responds that generally applicable laws are "one large step" removed from laws aimed at specific religious practices. The First Amendment, however, does not distinguish between laws that are generally applicable and laws that target particular religious practices. Indeed, few States would be so naive as to enact a law directly prohibiting or burdening a religious practice as such. Our free exercise cases have all concerned generally applicable laws that had the effect of significantly burdening a religious practice. If the First Amendment is to have any vitality, it ought not be construed to cover only the extreme and hypothetical situation in which a State directly targets a religious practice. . . .

To say that a person's right to free exercise has been burdened, of course, does not mean that he has an absolute right to engage in the conduct. Under our established First Amendment jurisprudence, we have recognized that the freedom to act, unlike the freedom to believe, cannot be absolute. Instead, we have respected both the First Amendment's express textual mandate and the governmental interest in regulation of conduct by requiring the Government to justify any substantial burden on religiously motivated conduct by a compelling state interest and by means narrowly tailored to achieve that interest. The compelling interest test effectuates the First Amendment's command that religious liberty is an independent liberty, that it occupies a preferred position, and that the Court will not permit encroachments upon this liberty, whether direct or indirect, unless required by clear and compelling governmental interests "of the highest order." . . .

The Court attempts to support its narrow reading of the Clause by claiming that "[w]e have never held that an individual's religious beliefs excuse him from compliance with an otherwise valid law prohibiting conduct that the State is free to regulate." But as the Court later notes, as it must, in cases such as *Cantwell* and [*Wisconsin v.*] *Yoder* [1972] we have in fact interpreted the Free Exercise Clause to forbid application of a generally applicable prohibition to religiously motivated conduct. Indeed, in *Yoder* we expressly rejected the interpretation the Court now adopts. . . .

The Court endeavors to escape from our decisions in *Cantwell* and *Yoder* by labeling them "hybrid" decisions, but there is no denying that both cases expressly relied on the Free Exercise Clause, and that we have consistently regarded those cases as part of the mainstream of our free exercise jurisprudence. Moreover, in each of the other cases cited by the Court to support its categorical rule, we rejected the particular constitutional claims before us only after carefully weighing the competing interests. See *Prince v. Massachusetts* (1944) (state interest in regulating children's activities justifies denial of religious exemption from child labor laws); *Braunfield v. Brown* (1961) (plurality opinion) (state interest in uniform day of rest justifies denial of religious exemption from Sunday closing law); *Gillette* [*v. United States* (1971)] (state interest in military affairs justifies denial of religious exemption from conscription laws); [*United States v.*] *Lee* [1982] (state interest in comprehensive social security system justifies denial of religious exemption from mandatory participation requirement). That we rejected the free exercise claims in those cases hardly calls into question the applicability of First Amendment doctrine in the first place. Indeed, it is surely unusual to judge the vitality of a constitutional doctrine by looking to the win-loss record of the plaintiffs who happen to come before us.

B

Respondents, of course, do not contend that their conduct is automatically immune from all governmental regulation simply because it is motivated by their sincere religious beliefs. The Court's rejection of that argument might therefore be regarded as merely harmless dictum. Rather, respondents invoke our traditional compelling interest test to argue that the Free Exercise Clause requires the State to grant them a limited exemption from its general criminal prohibition against the possession of peyote. The Court today, however, denies them even the opportunity to make that argument, concluding that "the sounder approach and the approach in accord with the vast majority of our precedents, is to hold the [compelling interest] test inapplicable to" challenges to general criminal prohibition.

In my view, however, the essence of a free exercise claim is relief from a burden imposed by government on religious practices or beliefs, whether the burden is imposed directly through laws that prohibit or compel specific religious practices, or indirectly through laws that, in effect, make abandonment of one's own religion or conformity to the religious beliefs of others the price of an equal place in the civil community. . . .

The Court today gives no convincing reason to depart from settled First Amendment jurisprudence. There is nothing talismanic about neutral laws of general applicability or general criminal prohibitions, for laws neutral toward religion can coerce a person to violate his religious conscience or intrude upon his religious duties just as effectively as laws aimed at religion. Although the Court suggests that the compelling interest test, as applied to generally applicable laws, would result in a "constitutional anomaly," the First Amendment unequivocally makes freedom of religion, like freedom from race discrimination and freedom of speech, a "constitutional nor[m]," not an "anomaly.". . .

Finally, the Court today suggests that the disfavoring of minority religions is an "unavoidable consequence" under our system of government and that accommodation of such religions must be left to the political process. In my view, however, the First Amendment was enacted precisely to protect the rights of those whose religious practices are not shared by the majority and may be viewed with hostility. The history of our free exercise doctrine amply demonstrates the harsh impact majoritarian rule has had on unpopular or emerging religious groups such as Jehovah's Witnesses and the Amish. . . .

III

The Court's holding today not only misreads settled First Amendment precedent; it appears to be unnecessary to this case. I would reach the same result applying our established free exercise jurisprudence.

A

There is no dispute that Oregon's criminal prohibition of peyote places a severe burden on the ability or respondents to freely exercise their religion. Peyote is a sacrament of the Native American Church and is regarded as vital to respondents' ability to practice their religion. . . . Under Oregon law, as construed by that State's highest court, members of the Native American Church must choose between carrying out the ritual embodying their religious beliefs and avoidance of criminal prosecution. That choice is, in my view, more than sufficient to trigger First Amendment scrutiny.

There is also no dispute that Oregon has a significant interest in enforcing laws that control the possession and use of controlled substances by its citizens. . . . In light of our recent decisions holding that the governmental interests in the collection of income tax, a comprehensive social security system, and military conscription, are compelling, respondents do not seriously dispute that Oregon has a compelling interest in prohibiting the possession of peyote by its citizens.

B

Thus, the critical question in this case is whether exempting respondents from the State's general criminal prohibition "will unduly interfere with fulfillment of the governmental interest.".... Although the question is close, I would conclude that uniform application of Oregon's criminal prohibition is "essential to accomplish" its overriding interest in preventing the physical harm caused by the use of a Schedule I controlled substance....

...I believe that granting a selective exemption in this case would seriously impair Oregon's compelling interest in prohibiting possession of peyote by its citizens. Under such circumstances, the Free Exercise Clause does not require the State to accommodate respondents' religiously motivated conduct....

I would therefore adhere to our established free exercise jurisprudence and hold that the State in this case has a compelling interest in regulating peyote use by its citizens and that accommodating respondents' religiously motivated conduct "will unduly interfere with fulfillment of the governmental interest." Accordingly, I concur in the judgment of the Court.

JUSTICE BLACKMUN, with whom JUSTICE BRENNAN and JUSTICE MARSHALL join, dissenting.

This Court over the years painstakingly has developed a consistent and exacting standard to test the constitutionality of a state statute that burdens the free exercise of religion. Such a statute may stand only if the law in general, and the State's refusal to allow a religious exemption in particular, are justified by a compelling interest that cannot be served by less restrictive means.

Until today, I thought this was a settled and inviolate principle of this Court's First Amendment jurisprudence. The majority, however, perfunctorily dismisses it as a "constitutional anomaly." As carefully detailed in JUSTICE O'CONNOR's concurring opinion, the majority is able to arrive at this view only by mischaracterizing this Court's precedents.... The Court views traditional free exercise as somehow inapplicable to criminal prohibitions (as opposed to conditions on receipt of benefits), and to state laws of general applicability (as opposed, presumably, to laws that expressly single out religious practices). The Court cites cases in which, due to various exceptional circumstances, we found strict scrutiny inapposite, to hint that the Court has repudiated that standard altogether. In short, it effectuates a wholesale overturning of settled law concerning the Religion Clauses of our Constitution. One hopes that the Court is aware of the consequences, and that its result is not a product of overreaction to the serious problems the country's drug crisis has generated.

This distorted view of our precedents leads the majority to conclude that strict scrutiny of a state law burdening the free exercise of religion is a "luxury" that a well-ordered society cannot afford, and that the repression of minority religions is an "unavoidable consequence of democratic government." I do not believe the Founders thought their dearly bought freedom from religious persecution a "luxury," but an essential element of liberty—and they could not have thought religious intolerance "unavoidable," for they drafted the Religion Clauses precisely to avoid that intolerance.

For these reasons, I agree with JUSTICE O'CONNOR's analysis of the applicable free exercise doctrine, and I join parts I and II of her opinion. As she points out, "the critical question in this case is whether exempting respondents from the State's general criminal prohibition 'will unduly interfere with fulfillment of the governmental interest.'" I do disagree, however, with her specific answer to that question.

I

In weighing respondents' clear interest in the free exercise of their religion against Oregon's asserted interest in enforcing its drug laws, it is important to articulate in precise terms the state interest involved. It is not the State's broad interest in fighting the critical "war on drugs" that must be weighed against respondents' claim, but the State's narrow interest in refusing to make an exception for the religious, ceremonial use of peyote. . . .

The State's interest in enforcing its prohibition, in order to be sufficiently compelling to outweigh a free exercise claim, cannot be merely abstract or symbolic. The State cannot plausibly assert that unbending application of a criminal prohibition is essential to fulfill any compelling interest, if it does not, in fact, attempt to enforce that prohibition. In this case, the State actually has not evinced any concrete interest in enforcing its drug laws against religious users of peyote. Oregon has never sought to prosecute respondents, and does not claim that it has made significant enforcement efforts against other religious users of peyote. The State's asserted interests thus amounts only to the symbolic preservation of an unenforced prohibition. But a government interest in "symbolism, even symbolism for so worthy a cause as the abolition of unlawful drugs," *Treasury Employees v. Von Raab* (1989)

(SCALIA, J. dissenting), cannot suffice to abrogate the constitutional rights of individuals.

Similarly, this Court's prior decisions have not allowed a government to rely on mere speculation about potential harms, but have demanded evidentiary support for a refusal to allow a religious exception. . . .

The State proclaims an interest in protecting the health and safety of its citizens from dangers of unlawful drugs. It offers, however, no evidence that the religious use of peyote has ever harmed anyone. The factual findings of other courts cast doubt on the State's assumption that religious use of peyote is harmful. . . .

The fact that peyote is classified as a Schedule I controlled substance does not, by itself, show that any and all uses of peyote, in any circumstance, are inherently harmful and dangerous. The Federal Government, which created the classifications of unlawful drugs from which Oregon's drug laws are derived, apparently does not find peyote so dangerous as to preclude an exemption for religious use. Moreover, other Schedule I drugs have lawful uses. . . .

The carefully circumscribed ritual context in which respondents used peyote is far removed from the irresponsible and unrestricted recreational use of unlawful drugs. The Native American Church's internal restrictions on, and supervision of, its members' use of peyote substantially obviate the State's health and safety concerns. . . .

Moreover, just as in *Yoder,* the values and interests of those seeking a religious exemption in this case are congruent, to a great degree, with those the State seeks to promote through its drug laws. . . . Not only does the Church's doctrine forbid nonreligious use of peyote; it also generally advocates self-reliance, familial responsibility, and abstinence from alcohol. . . . Far from promoting the lawless and irresponsible use of drugs, Native American Church members' spiritual code exemplifies values that Oregon's drug laws are presumably intended to foster.

The State also seeks to support its refusal to make an exception for religious use of peyote by invoking its interest in abolishing drug trafficking. There is, however, practically no illegal traffic in peyote. . . . Also, the availability of peyote for religious use, even if Oregon were to allow an exemption from its criminal laws, would still be strictly controlled by federal regulations. . . . Peyote simply is not a popular drug; its distribution for use in religious rituals has nothing to do with the vast and violent traffic in illegal narcotics that plagues this country.

Finally, the State argues that granting an exception for religious peyote use would erode its interest in the uniform, fair, and certain enforcement of its drug laws. The State fears that, if it grants an exemption for religious peyote use, a flood of other claims to religious exemptions will follow. It would then be placed in a dilemma, it says, between allowing a patchwork of exemptions that would hinder its law enforcement efforts, and risking a violation of the Establishment Clause by arbitrarily limiting its religious exemptions. This argument, however, could be made in almost any free exercise case. . . .

The State's apprehension of a flood of other religious claims is purely speculative. Almost half the States, and the Federal Government, have maintained an exemption for religious peyote use for many years, and apparently have not found themselves overwhelmed by claims to other religious exemptions. Allowing an exemption for religious peyote use would not necessarily oblige the State to grant a similar exemption to other religious groups. The unusual circumstances that make the religious use of peyote compatible with the State's interests in health and safety and in preventing drug trafficking would not apply to other religious claims. . . .

III

Finally, although I agree with JUSTICE O'CONNOR that courts should refrain from delving into questions of whether, as a matter of religious doctrine, a particular practice is "central" to the religion, I do not think this means that the courts must turn a blind eye to the severe impact of a State's restrictions on the adherents of a minority religion. . . .

Respondents believe, and their sincerity has *never* been at issue, that the peyote plant embodies their deity, and eating it is an act of worship and communion. Without peyote, they could not enact the essential ritual of their religion. . . .

. . . Congress recognized that certain substances, such as peyote, "have religious significance because they are sacred, they have power, they heal, they are necessary to the exercise of the rites of the religion, they are necessary to the cultural integrity of the tribe, and therefore, religious survival." H. R. Rep. No. 95-1308, p. 2 (1978).

The American Indian Religious Freedom Act, in itself, may not create rights enforceable against government action restricting religious freedom, but this Court must scrupulously apply its free exercise analysis to the religious claims of Native Americans, however unorthodox they may be. Otherwise, both the First Amendment and the stated policy of Congress will offer to Native Americans merely an unfulfilled and hollow promise.

IV

For these reasons, I conclude that Oregon's interest in enforcing its drug laws against religious use of peyote is not sufficiently compelling to outweigh respondents' right to the free exercise of their religion. Since the State could not constitutionally enforce its criminal prohibition against respondents, the interests underlying the State's drug laws cannot justify its denial of unemployment benefits. . . .

I dissent.

□□□

No. 88-150

Missouri, et al., Petitioner v. Kalima Jenkins et al.

On writ of certiorari to the United States Court of Appeals for the Eighth Circuit

[April 18, 1990]

JUSTICE WHITE delivered the opinion of the Court.

The United States District Court for the Western District of Missouri imposed an increase in the property taxes levied by the Kansas City, Missouri, School District (KCMSD) to ensure funding for the desegregation of KCMSD's public schools. We granted certiorari to consider the State of Missouri's argument that the District Court lacked the power to raise local property taxes. For the reasons given below, we hold that the District Court abused its discretion in imposing the tax increase. We also hold, however, that the modifications of the District Court's order made by the Court of Appeals do satisfy equitable and constitutional principles governing the District Court's power.

[I and II Omitted]

III

We turn to the tax increase imposed by the District Court. The State urges us to hold that the tax increase violated Article III, the Tenth Amendment, and principles of federal/state comity. We find it unnecessary to reach the difficult constitutional issues, for we agree with the State that the tax increase contravened the principles of comity that must govern the exercise of the District Court's equitable discretion in this area.

It is accepted by all parties, as it was by the courts below, that the imposition of a tax increase by a federal court was an extraordinary event. In assuming for itself the fundamental and delicate power of taxation the District Court not only intruded on local authority but circumvented it altogether. Before taking such a drastic step the District Court was obliged to assure itself that no permissible alternative would have accomplished the required task. We have emphasized that although the "remedial powers of an equity court must be adequate to the task, . . . they are not unlimited," *Witcomb v. Chavis* (1971), and one of the most important considerations governing the exercise of equitable power is a proper respect for the integrity and function of local government institutions. Especially is this true where, as here, those institutions are ready, willing, and—but for the operation of state law curtailing their powers—able to remedy the deprivation of constitutional rights themselves.

The District Court believed that it had no alternative to imposing a tax increase. But there was an alternative, the very one outlined by the Court of Appeals: it could have authorized or required KCMSD to levy property taxes at a rate adequate to fund the desegregation remedy and could have enjoined the operation of state laws that would have prevented KCMSD from exercising this power. The difference between the two approaches is far more than a matter of form. Authorizing and directing local government institutions to devise and implement remedies not only protects the function of those institutions but, to the extent possible, also places the responsibility for solutions to the problems of segregation upon those who have themselves created the problems.

As *Brown v. Board of Education* (1955) observed, local authorities have the "primary responsibility for elucidating, assessing, and solving" the problems of desegregation. See also *Milliken v. Bradley* (1977). This is true as well of the problems of financing desegregation, for no matter has been more consistently placed upon the shoulders of local government than that of financing public schools. As was said in another context, "[t]he very complexity of the problems of financing and managing a . . . public school system suggests that 'there will be more than one constitutionally permissible method of solving them,' and that . . . 'the legislature's efforts to tackle the problems' should be entitled to respect." *San Antonio Independent School District v. Rodriguez* (1973) (quoting *Jefferson v. Hackney* (1972)). By no means should a district court grant local government *carte blanche*, . . . but local officials should at least have the opportunity to devise their own solutions to these problems. . . .

The District Court therefore abused its discretion in imposing the tax itself. The Court of Appeals should not have allowed the tax increase to stand and should have reversed the District Court in this respect. See *Langnes v. Green* (1931).

IV

We stand on different ground when we review the modifications to the District Court's order made by the Court of Appeals. . . . [T]he Court of Appeals held that the District Court in the future should authorize KCMSD to submit a levy to the state tax collection authorities adequate to fund its budget and should enjoin the operation of state laws that would limit or reduce the levy below that amount.

The State argues that the funding ordered by the District Court violates principles of equity and comity because the remedial order itself was excessive. As the State puts it, "[t]he only reason that the court below needed to consider an unprecedented tax increase was the equally unprecedented cost of its remedial programs." We think this argument aims at the scope of the remedy rather than the manner in which the remedy is to be funded and thus falls outside our limited grant of certiorari in this case. As we denied certiorari on the first question presented by the State's petition, which did challenge the scope of the remedial order, we must resist the State's efforts to argue that point now. We accept, without approving or disapproving, the Court of Appeals conclusion that the District Court's remedy was proper. See *Cone v. West Virginia Pulp & Paper Co.* (1947).

The State has argued here that the District Court, having found the State and KCMSD jointly and severally liable, should have allowed any monetary obligations that KCMSD could not meet to fall on the State rather than interfere with state law to permit KCMSD to meet them. Under the circumstances of this case, we cannot say it was an abuse of discretion for the District Court to rule that KCMSD should be responsible for funding its share of the remedy. The State strenuously opposed efforts by respondents to make it responsible for the cost of implementing the order and had secured a reversal of the District Court's earlier decision placing on it all of the cost of substantial portions of the order. The District Court declined to require the State to pay for KCMSD's obligations because it believed that the Court of Appeals had ordered it to allocate the costs between the two governmental entities. Furthermore, if the District Court had chosen the route now suggested by the State, implementation of the remedial order might have been delayed if the State resisted efforts by KCMSD to obtain contribution.

It is true that in *Milliken v. Bradley*, we stated that the enforcement of a money judgment against the State did not violate principles of federalism because "[t]he District Court . . . neither attempted to restructure local governmental entities nor . . . mandat[ed] a particular method or structure of state or local financing." But we did not there state that a District Court could never set aside state laws preventing local governments from raising funds sufficient to satisfy their constitutional obligations just because those funds could also be obtained from the States. . . .

We turn to the constitutional issues. The modifications ordered by the Court of Appeals cannot be assailed as invalid under the Tenth Amendment. "The Tenth Amendment's reservation of nondelegated powers to the States is not implicated by a federal-court judgment enforcing the express prohibitions of unlawful state conduct enacted by the Fourteenth Amendment.". . .

Finally, the State argues that an order to increase taxes cannot be sustained under the judicial power of Article III. Whatever the merits of this argument when applied to the District Court's own order increasing taxes, a point we have not reached, a court order directing a local government body to levy its own taxes is plainly a judicial act within the power of a federal court. We held as much in *Griffin v. Prince Edward County School Bd.* [1964], where we stated that a District Court, faced with a county's attempt to avoid desegregation of the public schools by refusing to operate those schools, could "require the [County] Supervisors to exercise the power that is theirs to levy taxes to raise funds adequate to reopen, operate, and maintain without racial discrimination a public school system. . . ." *Griffin* followed a long and venerable line of cases in which this Court held that federal courts could issue the writ of mandamus to compel local governmental bodies to levy taxes adequate to satisfy their debt obligations. . . .

The State maintains, however, that even under these cases, the federal judicial power can go no further than to require local governments to levy taxes *as authorized under state law.* In other words, the State argues that federal courts cannot set aside state-imposed limitations on local taxing authority because to do so is to do more than to require the local government "to exercise the power *that is theirs.*" We disagree. . . .

. . . Here the KCMSD may be ordered to levy taxes despite the statutory limitations on its authority in order to compel the discharge of an obligation imposed on KCMSD by the Fourteenth Amendment. To hold otherwise would fail to take account of the obligations of local governments, under the Supremacy Clause, to fulfill the requirements that the Constitution imposes on them. However wide the discretion of local authorities in fashioning desegregation remedies may be, "if a state-imposed limitation on a school authority's discretion operates to inhibit or obstruct the operation of a unitary school system or impede the disestablishing of a dual school system, it must fall; state policy must give way when it operates to hinder vindication of federal constitutional guarantees." *North Carolina State Bd. of Education v. Swann* (1971). Even though a particular remedy may not be required in every case to vindicate constitutional guarantees, where (as here) it has been found that a particular remedy is required, the State cannot hinder the process by preventing a local government from implementing that remedy.

Accordingly, the judgment of the Court of Appeals is affirmed insofar as it required the District Court to modify its funding order and reversed insofar as it allowed the tax increase imposed by the District Court to stand. The case is remanded for further proceedings consistent with this opinion.

It is so ordered.

JUSTICE KENNEDY, with whom THE CHIEF JUSTICE, JUSTICE O'CONNOR, and JUSTICE SCALIA join, concurring in part and concurring in the judgment.

In agreement with the Court that we have jurisdiction to decide this case, I join Part II of the opinion. I agree also that the District Court exceeded its authority by attempting to impose a tax. The Court is unanimous in its holding, that the Court of Appeals' judgment affirming "the actions that the [district] court has taken to this point" must be reversed. This is consistent with our precedents and the basic principles defining judicial power.

In my view, however, the Court transgresses these same principles when it goes further, much further, to embrace by broad dictum an expansion of power in the federal judiciary beyond all precedent. Today's casual embrace of taxation imposed by the unelected, life-tenured federal judiciary disregards fundamental precepts for the democratic control of public institutions. I cannot acquiesce in the majority's statements on this point, and should there arise an actual dispute over the collection of taxes as here contemplated in a case that is not, like this one, premature, we should not confirm the outcome of premises adopted with so little constitutional justification. The Court's statements, in my view, cannot be seen as necessary for its judgment, or as precedent for the future, and I cannot join Parts III and IV of the Court's opinion.

I

Some essential litigation history is necessary for a full understanding of what is at stake here and what will be wrought if the implications of all the Court's statements are followed to the full extent. The District Court's remedial plan was proposed for the most part by the Kansas City, Missouri, School District (KCMSD) itself, which is in name a defendant in the suit. Defendants, and above all defendants that are public entities, act in the highest and best tradition of our legal system when they acknowledge fault and cooperate to suggest remedies. But in the context of this dispute, it is of vital importance to note that the KCMSD demonstrated little concern for the fiscal consequences of the remedy that it helped design.

As the District Court acknowledged, the plaintiffs and the KCMSD pursued a "friendly adversary" relationship. Throughout the remedial phase of the litigation, the KCMSD proposed ever more expensive capital improvements with the agreement of the plaintiffs, and the State objected. Some of these improvements involved basic repairs to deteriorating facilities within the school system. The KCMSD, however, devised a broader concept for district-wide improvement, and the District Court approved it. The plan involved a variation of the magnet school concept. Magnet schools ... offer special programs, often used to encourage voluntary movement of students within the district in a pattern that aids desegregation.

Although we have approved desegregation plans involving magnet schools of this conventional definition ... the District Court found this insufficient. Instead, the court and the KCMSD decided to make a magnet of the district as a whole. The hope was to draw new nonminority students from outside the district. The KCMSD plan adopted by the Court provided that "every senior high school, every middle school, and approximately one-half of the elementary schools in the KCMSD will become magnet schools by the school year 1991-92." The plan was intended to "improve the quality of education of all KCMSD students." The District Court was candid to acknowledge that the "long term goal of this Court's remedial order is to make available to *all* KCMSD students educational opportunities equal to or greater than those presently available in the average Kansas City, Missouri metropolitan suburban school district."

It comes as no surprise that the cost of this approach to the remedy far exceeded KCMSD's budget, or for that matter, its authority to tax. A few examples are illustrative. Programs such as a "performing arts middle school," a "technical magnet high school" that "will offer programs ranging from heating and air conditioning to cosmetology and robotics," were approved. The plan also included a "25 acre farm and 25 acre wildland area" for science study. The Court rejected various proposals by the State to make "capital improvements necessary to eliminate health and safety hazards and to provide a good learning environment," because these proposals failed to "consider the criteria of suburban comparability." The District Court stated: "This 'patch and repair' approach proposed by the State would not achieve suburban comparability or the visual attractiveness sought by the Court as it would result in floor coverings with unsightly sections of mismatched carpeting and tile, and individual walls possessing different shades of paint." Finding that construction of new schools would result in more "attractive" facilities than renovation of existing ones, the District Court approved new construction at a cost ranging from $61.80 per square foot to $95.70 per square foot as distinct from renovation at $45 per square foot.

By the time of the order at issue here, the District Court's remedies included some "$260 million in capital improvements and a magnet-school plan costing over $200 million." *Missouri v. Jenkins* (1989). And the remedial orders grew more expensive as shortfalls in revenue became more severe. As the Eighth Circuit judges dissenting from denial of rehearing in banc put it: "The remedies ordered go far beyond anything previously seen in a school desegregation case. The sheer immensity of the programs encompassed by the district court's order—the large number of magnet schools and the quantity of capital renovations and new construction—are concededly without parallel in any other school district in the country."

The judicial taxation approved by the Eighth Circuit is also without parallel. Other Circuits that have faced funding problems arising from remedial decrees have concluded that, while courts have undoubted power to order that schools operate in compliance with the Constitution, the manner and methods of school financing are beyond federal judicial authority. . . .

Unlike these other courts, the Eighth Circuit has endorsed judicial taxation. . . . The case before us represents the first in which a lower federal court has in fact upheld taxation to fund a remedial decree.

For reasons explained below, I agree with the Court that the Eighth Circuit's judgment affirming the District Court's direct levy of a property tax must be reversed. I cannot agree, however, that we "stand on different ground when we review the modifications to the District Court's order made by the Court of Appeals." At the outset, it must be noted that the Court of Appeals made no "modifications" to the District Court's order. Rather, it affirmed "the actions that the court has taken to this point." It is true that the Court of Appeals went on "to consider the procedures which the district court should use *in the future*." ([E]mphasis added.). . . .

The premise of the Court's analysis, I submit, is infirm. Any purported distinction between direct imposition of a tax by the federal court and an order commanding the school district to impose the tax is but a convenient formalism where the court's action is predicated on elimination of state law limitations on the school district's taxing authority. . . .

Whatever taxing power the KCMSD may exercise outside the boundaries of state law would derive from the federal court. The Court never confronts the judicial authority to issue an order for this purpose. Absent a change in state law, the tax is imposed by federal authority under a federal decree. The question is whether a district court possesses a power to tax under federal law, either directly or through delegation to the KCMSD.

II

Article III of the Constitution states that "[t]he judicial Power of the United States, shall be vested in one supreme Court, and in such inferior Courts as the Congress may from time to time ordain and establish." The description of the judicial power nowhere includes the word "tax" or anything that resembles it. This reflects the Framers' understanding that taxation was not a proper area for judicial involvement. . . .

Our cases throughout the years leave no doubt that taxation is not a judicial function. . . . The order at issue here . . . has the purpose and direct effect of extracting money from persons who have had no presence or representation in the suit. For this reason, the District Court's direct order imposing a tax was more than an abuse of discretion, for any attempt to collect the taxes from the citizens would have been a blatant denial of due process.

. . . A true exercise of judicial power provides due process of another sort. Where money is extracted from parties by a court's judgment, the adjudication itself provides the notice and opportunity to be heard that due process demands before a citizen may be deprived of property.

The order here provides neither of these protections. . . .

. . . [T]oday's case is not an instance of one branch of the Federal Government invading the province of another. It is instead one that brings the weight of federal authority upon a local government and a State. This does not detract, however, from the fundamental point that the judiciary is not free to exercise all federal power; it may exercise only the judicial power. And the important effects of the taxation order discussed here raise additional federalism concerns that counsel against the Court's analysis.

In perhaps the leading case concerning desegregation remedies, *Milliken v. Bradley* (1977), we upheld a prospective remedial plan, not a "money judgment," against a State's claim that principles of federalism had been ignored in the plan's implementation. In so doing the Court emphasized that the District Court had "neither attempted to restructure local governmental entities nor to mandate a particular method or structure of state or local financing." No such assurances emerge from today's decision, which endorses federal court intrusion into these precise matters. . . .

The power of taxation is one that the federal judiciary does not possess. In our system "the legislative department alone has access to the pockets of the people," The Federalist, No. 48, 334 (J. Cooke ed. 1961) (J. Madison), for it is the legislature that is accountable to them and represents their will. The authority that would levy the tax at issue here shares none of these qualities. Our federal judiciary, by design, is not representative or responsible to the people in a political sense; it is independent. Federal judges do not depend on the popular will for their office. They may not even share the burden of taxes they attempt to impose, for they may live outside the jurisdiction their orders affect. And federal judges have no fear that the competition for scarce public resources could result in a diminution of their salaries. It is not surprising that imposition of taxes by an authority so insulated from public communication or control can lead to deep feelings of frustration, powerlessness, and anger on the part of taxpaying citizens: . . .

At bottom, today's discussion seems motivated by the fear that failure to endorse judicial taxation power might in some extreme circumstance leave a court unable to remedy a constitutional violation. As I discuss below, I do not think this possibility is in reality a significant one. More important, this possibility is nothing more or less than the necessary consequence of *any* limit on judicial power. If, however, judicial discretion is to provide the sole limit on judicial remedies, that discretion must counsel restraint. Ill-considered entry into the volatile field of taxation is a step that may place at risk the legitimacy that justifies judicial independence.

III

One of the most troubling aspects of the Court's opinion is that discussion of the important constitutional issues of judicial authority to tax need never have been undertaken to decide this case. Even were I willing to accept the Court's proposition that a federal court might in some extreme case authorize taxation, this case is not the one. The suggestion that failure to approve judicial taxation here would leave constitutional rights unvindicated rests on a presumption that the District Court's remedy is the *only* possible cure for the constitutional violations it found. Neither our precedents nor the record support this view. In fact, the taxation power is sought here on behalf of a remedial order unlike any before seen.

It cannot be contended that interdistrict comparability, which was the ultimate goal of the District Court's orders, is itself a constitutional command. We have long since determined that "unequal expenditures between children who happen to reside in different districts" do not violate the Equal Protection Clause. *San Antonio Independent School Dist. v. Rodriguez* (1973). The District Court in this case found, and the Court of Appeals affirmed, that there was no interdistrict constitutional violation that would support mandatory interdistrict relief. . . . The State's complaint that this suit represents the attempt of a school district that could not obtain public support for increased spending to enlist the District Court to finance its educational policy cannot be dismissed out of hand. . . .

This Court has never approved a remedy of the type adopted by the District Court. There are strong arguments against the validity of such a plan. A remedy that uses the quality of education as a lure to attract nonminority students will place the District Court at the center of controversies over educational philosophy that by tradition are left to this Nation's communities. . . .

The prudence we have required in other areas touching on federal court intrusion in local government . . . is missing here. Even on the assumption that a federal court might order taxation in an extreme case, the unique nature of the taxing power would demand that this remedy be used as a last resort. In my view, a taxation order should not even be considered, and this Court need never have addressed the question, unless there has been a finding that without the particular remedy at issue the constitutional violation will go unremedied. By this I do not mean that the remedy is, as we assume this one was, within the broad discretion of the district court. Rather, as a prerequisite to considering a taxation order, I would require a finding that any remedy less costly than the one at issue would so plainly leave the violation unremedied that its implementation would itself be an abuse of discretion. There is no showing in this record that, faced with the revenue shortfall, the District Court gave due consideration to the possibility that another remedy among the "wide range of possibilities" would have addressed the constitutional violations without giving rise to a funding crisis. . . .

IV

This case is a stark illustration of the ever-present question whether ends justify means. Few ends are more important than enforcing the guarantee of equal educational opportunity for our Nation's children. But rules of taxation that override state political structures not themselves subject to any constitutional infirmity raise serious questions of federal authority, questions compounded by the odd posture of a case in which the Court assumes the validity of a novel conception of desegregation remedies we never before have approved. The historical record of voluntary compliance with the decree of *Brown v. Board of Education* [1955] is not a proud chapter in our constitutional history, and the judges of the District Courts and Courts of Appeals have been courageous and skillful in implementing its mandate. But courage and skill must be exercised with due regard for the proper and historic role of the courts.

I do not acknowledge the troubling departures in today's majority opinion as either necessary or appropriate to ensure full compliance with the Equal Protection Clause and its mandate to eliminate the cause and effects of racial discrimination in the schools. Indeed, while this case happens to arise in the compelling context of school desegregation, the principles involved are not limited to that context. There is no obvious limit to today's discussion that would prevent judicial taxation in cases involving prisons, hospitals, or other public institutions, or indeed to pay a large damages award levied against a municipality. . . . This assertion of judicial power in one of the most sensitive of policy areas, that involving taxation, begins a process that over time could threaten fundamental alteration of the form of government our Constitution embodies.

James Madison observed: "Justice is the end of government. It is the end of civil society. It ever has been, and ever will be pursued, until it be obtained, or until liberty be lost in the pursuit." The Federalist, No. 51, p. 352 (J. Cooke ed. 1961). In pursuing the demand of justice for racial equality, I fear that the Court today loses sight of other basic political liberties guaranteed by our constitutional system, liberties that can coexist with a proper exercise of judicial remedial powers adequate to correct constitutional violations.

□□□

No. 88-1597

Board of Education of the Westside Community Schools, etc., et al., Petitioners v. Bridget C. Mergens, by and through her next friend, Daniel N. Mergens, et al.

On writ of certiorari to the United States Court of Appeals for the Eighth Circuit

[June 4, 1990]

JUSTICE O'CONNOR delivered the opinion of the Court, except as to Part III.

This case requires us to decide whether the Equal Access Act, 89 Stat. 1302, 20 U.S.C. §§ 4071-4074, prohibits Westside High School from denying a student religious group permission to meet on school premises during noninstructional time, and if so, whether the Act, so construed, violates the Establishment Clause of the First Amendment.

I

Respondents are current and former students at Westside High School, a public secondary school in Omaha, Nebraska. At the time this suit was filed, the school enrolled about 1,450 students and included grades 10 to 12; in the 1987-1988 school year, ninth graders were added. Westside High School is part of the Westside Community School System, an independent public school district. Petitioners are the Board of Education of Westside Community Schools (District 66); Wayne W. Meier, the president of the school board; James E. Findley, the principal of Westside High School; Kenneth K. Hanson, the superintendent of schools for the school district; and James A. Tangdell, the assistant superintendent of schools for the school district.

Students at Westside High School are permitted to join various student groups and clubs, all of which meet after school hours on school premises. The students may choose from approximately 30 recognized groups on a voluntary basis. . . .

School Board Policy 5610 concerning "Student Clubs and Organizations" recognizes these student clubs as a "vital part of the total education program as a means of developing citizenship, wholesome attitudes, good human relations, knowledge and skills." Board Policy 5610 also provides that each club shall have faculty sponsorship and that "clubs and organizations shall not be sponsored by any political or religious organization, or by any organization which denies membership on the basis of race, color, creed, sex or political belief." Board Policy 6180 on "Recognition of Religious Beliefs and Customs" requires that "[s]tudents adhering to a specific set of religious beliefs or holding to little or no belief shall be alike respected." In addition, Board Policy 5450 recognizes its students' "Freedom of Expression," consistent with the authority of the board.

There is no written school board policy concerning the formation of student clubs. Rather, students wishing to form a club present their request to a school official who determines whether the proposed club's goals and objectives are consistent with school board policies and with the school district's "Mission and Goals"—a broadly worded "blueprint" that expresses the district's commitment to teaching academic, physical, civic, and personal skills and values.

In January 1985, respondent Bridget Mergens met with Westside's principal, Dr. Findley, and requested permission to form a Christian club at the school. The proposed club would have the same privileges and meet on the same terms and conditions as other Westside student groups, except that the proposed club would not have a faculty sponsor. According to the students' testimony at trial, the club's purpose would have been, among other things, to permit the students to read and discuss the Bible, to have fellowship, and to pray together. Membership would have been voluntary and open to all students regardless of religious affiliation.

Findley denied the request, as did associate superintendent Tangdell. In February 1985, Findley and Tangdell informed Mergens that they had discussed the matter with superintendent Hanson and that he had agreed that her request should be denied. The school officials explained that school policy required all student clubs to have a faculty sponsor, which the proposed religious club would not or could not have, and that a religious club at the school would violate the Establishment Clause. In March 1985, Mergens appealed the denial of her request to the Board of Education, but the board voted to uphold the denial.

Respondents, by and through their parents as next friends, then brought this suit in the United States District Court for the District of Nebraska seeking declaratory and injunctive relief. They alleged that petitioners' refusal to permit the proposed club to meet at Westside violated the Equal Access Act, 20 U.S.C. §§ 4071-4974, which prohibits public secondary schools that receive federal financial assistance and that maintain a "limited open forum" from denying "equal access" to students who wish to meet within the forum on the basis of the content of the speech at such meetings, § 4071(a). Respondents further alleged that petitioners' actions denied them their First and Fourteenth Amendment rights to freedom of speech, association, and the free exercise of religion. Petitioners responded that the Equal Access Act did not apply to Westside and that, if the Act did apply, it violated the Establishment Clause of the first Amendment and was therefore unconstitutional. The United States intervened . . . to defend the constitutionality of the Act.

The District Court entered judgment for petitioners. The court held that the Act did not apply in this case because Westside did not have a "limited open forum" as defined by the Act—all of Westside's student clubs, the court concluded, were curriculum-related and tied to the educational function of the school. . . .

The United States Court of Appeals for the Eighth Circuit reversed. The Court of Appeals held that the District Court erred in concluding that all the existing student clubs at Westside were curriculum-related. The Court of Appeals noted that the "broad interpretation" advanced by the Westside school officials "would make the [Equal Access Act] meaningless" and would allow any school to "arbitrarily deny access to school facilities to any unfavored student club on the basis of its speech content," which was "exactly the result that Congress sought to prohibit by enacting the [Act]." The Court of Appeals instead found that "[m]any of the student clubs at WHS, including the chess club, are noncurriculum-related.". . . Accordingly, because it found that Westside maintained a limited open forum under the Act, the Court of Appeals concluded that the Act applied to "forbi[d] discrimination against [respondents'] proposed club on the basis of its religious content."

The Court of Appeals then rejected petitioners' contention that the Act violated the Establishment Clause. . . .

We granted certiorari and now affirm.

II

A

In *Widmar v. Vincent* (1981), we invalidated, on free speech grounds, a state university regulation that prohibited student use of school facilities " 'for purposes of religious worship or religious teaching.' " In doing so, we held that an "equal access" policy would not violate the Establishment Clause under our decision in *Lemon v. Kurtzman* (1971). In particular, we held that such a policy would have a secular purpose, would not have the primary effect of advancing religion, and would not result in excessive entanglement between government and religion. We noted, however, that "[u]niversity students are, of course, young adults. They are less impressionable than younger students and should be able to appreciate that the University's policy is one of neutrality toward religion."

In 1984, Congress extended the reasoning of *Widmar* to public secondary schools. Under the Equal Access Act, a public secondary school with a "limited open forum" is prohibited from discriminating against students who wish to conduct a meeting within that forum on the basis of the "religious, political, philosophical, or other content of the speech at such meetings.".... A "limited open forum" exists whenever a public secondary school "grants an offering to or opportunity for one or more noncurriculum related student groups to meet on school premises during noninstructional time." "Meeting" is defined to include "those activities of student groups which are permitted under a school's limited open forum and are not directly related to the school curriculum." "Noninstructional time" is defined to mean "time set aside by the school before actual classroom instruction begins or after actual classroom instruction ends." Thus, even if a public secondary school allows only one "noncurriculum related student group" to meet, the Act's obligations are triggered and the school may not deny other clubs, on the basis of the content of their speech, equal access to meet on school premises during noninstructional time.

The Act further specifies that "[s]chools shall be deemed to offer a fair opportunity to students who wish to conduct a meeting within its limited open forum" if the school uniformly provides that the meetings are voluntary and student-initiated; are not sponsored by the school, the government, or its agents or employees; do not materially and substantially interfere with the orderly conduct of educational activities within the school; and are not directed, controlled, conducted, or regularly attended by "nonschool persons."....

Finally, the Act does not "authorize the United States to deny or withhold Federal financial assistance to any school" or "limit the authority of the school, its agents or employees, to maintain order and discipline of school premises, to protect the well-being of students and faculty, and to assure that attendance of students at the meetings is voluntary."

B

The parties agree that Westside High School receives federal financial assistance and is a public secondary school within the meaning of the Act. The Act's obligation to grant equal access to student groups is therefore triggered if Westside maintains a "limited open forum"—i.e., if it permits one or more "noncurriculum related student groups" to meet on campus before or after classes.

Unfortunately, the Act does not define the crucial phrase "noncurriculum related student group." Our immediate task is therefore one of statutory interpretation. We begin, of course, with the language of the statute. The common meaning of the term "curriculum" is "the whole body of courses offered by an educational institution or one of its branches.". . . Any sensible interpretation of "noncurriculum related student group" must therefore be anchored in the notion that such student groups are those that are not related to the body of courses offered by the school. The difficult question is the degree of "unrelatedness to the curriculum" required for a group to be considered "noncurriculum related."

The Act's definition of the sort of "meeting[s]" that must be accommodated under the statute sheds some light on this question. "[T]he term 'meeting' includes those activities of student groups which are . . . not *directly related* to the school curriculum." ([E]mphasis added.) Congress's use of the phrase "directly related" implies that student groups directly related to the subject matter of courses offered by the school do not fall within the "noncurriculum related" category and would therefore be considered "curriculum related."

The logic of the Act also supports this view, namely, that a curriculum-related student group is one that has more than just a tangential or attenuated relationship to courses offered by the school. Because the purpose of granting equal access is to prohibit discrimination between religious or political clubs on the one hand and other non-curriculum-related student groups on the other, the Act is premised on the notion that a religious or political club is itself likely to be a non-curriculum-related student group. It follows, then, that a student group that is "curriculum related" must at least have a more direct relationship to the curriculum than a religious or political club would have.

Although the phrase "noncurriculum related student group" nevertheless remains sufficiently ambiguous that we might normally resort to legislative history, we find the legislative history on this issue less than helpful.... During congressional debate on the subject, legislators referred to a number of different definitions, and thus both petitioners and respondents can cite to legislative history favoring their interpretation of the phrase....

We think it significant, however, that the Act, which was passed by wide, bipartisan majorities in both the House and the Senate, reflects at least some consensus on a broad legislative purpose. The committee reports indicate that the Act was intended to address perceived widespread discrimination against religious speech in public schools, and, as the language of the Act indicates, its sponsors contemplated that the Act would do more than merely validate the status quo. The committee reports also show that the Act was enacted in part in response to two federal appellate court decisions holding that student religious groups could not, consistent with the Establishment Clause, meet on school premises during noninstructional time....

In light of this legislative purpose, we think that the term "noncurriculum related student group" is best interpreted broadly to mean any student group that does not *directly* relate to the body of courses offered by the school In our view, ... a French club would directly relate to the curriculum if a school taught French in a regularly offered course or planned to teach the subject in the near future....

On the other hand, unless a school could show that groups such as a chess club, a stamp collecting club, or a community service club fell within our description of groups that directly relate to the curriculum, such groups would be "noncurriculum related student groups" for the purposes of the Act. The existence of such groups would create a "limited open forum" under the Act and would prohibit the school from denying equal access to any other student group on the basis of the content of that group's speech. Whether a specific student group is a "noncurriculum related student group" will therefore depend on a particular school's curriculum, but such determinations would be subject to factual findings well within the competence of trial courts to make....

C

The parties in this case focus their dispute on 10 of Westside's approximately 30 voluntary student clubs: Interact (a service club related to Rotary International); Chess; Subsurfers (a club for students interested in scuba diving); National Honor Society; Photography; Welcome to Westside (a club to introduce new students to the school); Future Business Leaders of America; Zonta (the female counterpart to Interact); Student Advisory Board (student government); and Student Forum (student government). Petitioners contend that all of these student activities are curriculum-related because they further the goals of particular aspects of the school's curriculum. . . .

To the extent that petitioners contend that "curriculum related" means anything remotely related to abstract educational goals, however, we reject that argument. To define "curriculum related" in a way that results in almost no schools having limited open fora, or in a way that permits schools to evade the Act by strategically describing existing student groups, would render the Act merely hortatory. . . .

Although our definition of "noncurriculum related student activities" looks to a school's actual practice rather than its stated policy, we note that our conclusion is also supported by the school's own description of its student activities. . . . [T]he school states that Band "is included in our regular curriculum"; Choir "is a course offered as part of the curriculum"; Distributive Education "is an extension of the Distributive Education class"; International Club is "developed through our foreign language classes"; Latin Club is "designed for those students who are taking Latin as a foreign language"; Student Publications "includes classes offered in preparation of the yearbook (Shield) and the student newspaper (Lance)"; Dramatics "is an extension of a regular academic class"; and Orchestra "is an extension of our regular curriculum." These descriptions constitute persuasive evidence that these student clubs directly relate to the curriculum. By inference, however, the fact that the descriptions of student activities such as Subsurfers and chess do not include such references strongly suggests that those clubs do not, by the school's own admission directly relate to the curriculum. . . .

. . . Given that the Act explicitly prohibits denial of "equal access . . . to . . . any students who wish to conduct a meeting within [the school's] limited open forum" on the basis of the religious content of the speech at such meetings, § 4071(a), we hold that Westside's denial of respondents' request to form a Christian club denies them "equal access" under the Act.

Because we rest our conclusion on statutory grounds, we need not decide—and therefore express no opinion on—whether the First Amendment requires the same result.

III

Petitioners contend that even if Westside has created a limited open forum within the meaning of the Act, its denial of official recognition to the proposed Christian club must nevertheless stand because the Act violates the Establishment Clause of the First Amendment, as applied to the States through the Fourteenth Amendment. Specifically, petitioners maintain that because the school's recognized student activities are an integral part of its educational mission, official recognition of respondents' proposed club would effectively incorporate religious activities into the school's official program, endorse participation in the religious club, and provide the club with an official platform to proselytize other students.

We disagree. In *Widmar,* we applied the three-part *Lemon* test to hold that an "equal access" policy, at the university level, does not violate the Establishment Clause. We concluded that "an open-forum policy, including nondiscrimination against religious speech, would have a secular purpose," and would in fact *avoid* entanglement with religion. ("[T]he University would risk greater 'entanglement' by attempting to enforce its exclusion of 'religious worship' and 'religious speech.'") We also found that although incidental benefits accrued to religious groups who used university facilities, this result did not amount to an establishment of religion. First, we stated that a university's forum does not "confer any imprimatur of state approval on religious sects or practices." Indeed, the message is one of neutrality rather than endorsement; if a State refused to let religious groups use facilities open to others, then it would demonstrate not neutrality but hostility toward religion. . . .

We think the logic of *Widmar* applies with equal force to the Equal Access Act. As an initial matter, the Act's prohibition of discrimination on the basis of "political, philosophical, or other" speech as well as religious speech is a sufficient basis for meeting the secular purpose prong of the *Lemon* test. . . .

Petitioners' principal contention is that the Act has the primary effect of advancing religion. Specifically, petitioners urge that, because the student religious meetings are held under school aegis, and because the state's compulsory attendance laws bring the students together (and thereby provide a ready-made audience for student evangelists), an objective observer in the position of a secondary school student will perceive official school support for such religious meetings. . . .

We disagree. First, although we have invalidated the use of public funds to pay for teaching state-required subjects at parochial schools . . . there is a crucial difference between *government* speech endorsing religion, which the Establishment Clause forbids, and *private* speech endorsing religion, which the Free Speech and Free Exercise Clauses protect. We think that secondary school students are mature enough and are likely to understand that a school does not endorse or support student speech that it merely permits on a nondiscriminatory basis. . . .

Indeed, we note that Congress specifically rejected the argument that high school students are likely to confuse an equal access policy with state sponsorship of religion. . . .

Second, we note that the Act expressly limits participation by school officials at meetings of student religious groups and that any such meetings must be held during "noninstructional time.". . . To be sure, the possibility of *student* peer pressure remains, but there is little if any risk of official state endorsement or coercion where no formal classroom activities are involved and no school officials actively participate. . . .

Third, the broad spectrum of officially recognized student clubs at Westside, and the fact that Westside students are free to initiate and organize additional student clubs, counteract any possible message of official endorsement of or preference for religion or a particular religious belief. . . .

Petitioners' final argument is that by complying with the Act's requirement, the school risks excessive entanglement between government and religion. The proposed club, petitioners urge, would be required to have a faculty sponsor who would be charged with actively directing the activities of the group, guiding its leaders, and ensuring balance in the presentation of controversial ideas. Petitioners claim that this influence over the club's religious program would entangle the government in day-to-day surveillance of religion of the type forbidden by the Establishment Clause.

Under the Act, however, faculty monitors may not participate in any religious meetings, and nonschool persons may not direct, control, or regularly attend activities of student groups. Although the Act permits "[t]he assignment of a teacher, administrator, or other school employee to the meeting for custodial purposes," such custodial oversight of the student-initiated religious group, merely to ensure order and good behavior, does not impermissibly entangle government in the day-to-day surveillance or administration of religious activities. . . .

Accordingly, we hold that the Equal Access Act does not on its face contravene the Establishment Clause. Because we hold that petitioners have violated the Act, we do not decide respondents' claims under the Free Speech and Free Exercise Clauses. For the foregoing reasons, the judgment of the Court of Appeals is affirmed.

It is so ordered.

JUSTICE KENNEDY, with whom JUSTICE SCALIA joins, concurring in part and concurring in the judgment.

The Court's interpretation of the statutory term "noncurriculum related groups" is proper and correct, in my view, and I join Parts I and II of the Court's opinion. I further agree that the Act does not violate the Establishment Clause, and so I concur in the judgment; but my view of the analytic premise that controls the establishment question differs from that employed by the plurality. I write to explain why I cannot join all that is said in Part III of JUSTICE O'CONNOR's opinion.

I

A brief initial comment on the statutory issue is in order. The student clubs recognized by Westside school officials are a far cry from the groups given official recognition by university officials in *Widmar v. Vincent* (1981). As JUSTICE STEVENS points out in dissent, one of the consequences of the statute, as we now interpret it, is that clubs of a most controversial character might have access to the student life of high schools that in the past have given official recognition only to clubs of a more conventional kind.

It must be apparent to all that the Act has made a matter once left to the discretion of local school officials the subject of comprehensive regulation by federal law. This decision, however, was for Congress to make, subject to constitutional limitations. Congress having decided in favor of legislative intervention, it faced the task of formulating general statutory standards against the background protections of the Free Speech Clause, as well as the Establishment and Free Exercise Clauses. Given the complexities of our own jurisprudence in these areas, there is no doubt that the congressional task was a difficult one. While I can not pretend that the language Congress used in the Act is free from ambiguity in some of its vital provisions, the Court's interpretation of the phrase "noncurriculum related" seems to be to be the most rational and indeed the most plausible interpretation available, given the words and structure of the Act and the constitutional implications of the subject it addresses.

. . . [I]n the matter before us, the school has not attempted to comply with the statute through any means, and we have only to determine whether it is possible for the statute to be implemented in a constitutional manner.

II

I agree with the plurality that a school complying with the statute by satisfying the criteria in § 4071(c) does not violate the Establishment Clause. The accommodation of religion mandated by the Act is a neutral one, and in the context of this case it suffices to inquire whether the Act violates either one of two principles. The first is that the government cannot "give direct benefits to religion in such a degree that it in fact 'establishes a [state] religion or religious faith, or tends to do so.'" *County of Allegheny v. American Civil Liberties Union, Greater Pittsburgh Chapter* (1989). . . . Any incidental benefits that accompany official recognition of a religious club under the criteria set forth in the § 4071(c) do not lead to the establishment of religion under this standard. The

KVCC KALAMAZOO VALLEY COMMUNITY COLLEGE LIBRARY

second principle controlling the case now before us, in my view, is that the government cannot coerce any student to participate in a religious activity. The Act is consistent with this standard as well. Nothing on the face of the Act or in the facts of the case as here presented demonstrate that enforcement of the statute will result in the coercion of any student to participate in a religious activity. The Act does not authorize school authorities to require, or even to encourage, students to become members of a religious club or to attend a club's meetings; the meetings take place while school is not in session; and the Act does not compel any school employee to participate in, or to attend, a club's meetings or activities.

The plurality uses a different test, one which asks whether school officials, by complying with the Act, have endorsed religion. It is true that when government gives impermissible assistance to a religion it can be said to have "endorsed" religion; but endorsement cannot be the test. The word endorsement has insufficient content to be dispositive. And for reasons I have explained elsewhere . . . its literal application may result in neutrality in name but hostility in fact when the question is the government's proper relation to those who express some religious preference.

I should think it inevitable that a public high school "endorses" a religious club, in a common-sense use of the term, if the club happens to be one of many activities that the school permits students to choose in order to further the development of their intellect and character in an extracurricular setting. But no constitutional violation occurs if the school's action is based upon a recognition of the fact that membership in a religious club is one of many permissible ways for a student to further his or her own personal enrichment. The inquiry with respect to coercion must be whether the government imposes pressure upon a student to participate in a religious activity. This inquiry, of course, must be undertaken with sensitivity to the special circumstances that exist in a secondary school where the line between voluntary and coerced participation may be difficult to draw. No such coercion, however, has been shown to exist as a necessary result of this statute, either on its face or as respondents seek to invoke it on the facts of this case.

For these reasons, I join Parts I and II of the Court's opinion, and concur in the judgment.

JUSTICE MARSHALL, with whom JUSTICE BRENNAN joins, concurring in the judgment.

I agree with the majority that "noncurriculum" must be construed broadly to "prohibit schools from discriminating on the basis of the content of a student group's speech." As the majority demonstrates, such a construction "is consistent with Congress' intent to provide a low threshold for triggering the Act's requirements." In addition, to the extent that Congress intended the Act to track this Court's free speech jurisprudence, as the dissent argues, the majority's construction is faithful to our commitment to nondiscriminatory access to open fora in public schools. When a school allows student-initiated clubs not directly tied to the school's curriculum to use school facilities, it has "created a forum generally open to student groups" and is therefore constitutionally prohibited from enforcing a "content-based exclusion" of other student speech. In this respect, the Act as construed by the majority simply codifies in statute what is already constitutionally mandated: schools may not discriminate among student-initiated groups that seek access to school facilities for expressive purposes not directly related to the school's curriculum.

The Act's low threshold for triggering equal access, however, raises serious Establishment Clause concerns where secondary schools with fora that differ substantially from the forum in *Widmar* [*v. Vincent* (1981)] are required to grant access to student religious groups. Indeed, as applied in the present case, the Act mandates a religious group's access to a forum that is dedicated to promoting fundamental values and citizenship as defined by the school. The Establishment Clause does not forbid the operation of the Act in such circumstances, but it does require schools to change their relationship to their fora so as to disassociate themselves effectively from religious clubs' speech. Thus, although I agree with the plurality that the Act as applied to Westside *could* withstand Establishment Clause scrutiny, I write separately to emphasize the steps Westside must take to avoid appearing to endorse the Christian Club's goals. The plurality's Establishment Clause analysis pays inadequate attention to the differences between this case and *Widmar* and dismisses too lightly the distinctive pressures created by Westside's highly structured environment.

I

A

This case involves the intersection of two First Amendment guarantees—the Free Speech Clause and the Establishment Clause. We have long regarded free and open debate over matters of controversy as necessary to the functioning of our constitutional system. . . . That the Constitution requires toleration of speech over its suppression is no less true in our Nation's schools. . . .

But the Constitution also demands that the State not take action that has the primary effect of advancing religion. The introduction of religious speech into the public schools reveals the tension between these two constitutional commitments, because the failure of a school to stand apart from religious speech can convey a message that the school endorses rather than merely tolerates that speech. . . .

B

We addressed at length the potential conflict between toleration and endorsement of religious speech in *Widmar*. There, a religious study group sought the same access to university facilities that the university afforded to over 100 officially recognized student groups, including many political organizations. In those circumstances, we concluded that granting religious organizations similar access to the public forum would have neither the purpose nor the primary effect of advancing religion. The plurality suggests that our conclusion in *Widmar* controls this case. But the plurality fails to recognize that the wide-open and independent character of the student forum in *Widmar* differs substantially from the forum at Westside.

Westside currently does not recognize any student club that advocates a controversial viewpoint. Indeed, the clubs at Westside that trigger the Act involve scuba diving, chess, and counseling for special education students. As a matter of school policy, Westside encourages student participation in clubs based on a broad conception of its educational mission. . . .

The entry of religious clubs into such a realm poses a real danger that those clubs will be viewed as part of the school's effort to inculcate fundamental values. The school's message with respect to its existing clubs is not one of toleration but one of endorsement. . . .

II

Given these substantial risks posed by the inclusion of the proposed Christian Club within Westside's present forum, Westside must redefine its relationship to its club program. The plurality recognizes that such redefinition is necessary to avoid the risk of endorsement. . . . Finally, and perhaps most importantly, the plurality states that schools bear the responsibility for taking whatever further steps are necessary to make clear that their recognition of a religious club does not reflect their endorsement of the views of the club's participants. . . .

JUSTICE STEVENS, dissenting.

The dictionary is a necessary, and sometimes sufficient, aid to the judge confronted with the task of construing an opaque act of Congress. In a case like this, however, I believe we must probe more deeply to avoid a patently bizarre result. Can Congress really have intended to issue an order to every public high school in the nation stating, in substance, that if you sponsor a chess club, a scuba diving club, or a French club—without having formal classes in those subjects—you must also open your doors to every religious, political, or social organization, no matter how controversial or distasteful its views may be? I think not. . . .

I

. . . I believe that the distinctions between Westside's program and the University of Missouri's program suggest what is the best understanding of the Act: an extracurricular student organization is "noncurriculum related" if it has as its purpose (or as part of its purpose) the advocacy of partisan theological, political, or ethical views. A school that admits at least one such club has apparently made the judgment that students are better off if the student community is permitted to, and perhaps even encouraged to, compete along ideological lines. This pedagogical strategy may be defensible or even desirable. But it is wrong to presume that Congress endorsed that strategy—and dictated its nationwide adoption—simply because it approved the application of *Widmar* to high schools. And it seems absurd to presume that Westside has invoked the same strategy by recognizing clubs like Swim Timing Team and Subsurfers which, though they may not correspond directly to anything in Westside's course offerings, are no more controversial than a grilled cheese sandwich.

Accordingly, as I would construe the Act, a high school could properly sponsor a French club, a chess club, or a scuba diving club simply because their activities are fully consistent with the school's curricular mission. It would not matter whether formal courses in any of those subjects—or in directly subjects—were being offered as long as faculty encouragement of student participation in such groups would be consistent with both the school's obligation of neutrality and its legitimate pedagogical concerns. Nothing in *Widmar* implies that the existence of a French club, for example, would create a constitutional obligation to allow student members of the Ku Klux Klan or the Communist Party to have access to school facilities. More importantly, nothing in that case suggests that the constitutional issue should turn on whether French is being taught in a formal course while the club is functioning. . . .

. . . The statutory definition of what is "noncurriculum related" should depend on the constitutional concern that motivated our decision in *Widmar*.

. . . [T]he majority, although it agrees that Congress intended by this Act to endorse the application of *Widmar* to high schools, does not compare this case to *Widmar*. Instead, the Court argues from two other propositions: first, that Congress intended to prohibit discrimination against religious groups; and, second, that the statute must not be construed in a fashion that would allow school boards to circumvent its reach by definitional fiat. I am in complete agreement with both of these principles. I do not, however, believe that either yields the conclusion which the majority adopts.

First, as the majority correctly observes, Congress intended the Act to prohibit schools from excluding—or believing that they were legally obliged to exclude—religious student groups solely because the groups were religious. Congress was clearly concerned with two lines of decisions in the Courts of Appeals: one line prohibiting schools that wished to admit student-initiated religious groups from doing so and a second line allowing schools to exclude religious groups solely because of Establishment Clause concerns. . . . These cases, however, involve only schools which either desire to recognize religious student groups, or schools which, like the University of Missouri at Kansas City, purport to exclude religious groups from a forum that is otherwise conceded to be open. It is obvious that Congress need go no further than our *Widmar* decision to redress this problem, and equally obvious that the majority's expansive reading of "noncurriculum related" is irrelevant to the Congressional objective of ending discrimination against religious student groups.

Second, the majority is surely correct that a " 'limited open forum should be triggered by what a school does, not by what it says.' " If, however, it is the recognition of advocacy groups that signals the creation of such a forum, I see no danger that school administrators will be able to manipulate the Act to defeat Congressional intent. Indeed, it seems to me that it is the majority's own test that is suspect on this score. It would appear that the school could alter the "noncurriculum related" status of Subsurfers simply by, for example, including one day of scuba instruction in its swimming classes, or by requiring physical education teachers to urge student participation in the club, or even by soliciting regular comments from the club about how the school could better accommodate the club's interest within coursework. . . .

For all of these reasons, the argument for construing "noncurriculum related" by recourse to the facts of *Widmar,* and so by reference to the existence of advocacy groups, seems to me overwhelming. It provides a test that is both more simple and more easily administered than what the majority has crafted. . . .

II

My construction of the Act makes it unnecessary to reach the Establishment Clause question that the Court decides. It is nevertheless appropriate to point out that the question is much more difficult than the Court assumes. The Court focuses upon whether the Act might run afoul of the Establishment Clause because of the danger that some students will mistakenly believe that the student-initiated religious clubs are sponsored by the school. I believe that the majority's construction of the statute obliges it to answer a further question: whether the Act violates the Establishment Clause by authorizing religious organizations to meet on high school grounds even when the high school's teachers and administrators deem it unwise to admit controversial or partisan organizations of any kind.

Under the Court's interpretation of the Act, Congress has imposed a difficult choice on public high schools receiving federal financial assistance. If such a school continues to allow students to participate in such familiar and innocuous activities as a school chess or scuba diving club, it must also allow religious groups to make use of school facilities. Indeed, it is hard to see how a cheerleading squad or a pep club, among the most common student groups in American high schools, could avoid being "noncurriculum related" under the majority's test. The Act, as construed by the majority, comes perilously close to an outright command to allow organized prayer, and perhaps the kind of religious ceremonies involved in *Widmar,* on school premises. . . .

I tend to agree with the Court that the Constitution does not forbid a local school district, or Congress, from bringing organized religion into the schools so long as all groups, religious or not, are welcomed equally if "they do not break either the laws or the furniture." That Congress has such authority, however, does not mean that the concerns underlying the Establishment Clause are irrelevant when, and if, that authority is exercised. Certainly we should not rush to embrace the conclusion that Congress swept aside these concerns by the hurried passage of clumsily drafted legislation.

There is an additional reason, also grounded in constitutional structure, why the Court's rendering of the Act is unsatisfying: so construed, the Act alters considerably the balance between state and federal authority over education, a balance long respected by both Congress and this Court. . . .

The Court's construction of this Act, however, leads to a sweeping intrusion by the federal government into the operation of our public schools, and does so despite the absence of any indication that Congress intended to divest local school districts of their power to shape the educational environment. . . .

III

. . . I respectfully dissent.

□□□

Nos. 89-1433 and 89-1434

United States, Appellant v. Shawn D. Eichman,
David Gerald Blalock and Scott W. Tyler

On appeal from the United States District Court
for the District of Columbia

United States, Appellant v. Mark John Haggerty, Carlos Garza,
Jennifer Proctor Campbell and Darius Allen Strong

On appeal from the United States District Court for the
Western District of Washington

[June 11, 1990]

JUSTICE BRENNAN delivered the opinion of the Court.

In these consolidated appeals, we consider whether appellees' prosecution for burning a United States flag in violation of the Flag Protection Act of 1989 is consistent with the First Amendment. Applying our recent decision in *Texas v. Johnson* (1989), the District Courts held that the Act cannot constitutionally be applied to appellees. We affirm.

I

In No. 89-1433, the United States prosecuted certain appellees for violating the Flag Protection Act of 1989 by knowingly setting fire to several United States flags on the steps of the United States Capitol while protesting various aspects of the Government's domestic and foreign policy. In No. 89-1434, the United States prosecuted other appellees for violating the Act by knowingly setting fire to a United States flag while protesting the Act's passage. In each case, the respective appellees moved to dismiss the flag-burning charge on the ground that the Act, both on its face and as applied, violates the First Amendment. Both the United States District Court for the Western District of Washington and the United States District Court for the District of Columbia held the Act unconstitutional as applied to appellees and dismissed the charges. . . .

II

Last Term in *Johnson,* we held that a Texas statute criminalizing the desecration of venerated objects, including the United States flag, was unconstitutional as applied to an individual who had set such a flag on fire during a political demonstration. The Texas statute provided that "[a] person commits an offense if he intentionally or knowingly desecrates . . . [a] national flag," where "desecrate" meant to "deface, damage, or otherwise physically mistreat in a way that the actor knows will seriously offend one or more persons likely to observe or discover his action." We first held that Johnson's flag-burning was "conduct 'sufficiently imbued with elements of communication' to implicate the First Amendment." We next considered and rejected the State's contention that, under *United States v. O'Brien* (1968), we ought to apply the deferential standard with which we have reviewed Government regulations of conduct containing both speech and nonspeech elements where "the governmental interest is unrelated to the suppression of free expression." We reasoned that the State's asserted interest "in preserving the flag as a symbol of nationhood and national unity," was an interest "related 'to the suppression of free expression' within the meaning of *O'Brien*" because the State's concern with protecting the flag's symbolic meaning is implicated "only when a person's treatment of the flag communicates some message." We therefore subjected the statute to " 'the most exacting scrutiny,' " quoting *Boos v. Barry* (1988), and we concluded that the State's asserted interests could not justify the infringement on the demonstrator's First Amendment rights.

After our decision in *Johnson,* Congress passed the Flag Protection Act of 1989. The Act provides in relevant part:

"(a)(1) Whoever knowingly mutilates, defaces, physically defiles, burns, maintains on the floor or ground, or tramples upon any flag of the United States shall be fined under this title or imprisoned for not more than one year, or both.

"(2) This subsection does not prohibit any conduct consisting of the disposal of a flag when it has become worn or soiled.

"(b) As used in this section, the term 'flag of the United States' means any flag of the United States or any part thereof, made of any substance, of any size, in a form that is commonly displayed."

The Government concedes in this case, as it must, that appellees' flag-burning constituted expressive conduct, but invites us to reconsider our rejection in *Johnson* of the claim that flag-burning as a mode of expression, like obscenity or "fighting words," does not enjoy the full protection of the First Amendment. Cf. *Chaplinsky v. New Hampshire* (1942). This we decline to do. The only remaining question is whether the Flag Protection Act is sufficiently distinct from the Texas statute that it may constitutionally be applied to proscribe appellees' expressive conduct.

The Government contends that the Flag Protection Act is constitutional because, unlike the statute addressed in *Johnson,* the Act does not target expressive conduct on the basis of the content of its message. The Government asserts an interest in "protect[ing] the physical integrity of the flag under all circumstances" in order to safeguard the flag's identity " 'as the unique and unalloyed symbol of the Nation.' " The Act proscribes conduct (other than disposal) that damages or mistreats a flag, without regard to the actor's motive, his intended message, or the likely effects of his conduct on onlookers. By contrast, the Texas statute expressly prohibited only those acts of physical flag desecration "that the actor knows will seriously offend" onlookers, and the former federal statute prohibited only those acts of desecration that "cas[t] contempt upon" the flag.

Although the Flag Protection Act contains no explicit content-based limitation on the scope of prohibited conduct, it is nevertheless clear that the Government's asserted *interest* is "related 'to the suppression of free expression,' " and concerned with the content of such expression. The Government's interest in protecting the "physical integrity" of a privately owned flag rests upon a perceived need to preserve the flag's status as a symbol of our Nation and certain national ideals. But the mere destruction or disfigurement of a particular physical manifestation of the symbol, without more, does not diminish or otherwise affect the symbol itself in any way. For example, the secret destruction of a flag in one's own basement would not threaten the flag's recognized meaning. Rather, the Government's desire to preserve the flag as a symbol for certain national ideals is implicated "only when a person's treatment of the flag communicates [a] message" to others that is inconsistent with those ideals.

Moreover, the precise language of the Act's prohibitions confirms Congress' interest in the communicative impact of flag destruction. The Act criminalizes the conduct of anyone who "knowingly mutilates, defaces, physically defiles, burns, maintains on the floor or ground, or tramples upon any flag." Each of the specified terms—with the possible exception of "burns"—unmistakably connotes disrespectful treatment of the flag and suggests a focus on those acts likely to damage the flag's symbolic value. And the explicit exemption in § 700(a)(2) for disposal of "worn or soiled" flags protects certain acts traditionally associated with patriotic respect for the flag.

As we explained in *Johnson:* "[I]f we were to hold that a State may forbid flag-burning wherever it is likely to endanger the flag's symbolic role, but allow it wherever burning a flag promotes that role—as where, for example, a person ceremoniously burns a dirty flag—we would be . . . permitting a State to 'prescribe what shall be orthodox' by saying that one may burn the flag to convey one's attitude toward it and its referents only if one does not endanger the flag's representation of nationhood and national unity." Although Congress cast the Flag Protection Act in somewhat broader terms than the Texas statute at issue in *Johnson,* the Act still suffers from the same fundamental flaw: it suppresses expression out of concern for its likely communicative impact. . . . The Act therefore must be subjected to "the most exacting scrutiny," *Boos,* and for the reasons stated in *Johnson,* the Government's interest cannot justify its infringement on First Amendment rights. We decline the Government's invitation to reassess this conclusion in light of Congress' recent recognition of a purported "national consensus" favoring a prohibition on flagburning. Even assuming such a consensus exists, any suggestion that the Government's interest in suppressing speech becomes more weighty as popular opposition to that speech grows is foreign to the First Amendment.

III

...Government may create national symbols, promote them, and encourage their respectful treatment. But the Flag Protection Act goes well beyond this by criminally proscribing expressive conduct because of its likely communicative impact.

We are aware that desecration of the flag is deeply offensive to many. But the same might be said, for example, of virulent ethnic and religious epithets, vulgar repudiations of the draft, and scurrilous caricatures. "If there is a bedrock principle underlying the First Amendment, it is that the Government may not prohibit the expression of an idea simply because society finds the idea itself offensive or disagreeable." *Johnson.* Punishing desecration of the flag dilutes the very freedom that makes this emblem so revered, and worth revering. The judgments are

Affirmed.

JUSTICE STEVENS, with whom THE CHIEF JUSTICE, JUSTICE WHITE and JUSTICE O'CONNOR join, dissenting.

The Court's opinion ends where proper analysis of the issue should begin. Of course "the Government may not prohibit the expression of an idea simply because society finds the idea itself offensive or disagreeable." None of us disagrees with that proposition. But it is equally well settled that certain methods of expression may be prohibited if (a) the prohibition is supported by a legitimate societal interest that is unrelated to suppression of the ideas the speaker desires to express; (b) the prohibition does not entail any interference with the speaker's freedom to express those ideas by other means; and (c) the interest in allowing the speaker complete freedom of choice among alternative methods of expression is less important than the societal interest supporting the prohibition.

Contrary to the position taken by counsel for the flag burners in *Texas v. Johnson* (1989), it is now conceded that the Federal Government has a legitimate interest in protecting the symbolic value of the American flag. Obviously that value cannot be measured, or even described, with any precision. It has at least these two components: in times of national crisis, it inspires and motivates the average citizen to make personal sacrifices in order to achieve societal goals of overriding importance; at all times, it serves as a reminder of the paramount importance of pursuing the ideals that characterize our society.

The first question the Court should consider is whether the interest in preserving the value of that symbol is unrelated to suppression of the ideas that flag burners are trying to express. In my judgment the answer depends, at least in part, on what those ideas are. A flag burner might intend various messages. The flag burner may wish simply to convey hatred, contempt, or sheer opposition directed at the United States. This might be the case if the flag were burned by an enemy during time of war. A flag burner may also, or instead, seek to convey the depth of his personal conviction about some issue, by willingly provoking the use of force against himself. In so doing, he says that "my disagreement with certain policies is so strong that I am prepared to risk physical harm (and perhaps imprisonment) in order to call attention to my views." This second possibility apparently describes the expressive conduct of the flag burners in these cases. Like the protesters who dramatized their opposition to our engagement in Vietnam by publicly burning their draft cards—and who were punished for doing so—their expressive conduct is consistent with affection for this country and respect for the ideals that the flag symbolizes. There is at least one further possibility: a flag burner may intend to make an accusation against the integrity of the American people who disagree with him. By burning the embodiment of America's collective commitment to freedom and equality, the flag burner charges that the majority has forsaken that commitment—that continued respect for the flag is nothing more than hypocrisy. Such a charge may be made even if the flag burner loves the country and zealously pursues the ideals that the country claims to honor.

The idea expressed by a particular act of flag burning is necessarily dependent on the temporal and political context in which it occurs. In the 1960's it may have expressed opposition to the country's Vietnam policies, or at least to the compulsory draft. In *Texas v. Johnson,* it apparently expressed opposition to the platform of the Republican Party. In these cases, the respondents have explained that it expressed their opposition to racial discrimination, to the failure to care for the homeless, and of course to statutory prohibitions of flag burning. In any of these examples, the protesters may wish both to say that their own position is the only one faithful to liberty and equality, and to accuse their fellow citizens of hypocritical indifference to—or even of a selfish departure from—the ideals which the flag is supposed to symbolize. The ideas expressed by flag burners are thus various and often ambiguous.

The Government's legitimate interest in preserving the symbolic value of the flag is, however, essentially the same regardless of which of many different ideas may have motivated a particular act of flag burning. As I explained in my dissent in *Johnson*, the flag uniquely symbolizes the ideas of liberty, equality, and tolerance—ideas that Americans have passionately defended and debated throughout our history. The flag embodies the spirit of our national commitment to those ideals. The message thereby transmitted does not take a stand upon our disagreements, except to say that those disagreements are best regarded as competing interpretations of shared ideals. It does not judge particular policies, except to say that they command respect when they are enlightened by the spirit of liberty and equality. To the world, the flag is our promise that we will continue to strive for these ideals. To us, the flag is a reminder both that the struggle for liberty and equality is unceasing, and that our obligation of tolerance and respect for all of our fellow citizens encompasses those who disagree with us—indeed, even those whose ideas are disagreeable or offensive.

Thus, the Government may—indeed, it should—protect the symbolic value of the flag without regard to the specific content of the flag burners speech. The prosecution in this case does not depend upon the object of the defendants' protest. It is, moreover, equally clear that the prohibition does not entail any interference with the speaker's freedom to express his or her ideas by other means. It may well be true that other means of expression may be less effective in drawing attention to those ideas. . . .

This case therefore comes down to a question of judgment. Does the admittedly important interest in allowing every speaker to choose the method of expressing his or her ideas that he or she deems most effective and appropriate outweigh the societal interest in preserving the symbolic value of the flag? . . .

. . . The freedom of expression protected by the First Amendment embraces not only the freedom to communicate particular ideas, but also the right to communicate them effectively. That right, however, is not absolute—the communicative value of a well-placed bomb in the Capitol does not entitle it to the protection of the First Amendment.

Burning a flag is not, of course, equivalent to burning a public building. Assuming that the protester is burning his own flag, it causes no physical harm to other persons or to their property. The impact is purely symbolic, and it is apparent that some thoughtful persons believe that impact, far from depreciating the value of the symbol, will actually enhance its meaning. I most respectfully disagree. Indeed, what makes this case particularly difficult for me is what I regard as the damage to the symbol that has already occurred as a result of this Court's decision to place its stamp of approval on the act of flag burning. A formerly dramatic expression of protest is now rather commonplace. In today's marketplace of ideas, the public burning of a Vietnam draft card is probably less provocative than lighting a cigarette. Tomorrow flag burning may produce a similar reaction. There is surely a direct relationship between the communicative value of the act of flag burning and the symbolic value of the object being burned.

The symbolic value of the American flag is not the same today as it was yesterday. Events during the last three decades have altered the country's image in the eyes of numerous Americans, and some now have difficulty understanding the message that the flag conveyed to their parents and grandparents—whether born abroad and naturalized or native born. Moreover, the integrity of the symbol has been compromised by those leaders who seem to advocate compulsory worship of the flag even by individuals whom it offends. . . .

Given all these considerations, plus the fact that the Court today is really doing nothing more than reconfirming what it has already decided, it might be appropriate to defer to the judgment of the majority and merely apply the doctrine of *stare decisis* to the case at hand. That action, however, would not honestly reflect my considered judgment concerning the relative importance of the conflicting interests that are at stake. I remain persuaded that the considerations identified in my opinion in *Texas v. Johnson* are of controlling importance in this case as well.

Accordingly, I respectfully dissent.

□□□

Nos. 88-1872 and 88-2074

Cynthia Rutan, et al., Petitioners v. Republican Party of Illinois et al.; Mark Frech, et al., Petitioners v. Cynthia Rutan et al.

On writs of certiorari to the United States Court of Appeals for the Seventh Circuit

[June 21, 1990]

JUSTICE BRENNAN delivered the opinion of the Court.

To the victor belong only those spoils that may be constitutionally obtained. *Elrod v. Burns* (1976) and *Branti v. Finkel* (1980), decided that the First Amendment forbids government officials to discharge or threaten to discharge public employees solely for not being supporters of the political party in power, unless party affiliation is an appropriate requirement for the position involved. Today we are asked to decide the constitutionality of several related political patronage practices—whether promotion, transfer, recall, and hiring decisions involving low-level public employees may be constitutionally based on party affiliation and support. We hold that they may not.

I

The petition and cross-petition before us arise from a lawsuit protesting certain employment policies and practices instituted by Governor James Thompson of Illinois. On November 12, 1980, the Governor issued an executive order proclaiming a hiring freeze for every agency, bureau, board, or commission subject to his control. The order prohibits state officials from hiring any employee, filling any vacancy, creating any new position, or taking any similar action. It affects approximately 60,000 state positions. More than 5,000 of these become available each year as a result of resignations, retirements, deaths, expansion, and reorganizations. The order proclaims that *"no* exceptions" [emphasis added] are permitted without the Governor's "express permission after submission of appropriate requests to [his] office."

Requests for the Governor's "express permission" have allegedly become routine. Permission has been granted or withheld through an agency expressly created for this purpose, the Governor's Office of Personnel (Governor's Office). Agencies have been screening applicants under Illinois' civil service system, making their personnel choices, and submitting them as requests to be approved or disapproved by the Governor's Office. Among the employment decisions for which approvals have been required are new hires, promotions, transfers, and recalls after layoffs.

By means of the freeze, according to petitioners, the Governor has been using the Governor's Office to operate a political patronage system to limit state employment and beneficial employment-related decisions to those who are supported by the Republican Party. In reviewing an agency's request that a particular applicant be approved for a particular position, the Governor's Office has looked at whether the applicant voted in Republican primaries in past election years, whether the applicant has provided financial or other support to the Republican Party and its candidates, whether the applicant has promised to join and work for the Republican Party in the future, and whether the applicant has the support of Republican Party officials at state or local levels.

Five people (including the three petitioners) brought suit against various Illinois and Republican Party officials in the United States District Court for the Central District of Illinois. They alleged that they had suffered discrimination with respect to state employment because they had not been supporters of the State's Republican Party and that this discrimination violates the First Amendment. Cynthia B. Rutan has been working for the State since 1974 as a rehabilitation counselor. She claims that since 1981 she has been repeatedly denied promotions to supervisory positions for which she was qualified because she had not worked for or supported the Republican Party. Franklin Taylor, who operates road equipment for the Illinois Department of Transportation, claims that he was denied a promotion in 1983 because he did not have the support of the local Republican Party. Taylor also maintains that he was denied a transfer to an office nearer to his home because of opposition from the Republican Party chairmen in the counties in which he worked and to which he requested a transfer. James W. Moore claims that he has been repeatedly denied state employment as a prison guard because he did not have the support of Republican Party officials.

The two other plaintiffs, before the Court as cross-respondents, allege that they were not recalled after layoffs because they lacked Republican credentials. Ricky Standefer was a state garage worker who claims that he was not recalled, although his fellow employees were, because he had voted in a Democratic primary and did not have the support of the Republican Party. Dan O'Brien, formerly a dietary manager with the mental health department, contends that he was not recalled after a layoff because of his party affiliation and that he later obtained a lower paying position with the corrections department only after receiving support from the chairman of the local Republican Party.

The District Court dismissed the complaint with prejudice, under Federal Rule of Civil Procedure 12(b)(6), for failure to state a claim upon which relief could be granted. The United States Court of Appeals for the Seventh Circuit initially issued a panel opinion, but then reheard the appeal en banc. The court affirmed the District Court's decision in part and reversed in part. Noting that this Court had previously determined that the patronage practice of discharging public employees on the basis of their political affiliation violates the First Amendment, the Court of Appeals held that other patronage practices violate the First Amendment only when they are the "substantial equivalent of a dismissal." The court explained that an employment decision is equivalent to a dismissal when it is one that would lead a reasonable person to resign. The court affirmed the dismissal of Moore's claim because it found that basing hiring decision on political affiliation does not violate the First Amendment, but remanded the remaining claims for further proceedings.

Rutan, Taylor, and Moore petitioned this Court to review the constitutional standard set forth by the Seventh Circuit and the dismissal of Moore's claim. Respondents cross-petitioned this Court, contending that the Seventh Circuit's remand of four of the five claims was improper because the employment decisions alleged here do not, as a matter of law, violate the First Amendment. We granted certiorari to decide the important question whether the first Amendment's proscription of patronage dismissals recognized in *Elrod* (1976) and *Branti* (1980) extends to promotion, transfer, recall, or hiring decisions involving public employment positions for which party affiliation is not an appropriate requirement.

II

A

In *Elrod* we decided that a newly elected Democratic sheriff could not constitutionally engage in the patronage practice of replacing certain office staff with members of his own party "when the existing employees lack or fail to obtain requisite support from, or fail to affiliate with, that party." The plurality explained that conditioning public employment on the provision of support for the favored political party "unquestionably inhibits protected belief and association." It reasoned that conditioning employment on political activity pressures employees to pledge political allegiance to a party with which they prefer not to associate, to work for the election of political candidates they do not support, and to contribute money to be used to further policies with which they do not agree. . . . At the same time, employees are constrained from joining, working for or contributing to the political party and candidates of their own choice. "[P]olitical belief and association constitute the core of those activities protected by the First Amendment," the plurality emphasized. . . .

The Court then decided that the government interest generally asserted in support of patronage fail to justify this burden on First Amendment rights because patronage dismissals are not the least restrictive means for fostering those interests. See *Elrod*. . . . The plurality also found that a government can meet its need for politically loyal employees to implement its policies by the less intrusive measure of dismissing, on political grounds, only those employees in policymaking positions. . . .

Four years later, in *Branti*, we decided that the First Amendment prohibited a newly appointed public defender, who was a Democrat, from discharging assistant public defenders because they did not have the support of the Democratic Party. The Court rejected an attempt to distinguish the case from *Elrod*, deciding that it was immaterial whether the public defender had attempted to coerce employees to change political parties or had only dismissed them on the basis of their private political beliefs. . . .

B

We first address the claims of the four current or former employees. Respondents urge us to view *Elrod* and *Branti* as inapplicable because the patronage dismissals at issue in those cases are different in kind from failure to promote, failure to transfer, and failure to recall after layoff. Respondents initially contend that the employee petitioner's First Amendment rights have not been infringed because they have no entitlement to promotion, transfer, or rehire. We rejected just such an argument in *Elrod* and *Branti,* as both cases involved state workers who were employees at will with no legal entitlement to continued employment. In *Perry [v. Singermann,* 1972] we held explicitly that the plaintiff teacher's lack of a contractual or tenure right to reemployment was immaterial to his First Amendment claim. We explained the viability of his First Amendment claim as follows:

> "For at least a quarter-century, this Court has made clear that even though a person has no 'right' to a valuable governmental benefit and even though the government may deny him the benefit for any number of reasons, *there are some reasons upon which the government may not rely. It may not deny a benefit to a person on a basis that infringes his constitutionally protected interests—especially, his interest in freedom of speech.* For if the government could deny a benefit to a person because of his constitutionally protected speech or associations, his exercise of those freedoms would in effect be penalized and inhibited.... ([E]mphasis added.)

Likewise, we find the assertion here that the employee petitioners had no legal entitlement to promotion, transfer, or recall beside the points.

Respondents next argue that the employment decisions at issue here do not violate the First Amendment because the decisions are not punitive, do not in any way adversely affect the terms of employment, and therefore do not chill the exercise of protected belief and association by public employees. This is not credible. Employees who find themselves in dead-end positions due to their political backgrounds *are* adversely affected. They will feel a significant obligation to support political positions held by their superiors, and to refrain from acting on the political views they actually hold, in order to progress up the career ladder. Employees denied transfers to workplaces reasonably close to their homes until they join and work for the Republican Party will feel a daily pressure from their long commutes to do so. And employees who have been laid off may well feel compelled to engage in whatever political activity is necessary to regain regular paychecks and positions corresponding to their skill and experience.

... Unless these patronage practices are narrowly tailored to four other vital government interests, we must conclude that they impermissibly encroach on First Amendment freedoms....

We ... determine that promotions, transfers, and recalls after layoffs based on political affiliation or support are an impermissible infringement on the First Amendment rights of public employees. In doing so, we reject the Seventh Circuit's view of the appropriate constitutional standard by which to measure alleged patronage practices in government employment. The Seventh Circuit proposed that only those employment decisions that are the "substantial equivalent of a dismissal" violate a public employee's rights under the First Amendment. We find this test unduly restrictive because it fails to recognize that there are deprivations less harsh than dismissal that nevertheless press state employees and applicants to conform their beliefs and associations to some state-selected orthodoxy. . . .

Whether the four employees were in fact denied promotions, transfers, or rehire for failure to affiliate with and support the Republican Party is for the District Court to decide in the first instance. What we decide today is that such denials are irreconcilable with the Constitution. . . . Therefore, although we affirm the Seventh Circuit's judgment to reverse the District Court's dismissal of these claims and remand them for further proceedings, we do not adopt the Seventh Circuit's reasoning.

C

Petitioner James W. Moore presents the closely related question whether patronage hiring violates the First Amendment. Patronage hiring places burdens on free speech and association similar to those imposed by the patronage practices discussed above. A state job is valuable. Like most employment, it provides regular paychecks, health insurance, and other benefits. In addition, there may be openings with the State when business in the private sector is slow. There are also occupations for which the government is a major (or the only) source of employment, such as social workers, elementary school teachers, and prison guards. Thus, denial of a state job is a serious privation.

Nonetheless, respondents contend that the burden imposed is not of constitutional magnitude. Decades of decisions by this Court belie such a claim. . . .

Under our sustained precedent, conditioning hiring decisions on political belief and association plainly constitutes an unconstitutional condition, unless the government has a vital interest in doing so. . . . We find no such government interest here, for the same reasons that we found the government lacks justification for patronage promotions, transfers or recalls. . . .

If Moore's employment application was set aside because he chose not to support the Republican Party, as he asserts, then Moore's First Amendment rights have been violated. Therefore, we find that Moore's complaint was improperly dismissed.

III

. . . We affirm the Seventh Circuit insofar as it remanded Rutan's, Taylor's, Standefer's, and O'Brien's claims. However, we reverse the

Circuit Court's decision to uphold the dismissal of Moore's claim. All five claims are remanded for proceedings consistent with this opinion.

It is so ordered.

JUSTICE STEVENS, concurring.

While I join the Court's opinion, these additional comments are prompted by three propositions advanced by JUSTICE SCALIA in his dissent. First, he implies that prohibiting imposition of an unconstitutional condition upon eligibility for government employment amounts to adoption of a civil service system. Second, he makes the startling assertion that a long history of open and widespread use of patronage practices immunizes them from constitutional scrutiny. Third, he assumes that the decisions in *Elrod v. Burns* (1976) and *Branti v. Finkel* (1980) represented dramatic departures from prior precedent.

... Denying the Governor of Illinois the power to require every state employee, and every applicant for state employment, to pledge allegiance and service to the political party in power is a far cry from a civil service code. The question in this case is simply whether a Governor may adopt a rule that would be plainly unconstitutional if enacted by the General Assembly of Illinois.

Second, JUSTICE SCALIA asserts that "when a practice not expressly prohibited by the text of the Bill of Rights bears the endorsement of a long tradition of open, widespread, and unchallenged use that dates back to the beginning of the Republic, we have no proper basis for striking it down." The argument that traditional practices are immune from constitutional scrutiny is advanced in two plurality opinions that JUSTICE SCALIA has authored, but not by any opinion joined by a majority of the Members of the Court....

With respect to JUSTICE SCALIA's view that until *Elrod v. Burns* was decided in 1975, it was unthinkable that patronage could be unconstitutional, it seems appropriate to point out ... that they were firmly grounded in several decades of decisions of this Court....

... JUSTICE SCALIA would weigh the supposed general state interest in patronage hiring against the aggregated interests of the many employees affected by the practice. This defense of patronage obfuscates the critical distinction between partisan interest and the public interest. It assumes that governmental power and public resources—in this case employment opportunities—may appropriately be used to subsidize partisan activities even when the political affiliation of the employee or the job applicant is entirely unrelated to his or her public service. The premise on which this position rests would justify the use of public funds to compensate party members for their campaign work, or conversely, a legislative enactment denying public employment to nonmembers of the majority party. If such legislation is unconstitutional—as it clearly would be—an equally pernicious rule promulgated by the Executive must also be invalid.

JUSTICE SCALIA argues that distinguishing "inducement and compulsion" reveals that a patronage system's impairment of the speech and associational rights of employees and would-be employees is insignificant. This analysis contradicts the harsh reality of party discipline that is the linchpin of his theory of patronage. . . . More importantly, it rests on the long-rejected fallacy that a privilege may be burdened by unconstitutional conditions. There are a few jobs for which an individual's race or religion may be relevant; there are many jobs for which political affiliation is relevant to the employee's ability to function effectively as part of a given administration. In those cases—in other words, cases in which "the efficiency of the public service" would be advanced by hiring workers who are loyal to the Governor's party—such hiring is permissible under the holdings in *Elrod* and *Branti*. This case, however, concerns jobs in which race, religion, and political affiliation are all equally and entirely irrelevant to the public service to be performed. . . .

JUSTICE SCALIA, with whom THE CHIEF JUSTICE and JUSTICE KENNEDY join, and with whom JUSTICE O'CONNOR joins as to Parts II and III, dissenting.

Today the Court establishes the constitutional principle that party membership is not a permissible factor in the dispensation of government jobs, except for those jobs for the performance of which party affiliation is an "appropriate requirement." It is hard to say precisely (or even generally) what that exception means, but if there is any category of jobs for whose performance party affiliation is not an appropriate requirement, it is the job of being a judge, where partisanship is not only unneeded but positively undesirable. It is, however, rare that a federal administration of one party will appoint a judge from another party. And it has always been rare. Thus, the new principle that the Court today announces will be enforced by a corps of judges (the Members of this Court included) who overwhelmingly owe their office to its violation. Something must be wrong here, and I suggest it is the Court.

The merit principle for government employment is probably the most favored in modern America, having been widely adopted by civil-service legislation at both the state and federal levels. But there is another point of view, described in characteristically Jacksonian fashion by an eminent practitioner of the patronage system, George Washington Plunkitt of Tammany Hall:

> "I ain't up on sillygisms, but I can give you some arguments that nobody can answer.
> "First, this great and glorious country was built up by political parties; second, parties can't hold together if their workers don't get offices when they

win; third, if the parties go to pieces, the government they built up must go to pieces, too; fourth, then there'll be hell to pay." W. Riordon, Plunkitt of Tammany Hall 13 (1963).

It may well be that the Good Government Leagues of America were right, and that Plunkitt, James Michael Curley and their ilk were wrong; but that is not entirely certain. As the merit principle has been extended and its effects increasingly felt; as the Boss Tweeds, the Tammany Halls, the Pendergast Machines, the Byrd Machines and the Daley Machines have faded into history; we find that political leaders at all levels increasingly complain of the helplessness of elected government, unprotected by "party discipline," before the demands of small and cohesive interest-groups.

The choice between patronage and the merit principle—or, to be more realistic about it, the choice between the desirable mix of merit and patronage principles in widely varying federal, state, and local political contexts—is not so clear that I would be prepared, as an original matter, to chisel a single, inflexible prescription into the Constitution. Fourteen years ago, in *Elrod v. Burns* [1976], the Court did that. *Elrod* was limited however, as was the later decision of *Branti v. Finkel* [1980], to patronage firings, leaving it to state and federal legislatures to determine when and where political affiliation could be taken into account in hirings and promotions. Today the Court makes its constitutional civil-service reform absolute, extending to all decisions regarding government employment. Because the first amendment has never been thought to require this disposition, which may well have disastrous consequences for out political system, I dissent.

I

The restrictions that the Constitution places upon the government in its capacity as lawmaker, *i.e.,* as the regulator of private conduct, are not the same as the restrictions that it places upon the government in its capacity as employer. We have recognized this in many contexts, with respect to many different constitutional guarantees. Private citizens perhaps cannot be prevented from wearing long hair, but policemen can. *Kelley v. Johnson* (1976). Private citizens cannot have their property searched without probable cause, but in many circumstances government employees can. *O'Connor v. Ortega* (1987). . . . Private citizens cannot be punished for speech of merely private concern, but government employees can be fired for that reason. *Connick v. Myers* (1983). . . .

Once it is acknowledged that the Constitution's prohibition against laws "abridging the freedom of speech" does not apply to laws enacted in the government's capacity as employer the same way it does to laws enacted in the government's capacity as regulator of private conduct, it may sometimes be difficult to assess what employment practices are permissible and what are not. That seems to me not a difficult question, however, in the present context. The provisions of the Bill of Rights were designated to restrain transient majorities from impairing long-recognized personal liberties. They did not create by implication novel individual rights overturning accepted political norms. Thus, when a practice not expressly prohibited by the text of the Bill of Rights bears the endorsement of a long tradition of open, widespread, and unchallenged use that dates back to the beginning of the Republic, we have no proper basis for striking it down. Such a venerable and accepted tradition is not to be laid on the examining table and scrutinized for its conformity to some abstract principle of First-Amendment adjudication devised by this Court. . . .

[II omitted]

III

Even were I not convinced that *Elrod* and *Branti* were wrongly decided, I would hold that they should not be extended beyond their facts, viz., actual discharge of employees for their political affiliation. Those cases invalidated patronage firing in order to prevent the "restraint it places on freedoms of belief and association." *Elrod.* The loss of one's current livelihood is an appreciably greater constraint than such other disappointments as the failure to obtain a promotion or selection for an uncongenial transfer. Even if the "coercive" effect of the former has been held always to outweigh the benefits of party-based employment decisions, the "coercive" effect of the latter should not be. We have drawn a line between firing and other employment decisions in other contexts, see *Wygant v. Jackson Bd. of Education* (1986), and should do so here as well.

I would reject the alternative that the Seventh Circuit adopted in this case, which allows a cause of action if the employee can demonstrate that he was subjected to the "substantial equivalent of dismissal." The trouble with that seemingly reasonable standard is that it is so imprecise that it will multiply yet again the harmful uncertainty that *Branti* has already created. If *Elrod* and *Branti* are not to be reconsidered in light of their demonstrably unsatisfactory consequences, I would go no further than to allow a cause of action when the employee has lost his position, that is, his formal title and salary. That narrow ground alone is enough to resolve the constitutional claims in the present case. Since none of the plaintiffs has alleged loss of his position because of affiliation, I would affirm the Seventh Circuit's judgment insofar as it affirmed the dismissal of petitioners' claims, and would reverse the Seventh Circuit's judgment insofar as it reversed the dismissal of cross-respondent's claims.

The Court's opinion, of course, not only declines to confine *Elrod* and *Branti* to dismissals in the narrow sense I have proposed, but, unlike the Seventh Circuit, even extends those opinions beyond "constructive" dismissals—indeed, even beyond adverse treatment of current employees—to all hiring decisions. In the long run there may be cause to rejoice in that extension. When the courts are flooded with litigation under that most unmanageable of standards *(Branti)* brought by that most persistent and tenacious of suitors (the disappointed office-seeker) we may be moved to reconsider our intrusion into this entire field.

In the meantime, I dissent.

□□□

No. 88-1503

Nancy Beth Cruzan, by her parents and co-guardians, Lester L. Cruzan, et ux., Petitioners v. Director, Missouri Department of Health, et al.

On writ of certiorari to the Supreme Court of Missouri

[June 25, 1990]

CHIEF JUSTICE REHNQUIST delivered the opinion of the Court.

... In this Court, the question is simply and starkly whether the United States Constitution prohibits Missouri from choosing the rule of decision which it did. This is the first case in which we have been squarely presented with the issue of whether the United States Constitution grants what is in common parlance referred to as a "right to die." We follow the judicious counsel of our decision in *Twin City Bank v. Nebeker* (1987), where we said that in deciding "a question of such magnitude and importance ... it is the [better] part of wisdom not to attempt, by any general statement, to cover every possible phase of the subject."

The Fourteenth Amendment provides that no State shall "deprive any person of life, liberty, or property, without due process of law." The principle that a competent person has a constitutionally protected liberty interest in refusing unwanted medical treatment may be inferred from our prior decisions. In *Jacobson v. Massachusetts* (1905), for instance, the Court balanced an individual's liberty interest in declining an unwanted smallpox vaccine against the State's interest in preventing disease....

Just this Term, in the course of holding that a State's procedures for administering antipsychotic medication to prisoners were sufficient to satisfy due process concerns, we recognized that prisoners possess "a significant liberty interest in avoiding the unwanted administration of antipsychotic drugs under the Due Process Clause of the Fourteenth Amendment." *Washington v. Harper* (1990). . . . Still other cases support the recognition of a general liberty interest in refusing medical treatment. . . .

But determining that a person has a "liberty interest" under the Due Process Clause does not end the inquiry; "whether respondent's constitutional rights have been violated must be determined by balancing his liberty interests against the relevant state interests." *Youngberg v. Romeo* (1982). See also *Mills v. Rogers* (1982).

Petitioners insist that under the general holdings of our cases, the forced administration of life-sustaining medical treatment, and even of artificially-delivered food and water essential to life, would implicate a competent person's liberty interest. Although we think the logic of the cases discussed above would embrace such a liberty interest, the dramatic consequences involved in refusal of such treatment would inform the inquiry as to whether the deprivation of that interest is constitutionally permissible. But for purposes of this case, we assume that the United States Constitution would grant a competent person a constitutionally protected right to refuse lifesaving hydration and nutrition.

Petitioners go on to assert that an incompetent person should possess the same right in this respect as is possessed by a competent person. They rely primarily on our decisions in *Parham v. J. R.* [1979] and *Youngberg v. Romeo* (1982). In *Parham,* we held that a mentally disturbed minor child had a liberty interest in "not being confined unnecessarily for medical treatment," but we certainly did not intimate that such a minor child, after commitment, would have a liberty interest in refusing treatment. In *Youngberg,* we held that a seriously retarded adult had a liberty interest in safety and freedom from bodily restraint. *Youngberg,* however, did not deal with decisions to administer or withhold medical treatment.

The difficulty with petitioners' claim is that in a sense it begs the question: an incompetent person is not able to make an informed and voluntary choice to exercise a hypothetical right to refuse treatment or any other right. Such a "right" must be exercised for her, if at all, by some sort of surrogate. Here, Missouri has in effect recognized that under certain circumstances a surrogate may act for the patient in electing to have hydration and nutrition withdrawn in such a way as to cause death, but it has established a procedural safeguard to assure that the action of the surrogate conforms as best it may to the wishes expressed by the patient while competent. Missouri requires that evidence of the incompetent's wishes as to the withdrawal of treatment be proved by clear and convincing evidence. The question, then, is whether the United States Constitution forbids the establishment of this procedural requirement by the State. We hold that it does not.

Whether or not Missouri's clear and convincing evidence requirement comports with the United States Constitution depends in part on
what interests the State may properly seek to protect in this situation.
Missouri relies on its interest in the protection and preservation of human
life, and there can be no gainsaying this interest. As a general matter, the
States—indeed, all civilized nations—demonstrate their commitment to
life by treating homicide as serious crime. Moreover, the majority of States
in this country have laws imposing criminal penalties on one who assists
another to commit suicide. We do not think a State is required to remain
neutral in the face of an informed and voluntary decision by a physically-
able adult to starve to death.

But in the context presented here, a State has more particular
interests at stake. The choice between life and death is a deeply personal
decision of obvious and overwhelming finality. We believe Missouri may
legitimately seek to safeguard the personal element of this choice through
the imposition of heightened evidentiary requirements. It cannot be
disputed that the Due Process Clause protects an interest in life as well as
an interest in refusing life-sustaining medical treatment. Not all incompetent patients will have loved ones available to serve as surrogate
decisionmakers. And even where family members are present, "[t]here
will, of course, be some unfortunate situations in which family members
will not act to protect a patient." *In re Jobes* (1987). A State is entitled to
guard against potential abuses in such situations. Similarly, a State is
entitled to consider that a judicial proceeding to make a determination
regarding an incompetent's wishes may very well not be an adversarial
one, with the added guarantee of accurate factfinding that the adversary
process brings with it. Finally, we think a State may properly decline to
make judgments about the "quality" of life that a particular individual
may enjoy, and simply assert an unqualified interest in the preservation of
human life to be weighed against the constitutionally protected interests of
the individual.

In our view, Missouri has permissibly sought to advance these
interests through the adoption of a "clear and convincing" standard of
proof to govern such proceedings. . . .

We think it self-evident that the interests at stake in the instant
proceedings are more substantial, both on an individual and societal level,
than those involved in a run-of-the-mine civil dispute. But not only does
the standard of proof reflect the importance of a particular adjudication, it
also serves as "a societal judgment about how the risk of error should be
distributed between the litigants." *Santosky* [*v. Kramer* (1982).] The more
stringent the burden of proof a party must bear, the more that party bears
the risk of an erroneous decision. We believe that Missouri may
permissibly place an increased risk of an erroneous decision on those
seeking to terminate an incompetent individual's life-sustaining treatment.

An erroneous decision not to terminate results in a maintenance of the status quo; the possibility of subsequent developments such as advancements in medical science, the discovery of new evidence regarding the patient's intent, charges in the law, or simply the unexpected death of the patient despite the administration of life-sustaining treatment, at least create the potential that a wrong decision will eventually be corrected or its impact mitigated. An erroneous decision to withdraw life-sustaining treatment, however, is not susceptible of correction. . . .

It is also worth nothing that most, if not all, States simply forbid oral testimony entirely in determining the wishes of parties in transactions which, while important, simply do not have the consequences that a decision to terminate a person's life does. At common law and by statute in most States, the parole evidence rule prevents the variations of the terms of a written contract by oral testimony. The statute of frauds makes unenforceable oral contracts to leave property by will, and statutes regulating the making of wills universally require that those instruments be in writing. There is no doubt that statutes requiring wills to be in writing, and statutes of frauds which require that a contract to make a will be in writing, on occasion frustrate the effectuation of the intent of a particular decedent, just as Missouri's requirement of proof in this case may have frustrated the effectuation of the not-fully-expressed desires of Nancy Cruzan. But the Constitution does not require general rules to work faultlessly; no general rule can.

In sum, we conclude that a State may apply a clear and convincing evidence standard in proceedings where a guardian seeks to discontinue nutrition and hydration of a person diagnosed to be in a persistent vegetative state. We note that many courts which have adopted some sort of substituted judgment procedure in situations like this, whether they limit consideration of evidence to the prior expressed wishes of the incompetent individual, or whether they allow more general proof of what the individual's decision would have been, require a clear and convincing standard of proof for such evidence.

The Supreme Court of Missouri held that in this case the testimony adduced at trial did not amount to clear and convincing proof of the patient's desire to have hydration and nutrition withdrawn. In so doing, it reversed a decision of the Missouri trial court which had found that the evidence "suggest[ed]" Nancy Cruzan would not have desired to continue such measures, but which had not adopted the standard of "clear and convincing evidence" enunciated by the Supreme Court. The testimony adduced at trial consisted primarily of Nancy Cruzan's statements made to a housemate about a year before her accident that she would not want to live should she face life as a "vegetable," and other observations to the same effect. The observations did not deal in terms with withdrawal of medical treatment or of hydration and nutrition. We cannot say that the

Supreme Court of Missouri committed constitutional error in reaching the conclusion that it did.

Petitioners alternatively contend that Missouri must accept the "substituted judgment" of close family members even in the absence of substantial proof that their views reflect the views of the patient. They rely primarily upon our decisions in *Michael H. v. Gerald D.* (1989) and *Parham v. J. R.* (1979). But we do not think these cases support their claim. In *Michael H.,* we *upheld* the constitutionality of California's favored treatment of traditional family relationships; such a holding may not be turned around into a constitutional requirement that a State *must* recognize the primacy of those relationships in a situation like this. And in *Parham,* where the patient was a minor, we also *upheld* the constitutionality of a state scheme in which parents made certain decisions for mentally ill minors. Here again petitioners would seek to turn a decision which allowed a State to rely on family decisionmaking into a constitutional requirement that the State recognize such decisionmaking. But constitutional law does not work that way.

No doubt is engendered by anything in this record but that Nancy Cruzan's mother and father are loving and caring parents. If the State were required by the United States Constitution to repose a right of "substituted judgment" with anyone, the Cruzans would surely qualify. But we do not think the Due Process Clause requires the State to repose judgment on these matters with anyone but the patient herself. Close family members may have a strong feeling—a feeling not at all ignoble or unworthy, but not entirely disinterested, either—that they do not wish to witness the continuation of the life of a loved one which they regard as hopeless, meaningless, and even degrading. But there is no automatic assurance that the view of close family members will necessarily be the same as the patient's would have been had she been confronted with the prospect of her situation while competent. All of the reasons previously discussed for allowing Missouri to require clear and convincing evidence of the patient's wishes lead us to conclude that the State may choose to defer only to those wishes, rather than confide the decision to close family members.

The judgment of the Supreme Court of Missouri is

Affirmed.

JUSTICE O'CONNOR, concurring.

... [T]he Court does not today decide the issue whether a State must also give effect to the decisions of a surrogate decisionmaker. In my view, such a duty may well be constitutionally required to protect the patient's liberty interest in refusing medical treatment. Few individuals provide explicit oral or written instructions regarding their intent to refuse medical treatment should they become incompetent. States which decline to consider any evidence other than such instructions may frequently fail to honor a patient's intent. Such failures might be avoided if the State considered an equally probative source of evidence: the patient's appointment of a proxy to make health care decisions on her behalf. Delegating the authority to make medical decisions to a family member or friend is becoming a common method of planning for the future. Several States have recognized the practical wisdom of such a procedure by enacting durable power of attorney statutes that specifically authorize an individual to appoint a surrogate to make medical treatment decisions. Some state courts have suggested that an agent appointed pursuant to a general durable power of attorney statute would also be empowered to make health care decisions on behalf of the patient. Other States allow an individual to designate a proxy to carry out the intent of a living will. These procedures for surrogate decisionmaking, which appear to be rapidly gaining in acceptance, may be a valuable additional safeguard of the patient's interest in directing his medical care. . . .

Today's decision, holding only that the Constitution permits a State to require clear and convincing evidence of Nancy Cruzan's desire to have artificial hydration and nutrition withdrawn, does not preclude a future determination that the Constitution requires the States to implement the decisions of a patient's duly appointed surrogate. Nor does it prevent States from developing other approaches for protecting an incompetent individual's liberty interest in refusing medical treatment. As is evident from the Court's survey of state court decisions, no national consensus has yet emerged on the best solution for this difficult and sensitive problem. Today we decide only that one State's practice does not violate the Constitution; the more challenging task of crafting appropriate procedures for safeguarding incompetents' liberty interests is entrusted to the "laboratory" of the States. . . .

JUSTICE SCALIA, concurring.

The various opinions in this case portray quite clearly the difficult, indeed agonizing, questions that are presented by the constantly increasing power of science to keep the human body alive for longer than any reasonable person would want to inhabit it. The States have begun to grapple with these problems through legislation. I am concerned, from the tenor of today's opinions, that we are poised to confuse that enterprise as successfully as we have confused the enterprise of legislating concerning abortion—requiring it to be conducted against a background of federal constitutional imperatives that are unknown because they are being newly crafted from Term to Term. That would be a great misfortune.

While I agree with the Court's analysis today, and therefore join in its opinion, I would have preferred that we announce, clearly and promptly, that the federal courts have no business in this field; that American law has always accorded the State the power to prevent, by force if necessary, suicide—including suicide by refusing to take appropriate measures necessary to preserve one's life; that the point at which life becomes "worthless," and the point at which the means necessary to preserve it become "extraordinary" or "inappropriate," are neither set forth in the Constitution nor known to the nine Justices of this Court any better than they are known to nine people picked at random from the Kansas City telephone directory; and hence, that even when it *is* demonstrated by clear and convincing evidence that a patient no longer wishes certain measures to be taken to preserve her life, it is up to the citizens of Missouri to decide, through their elected representatives, whether that wish will be honored. . . .

JUSTICE BRENNAN, with whom JUSTICE MARSHALL and JUSTICE BLACKMUN join, dissenting.

> "Medical technology has effectively created a twilight zone of suspended animation where death commences while life, in some form, continues. Some patients, however, want no part of a life sustained only by medical technology. Instead, they prefer a plan of medical treatment that allows nature to take its course and permits them to die with dignity."

. . . Nancy Cruzan has dwelt in that twilight zone for six years. She is oblivious to her surroundings and will remain so. Her body twitches only reflexively, without consciousness. The areas of her brain that once thought, felt, and experienced sensations have degenerated badly and are continuing to do so. The cavities remaining are filling with cerebrospinal fluid. The " 'cerebral cortical atrophy is irreversible, permanent, progressive and ongoing.' " "Nancy will never interact meaningfully with her environment again. She will remain in a persistent vegetative state until her death." Because she cannot swallow, her nutrition and hydration are delivered through a tube surgically implanted in her stomach.

A grown woman at the time of the accident, Nancy had previously expressed her wish to forgo continuing medical care under circumstances such as these. Her family and her friends are convinced that this is what she would want. A guardian ad litem appointed by the trial court is also convinced that this is what Nancy would want. Yet the Missouri Supreme Court, alone among state courts deciding such a question, has determined that an irreversibly vegetative patient will remain a passive prisoner of medical technology—for Nancy, perhaps for the next 30 years.

Today the Court, while tentatively accepting that there is some degree of constitutionally protected liberty interest in avoiding unwanted medical treatment, including life-sustaining medical treatment such as artificial nutrition and hydration, affirms the decision of the Missouri

Supreme Court. The majority opinion, as I read it, would affirm that decision on the ground that a State may require "clear and convincing" evidence of Nancy Cruzan's prior decision to forgo life-sustaining treatment under circumstances such as hers in order to ensure that her actual wishes are honored. Because I believe that Nancy Cruzan has a fundamental right to be free of unwanted artificial nutrition and hydration, which right is not outweighed by any interests of the State, and because I find that the improperly biased procedural obstacles imposed by the Missouri Supreme Court impermissibly burden that right, I respectfully dissent. Nancy Cruzan is entitled to choose to die with dignity.

I

[A Omitted]

B

The starting point for our legal analysis must be whether a competent person has a constitutional right to avoid unwanted medical care. Earlier this Term, this Court held that the Due Process Clause of the Fourteenth Amendment confers a significant liberty interest in avoiding unwanted medical treatment. *Washington v. Harper* (1990). Today, the Court concedes that our prior decisions "support the recognition of a general liberty interest in refusing medical treatment." The Court, however, avoids discussing either the measure of that liberty interest or its application by assuming, for purposes of this case only, that a competent person has a constitutionally protected liberty interest in being free of unwanted artificial nutrition and hydration. . . .

II

A

The right to be free from unwanted medical attention is a right to evaluate the potential benefit of treatment and its possible consequences according to one's own values and to make a personal decision whether to subject oneself to the intrusion. For a patient like Nancy Cruzan, the sole benefit of medical treatment is being kept metabolically alive. Neither artificial nutrition nor any other form of medical treatment available today can cure or in any way ameliorate her condition. Irreversibly vegetative patients are devoid of thought, emotion and sensation; they are permanently and completely unconscious. As the President's Commission [for the Study of Ethical Problems in Medicine and Biomedical and Behavioral Research, "Deciding to Forego Life-Sustaining Treatment" (1983)] concluded in approving the withdrawal of life support equipment from irreversibly vegetative patients:

> "[T]reatment ordinarily aims to benefit a patient through preserving life, relieving pain and suffering, protecting against disability, and returning maximally effective functioning. If a prognosis of permanent unconsciousness is correct, however, continued treatment cannot confer such benefits. Pain and suffering are absent, as are joy, satisfaction, and pleasure. Disability is total and no return to an even minimal level of social or human functioning is possible."

There are also affirmative reasons why someone like Nancy might choose to forgo artificial nutrition and hydration under these circumstances. Dying is personal. And it is profound. For many, the thought of an ignoble end, steeped in decay, is abhorrent. . . .

Such conditions are, for many, humiliating to contemplate, as is visiting a prolonged and anguished vigil on one's parents, spouse, and children. A long, drawn-out death can have a debilitating effect on family members. For some, the idea of being remembered in their persistent vegetative states rather than as they were before their illness or accident may be very disturbing.

B

Although the right to be free of unwanted medical intervention, like other constitutionally protected interests, may not be absolute, no State interest could outweigh the rights of an individual in Nancy Cruzan's position. Whatever a State's possible interests in mandating life-support treatment under other circumstances, there is no good to be obtained here by Missouri's insistence that Nancy Cruzan remain on life-support systems if it is indeed her wish not to do so. Missouri does not claim, nor could it, that society as a whole will be benefited by Nancy's receiving medical treatment. No third party's situation will be improved and no harm to others will be averted.

The only state interest asserted here is a general interest in the preservation of life. But the State has no legitimate general interest in someone's life, completely abstracted from the interest of the person living that life, that could outweigh the person's choice to avoid medical treatment. . . . Thus, the State's general interest in life must accede to Nancy Cruzan's particularized and intense interest in self-determination in her choice of medical treatment. There is simply nothing legitimately within the State's purview to be gained by superseding her decision. . . .

III

This is not to say that the State has no legitimate interests to assert here. As the majority recognizes, Missouri has a *parens patriae* interest in providing Nancy Cruzan, now incompetent, with as accurate as possible a determination of how she would exercise her rights under these circumstances. Second, if and when it is determined that Nancy Cruzan would want to continue treatment, the State may legitimately assert an interest in providing that treatment. But *until* Nancy's wishes have been determined, the only state interest that may be asserted is an interest in safeguarding the accuracy of that determination.

Accuracy, therefore, must be our touchstone. Missouri may constitutionally impose only those procedural requirements that serve to enhance the accuracy of a determination of Nancy Cruzan's wishes or are at least consistent with an accurate determination. The Missouri "safeguard" that the Court upholds today does not meet that standard. The determination needed in this context is whether the incompetent person would choose to live in a persistent vegetative state on life-support or to avoid this medical treatment. Missouri's rule of decision imposes a markedly asymmetrical evidentiary burden. Only evidence of specific statements of treatment choice made by the patient when competent is admissible to support a finding that the patient ... would wish to avoid further medical treatment. Moreover, this evidence must be clear and convincing. No proof is required to support a finding that the incompetent person would wish to continue treatment. . . .

[A omitted]

B

Even more than its heightened evidentiary standard, the Missouri court's categorical exclusion of relevant evidence dispenses with any semblance of accurate factfinding. The court adverted to no evidence supporting its decision, but held that no clear and convincing, inherently reliable evidence had been presented to show that Nancy would want to avoid further treatment. In doing so, the court failed to consider statements Nancy had made to family members and a close friend. The court also failed to consider testimony from Nancy's mother and sister that they were certain that Nancy would want to discontinue to artificial nutrition and hydration, even after the court found that Nancy's family was loving and without malignant motive. The court also failed to consider the conclusions of the guardian ad litem ... that there was clear and convincing evidence that Nancy would want to discontinue medical treatment and that this was in her best interests. The court did not specifically define what kind of evidence it would consider clear and convincing, but its general discussion suggests that only a living will or equivalently formal directive from the patient when competent would meet this standard.

Too few people execute living wills or equivalently formal directives for such an evidentiary rule to ensure adequately that the wishes of incompetent persons will be honored. While it might be a wise social policy to encourage people to furnish such instructions, no general conclusion about a patient's choice can be drawn from the absence of formalities. The probability of becoming irreversibly vegetative is so low that many people may not feel an urgency to marshal formal evidence of their preferences. Some may not wish to dwell on their own physical deterioration and mortality. Even someone with a resolute determination to avoid life-support under circumstances such as Nancy's would still need to know that such things as living wills exist and how to execute one. . . .

The testimony of close friends and family members, on the other hand, may often be the best evidence available of what the patient's choice would be. It is they with whom the patient most likely will have discussed such questions and they who know the patient best. . . .

C

. . . Even if the Court had ruled that Missouri's rule of decision is unconstitutional, as I believe it should have, States would nevertheless remain free to fashion procedural protections to safeguard the interests of incompetents under these circumstances. The Constitution provides merely a framework here: protections must be genuinely aimed at ensuring decisions commensurate with the will of the patient, and must be reliable as instruments to that end. Of the many States which have instituted such protections, Missouri is virtually the only one to have fashioned a rule that lessens the likelihood of accurate determinations. . . .

D

Finally, I cannot agree with the majority that where it is not possible to determine what choice an incompetent patient would make, a State's role as *parens patriae* permits the State automatically to make that choice itself. . . . A State's legitimate interest in safeguarding a patient's choice cannot be furthered by simply appropriating it. . . .

A State's inability to discern an incompetent patient's choice still need not mean that a State is rendered powerless to protect that choice. But I would find that the Due Process Clause prohibits a State from doing more than that. A State may ensure that the person who makes the decision on the patient's behalf is the one whom the patient himself would have selected to make that choice for him. And a State may exclude from consideration anyone having improper motives. But a State generally must either repose the choice with the person whom the patient himself would most likely have chosen as proxy or leave the decision to the patient's family. . . .

JUSTICE STEVENS, dissenting.

Our Constitution is born of the proposition that all legitimate governments must secure the equal right of every person to "Life, Liberty, and the pursuit of Happiness." In the ordinary case we quite naturally assume that these three ends are compatible, mutually enhancing, and perhaps even coincident.

The Court would make an exception here. It permits the State's abstract, undifferentiated interest in the preservation of life to overwhelm the best interests of Nancy Beth Cruzan, interests which would, according to an undisputed finding, be served by allowing her guardians to exercise her constitutional right to discontinue medical treatment. Ironically, the Court reaches this conclusion despite endorsing three significant propositions which should save it from any such dilemma. First, a competent individual's decision to refuse life-sustaining medical procedures is an aspect of liberty protected by the Due Process Clause of the Fourteenth Amendment. Second, upon a proper evidentiary showing, a qualified guardian may make that decision on behalf of an incompetent ward. Third, in answering the important question presented by this tragic case, it is wise "not to attempt by any general statement, to cover every possible phase of the subject." Together, these considerations suggest that Nancy Cruzan's liberty to be free from medical treatment must be understood in light of the facts and circumstances particular to her.

I would so hold: in my view the Constitution requires the State to care for Nancy Cruzan's life in a way that gives appropriate respect to her own best interests. . . .

□□□

Nos. 88-1125 and 88-1309

Jane Hodgson, et al., Petitioners v. Minnesota et al.
Minnesota, et al., Petitioners v. Jane Hodgson et al.

On writs of Certiorari to the United States Court of Appeals
for the Eighth Circuit

[June 25, 1990]

JUSTICE STEVENS announced the judgment of the Court and delivered the opinion of the Court with respect to Parts I, II, IV, and VII, an opinion with respect to Part III in which JUSTICE BRENNAN joins, an opinion with respect to Parts V and VI in which JUSTICE O'CONNOR joins, and a dissenting opinion with respect to Part VIII.

A Minnesota statute, Minn. Stat. §§ 114.343(2)-(7) (1988), provides, with certain exceptions, that no abortion shall be performed on a woman under 18 years of age until at least 48 hours after both of her parents have been notified. In subdivisions 2-4 of the statute the notice is mandatory unless (1) the attending physician certifies that an immediate abortion is necessary to prevent the woman's death and there is insufficient time to provide the required notice; (2) both of her parents have consented in writing; or (3) the woman declares that she is a victim of parental abuse or neglect, in which event notice of her declaration must be given to the proper authorities. The United States Court of Appeals for the Eighth Circuit, sitting en banc, unanimously held this provision unconstitutional. In No. 88-1309, we granted the State's petition to review that holding. Subdivision 6 of the same statute provides that if a court enjoins the enforcement of subdivision 2, the same notice requirement shall be effective unless the pregnant woman obtains a court order permitting the abortion to proceed. By a vote of 7-3, the Court of Appeals upheld the constitutionality of subdivision 6. In No. 88-1125, we granted the plaintiffs' petition to review that holding.

For reasons that follow, we now conclude that the requirement of notice to both of the pregnant minor's parents is not reasonably related to legitimate state interests and that subdivision 2 is unconstitutional. A different majority of the Court, for reasons stated in separate opinions, concludes that subdivision 6 is constitutional. Accordingly, the judgment of the Court of Appeals in its entirety is affirmed.

I

The parental notice statute was enacted in 1981 as an amendment to the Minors' Consent to Health Services Act. . . .

The 1981 amendment qualified the authority of an "unemancipated minor" to give effective consent to an abortion by requiring that either her physician or an agent notify "the parent" personally or by certified mail at least 48 hours before the procedure is performed. The term "parent" is defined in subdivision 3 to mean "both parents of the pregnant woman if they are both living." No exception is made for a divorced parent, a noncustodial parent, or a biological parent who never married or lived with the pregnant woman's mother. . . .

. . . If the pregnant minor can convince "any judge of a court of competent jurisdiction" that she is "mature and capable of giving informed consent to the proposed abortion," or that an abortion without notice to both parents would be in her best interest, the court can authorize the physician to proceed without notice. The statute provides that the bypass procedure shall be confidential, that it shall be expedited, that the minor has a right to court-appointed counsel, and that she shall be afforded free access to the court "24 hours a day, seven days a week." An order denying an abortion can be appealed on an expedited basis, but an order authorizing an abortion without notification is not subject to appeal.

II

This litigation was commenced on July 30, 1981, two days before the effective date of the parental notification statute. The plaintiffs include two Minnesota doctors who specialize in obstetrics and gynecology, four clinics providing abortion and contraceptive services in metropolitan areas in Minnesota, six pregnant minors representing a class of pregnant minors, and the mother of a pregnant minor. Plaintiffs alleged that the statute violated the Due Process and Equal Protection Clauses of the Fourteenth Amendment and various provisions of the Minnesota Constitution.

Based on the allegations in their verified complaint, the District Court entered a temporary restraining order enjoining the enforcement of subdivision 2 of the statute. After a hearing, the court entered a preliminary injunction which still remains in effect. The District Court refused, however, to rule on the validity of the judicial bypass procedure in advance of trial.

In 1986, after a 5-week trial, the District Court concluded that both the two-parent notification requirement and the 48-hour waiting period were invalid. . . . The court declared the entire statute unconstitutional and enjoined the defendants from enforcing it.

A three-judge panel of the Court of Appeals affirmed. . . .

The panel opinion was vacated and the Court of Appeals reheard the case en banc. The court unanimously and summarily rejected the State's submission that the two-parent notice requirement was constitutional without any bypass procedure. The majority concluded, however, that subdivision 6 of the statute was valid. . . .

III

. . . A woman's decision to beget or bear a child is a component of her liberty that is protected by the Due Process Clause of the Fourteenth Amendment to the Constitution. . . . As we stated in *Planned Parenthood of Central Missouri v. Danforth* (1976), the right to make this decision "do[es] not mature and come into being magically only when one attains the state-defined age of majority." Thus, the constitutional protection against unjustified state intrusion into the process of deciding whether or not to bear a child extends to pregnant minors as well as adult women.

In cases involving abortion, as in cases involving the right to travel or the right to marry, the identification of the constitutionally protected interest is merely the beginning of the analysis. State regulation of travel and of marriage is obviously permissible even though a State may not categorically exclude nonresidents from its borders, *Shapiro v. Thompson* (1969), or deny prisoners the right to marry, *Turner v. Safley* (1987). But the regulation of constitutionally protected decisions, such as where a person shall reside or whom he or she shall marry, must be predicated on legitimate state concerns other than disagreement with the choice the individual has made. In the abortion area, a State may have no obligation to spend its own money, or use its own facilities, to subsidize nontherapeutic abortions for minors or adults. A State's value judgment favoring childbirth over abortion may provide adequate support for decisions involving such allocation of public funds, but not for simply substituting a state decision for an individual decision that a woman has a right to make for herself. Otherwise, the interest in liberty protected by the Due Process Clause would be a nullity. A state policy favoring childbirth over abortion is not in itself a sufficient justification for overriding the woman's decision or for placing "obstacles—absolute or otherwise—in the pregnant woman's path to an abortion."

In these cases the State of Minnesota does not rest its defense of this statute on any such value judgment. Indeed, it affirmatively disavows that state interest as a basis for upholding this law. Moreover, it is clear that the state judges who have interpreted the statute in over 3,000 decisions implementing its bypass procedures have found no legislative intent to disfavor the decision to terminate a pregnancy. On the contrary, in all but a handful of cases they have approved such decisions. Because the Minnesota statute unquestionably places obstacles in the pregnant minor's path to an abortion, the State has the burden of establishing its constitutionality. Under any analysis, the Minnesota statute cannot be sustained if the obstacles it imposes are not reasonably related to legitimate state interests.

IV

The Court has considered the constitutionality of statutes providing for parental consent or parental notification in six abortion cases decided during the last 14 years. Although the Massachusetts statute reviewed in *Bellotti v. Baird* (1976) *(Bellotti I)* and *Bellotti II* [1979] required the consent of both parents, and the Utah statute reviewed in *H. L. v.*

Matheson (1981), required notice to "the parents," none of the opinions in any of those cases focused on the possible significance of making the consent or the notice requirement applicable to both parents instead of just one. In contrast, the arguments in these cases, as well as the extensive findings of the District Court, are directed primarily at that distinction. It is therefore appropriate to summarize these findings before addressing the constitutionality of the 48-hour waiting period or the two-parent notification requirement, particularly since none of the findings has been challenged in either this Court or the Court of Appeals. . . .

The District Court found—on the basis of extensive testimony at trial—that the two-parent notification requirement had particularly harmful effects on both the minor and the custodial parent when the parents were divorced or separated. Relations between the minor and absent parent were not reestablished as a result of the forced notification thereby often producing disappointment in the minor. . . . Moreover, "[t]he reaction of the custodial parent to the requirement of forced notification is often one of anger, resentment and frustration at the intrusion of the absent parent," and fear that notification will threaten the custody rights of the parent or otherwise promote intrafamily violence. Tragically, those fears were often realized. . . .

The District Court also found that the two-parent notification requirement had adverse effects in families in which the minor lives with both parents. These effects were particularly pronounced in the distressingly large number of cases in which family violence is a serious problem. The court found that many minors in Minnesota "live in fear of violence by family members" and "are, in fact, victims of rape, incest, neglect and violence." The District Court found that few minors can take advantage of the exception for a minor who declares that she is a victim of sexual or physical abuse because of the obligation to report the information to the authorities and the attendant loss of privacy. . . .

Scheduling petitions in the Minnesota court typically required minors to wait only two or three days for hearings. The District Court found, however, that the statutory waiting period of 48 hours was frequently compounded by a number of other factors that "commonly" created a delay of 72 hours, and, "in many cases" a delay of a week or more in effecting a decision to terminate a pregnancy. A delay of that magnitude increased the medical risk associated with the abortion procedure to "a statistically significant degree.". . .

V

Three separate but related interests—the interest in the welfare of the pregnant minor, the interest of the parents, and the interest of the family unit—are relevant to our consideration of the constitutionality of the 48-hour waiting period and the two-parent notification requirement.

The State has a strong and legitimate interest in the welfare of its young citizens, whose immaturity, inexperience, and lack of judgment may sometimes impair their ability to exercise their rights wisely. That interest, which justifies state-imposed requirements that a minor obtain his or her parent's consent before undergoing an operation, marrying, or entering military service, extends also to the minor's decision to terminate her pregnancy. Although the Court has held that parents may not exercise "an absolute, and possibly arbitrary, veto" over that decision, it has never challenged a State's reasonable judgment that the decision should be made after notification to and consultation with a parent. . . .

While the State has a legitimate interest in the creation and dissolution of the marriage contract, the family has a privacy interest in the upbringing and education of children and the intimacies of the marital relationship which is protected by the Constitution against undue state interference. . . . We have long held that there exists a "private realm of family life which the state cannot enter." *Prince v. Massachusetts* [1944]. . . .

VI

We think it is clear that a requirement that a minor wait 48 hours after notifying a single parent of her intention to get an abortion would reasonably further the legitimate state interest in ensuring that the minor's decision is knowing and intelligent. We have held that when a parent or another person has assumed "primary responsibility" for a minor's well-being, the State may properly enact "laws designed to aid discharge of that responsibility." *Ginsberg v. New York* (1968). To the extent that subdivision 2 of the Minnesota statute requires notification of only one parent, it does just that. The brief waiting period provides the parent the opportunity to consult with his or her spouse and a family physician, and it permits the parent to inquire into the competency of the doctor performing the abortion, discuss the religious or moral implications of the abortion decision, and provide the daughter needed guidance and counsel in evaluating the impact of the decision on her future. . . .

VII

It is equally clear that the requirement that *both* parents be notified, whether or not both wish to be notified or have assumed responsibility for the upbringing of the child, does not reasonably further any legitimate state interest. The usual justification for a parental consent or notification provision is that it supports the authority of a parent who is presumed to act in the minor's best interest and thereby assures that the minor's decision to terminate her pregnancy is knowing, intelligent, and deliberate. To the extent that such an interest is legitimate, it would be fully served by a requirement that the minor notify one parent who can then seek the counsel of his or her mate or any other party, when such advice and support is deemed necessary to help the child make a difficult decision. In the ideal family setting, of course, notice to either parent would normally constitute notice to both. A statute requiring two-parent notification would not further any state interest in those instances. In many families, however, the parent notified by the child would not notify the other parent. In those cases the State has no legitimate interest in questioning one parent's judgment that notice to the other parent would not assist the minor or in presuming that the parent who has assumed parental duties is incompetent to make decisions regarding the health and welfare of the child.

Not only does two-parent notification fail to serve any state interest with respect to functioning families, it disserves the state interest in protecting and assisting the minor with respect to dysfunctional families. The record reveals that in the thousands of dysfunctional families affected by this statute, the two-parent notice requirement proved positively harmful to the minor and her family. The testimony at trial established that this requirement . . . resulted in major trauma to the child, and often to a parent as well. . . .

VIII

The Court holds that the constitutional objection to the two-parent notice requirement is removed by the judicial bypass option provided in subdivision 6 of the Minnesota statute. I respectfully dissent from that holding. . . .

A judicial bypass that is designed to handle exceptions from a reasonable general rule, and thereby preserve the constitutionality of that rule, is quite different from a requirement that a minor—or a minor and one of her parents—must apply to a court for permission to avoid the application of a rule that is not reasonably related to legitimate state goals. A requirement that a minor acting with the consent of *both* parents apply to a court for permission to effectuate her decision clearly would constitute an unjustified official interference with the privacy of the minor and her family. The requirement that the bypass procedure must be invoked when the minor and one parent agree that the other parent should not be notified represents an equally unjustified governmental intrusion into the family's decisional process. . . .

The judgment of the Court of Appeals in its entirety is affirmed.

It is so ordered.

JUSTICE O'CONNOR, concurring in part and concurring in the judgment in part.

I

I join all but Parts III and VIII of JUSTICE STEVENS' opinion. While I agree with some of the central points made in Part III, I cannot join the broader discussion. I agree that the Court has characterized "[a] woman's decision to beget or to bear a child [as] a component of her liberty that is protected by the Due Process Clause of the Fourteenth Amendment to the Constitution." This Court extended that liberty interest to minors in *Bellotti v. Baird* (1979) and *Planned Parenthood of Central Missouri v. Danforth* (1976), albeit with some important limitations. . . .

It has been my understanding in this area that "[i]f the particular regulation does not 'unduly burde[n]' the fundamental right, . . . then our evaluation of that regulation is limited to our determination that the regulation rationally relates to a legitimate state purpose." *Akron v. Akron Center for Reproductive Health, Inc.* (1983) (O'CONNOR, J., dissenting); see also *Webster v. Reproductive Health Services* (1989) (O'CONNOR, J., concurring in part and concurring in judgment). It is with that understanding that I agree with JUSTICE STEVENS' statement that the "statute cannot be sustained if the obstacles it imposes are not reasonably related to legitimate state interests."

I agree with JUSTICE STEVENS that Minnesota has offered no sufficient justification for its interference with the family's decisionmaking processes created by subdivision 2—two-parent notification. Subdivision 2 is the most stringent notification statute in the country. . . .

The Minnesota exception to notification for minors who are victims of neglect or abuse is, in reality, a means of notifying the parents. As JUSTICE STEVENS points out, to avail herself of the neglect or abuse exception, the minor must report the abuse. A report requires the welfare agency to immediately "conduct an assessment." If the agency interviews the victim, it must notify the parent of the fact of the interview; if the parent is the subject of an investigation, he has a right of access to the record of the investigation. . . .

Minnesota's two-parent notice requirement is all the more unreasonable when one considers that only half of the minors in the state of Minnesota reside with both biological parents. . . . Given its broad sweep and its failure to serve the purposes asserted by the State in too many cases, I join the Court's striking of subdivision 2.

II

. . . Subdivision 6 passes constitutional muster because the interference with the internal operation of the family required by subdivision 2 simply does not exist where the minor can avoid notifying one or both parents by use of the bypass procedure.

JUSTICE MARSHALL, with whom JUSTICE BRENNAN and JUSTICE BLACKMUN join, concurring in part, concurring in the judgment in part, and dissenting in part.

I concur in Parts I, II, IV, and VII of JUSTICE STEVENS' opinion for the Court in No. 88-1309. Although I do not believe that the Constitution permits a State to require a minor to notify or consult with a parent before obtaining an abortion, I am in substantial agreement with the remainder of the reasoning in Part V of the Court's opinion. For the reasons stated by JUSTICE STEVENS, Minnesota's two-parent notification requirement is not even reasonably related to a legitimate state interest. Therefore, that requirement surely would not pass the strict scrutiny applicable to restrictions on a woman's fundamental right to have an abortion.

I dissent from the judgment of the Court in No. 89-1125, however, that the judicial bypass option renders the parental notification and 48-hour delay requirements constitutional. The bypass procedure cannot save those requirements because the bypass itself is unconstitutional both on its face and as applied. At the very least, this scheme substantially burdens a woman's right to privacy without advancing a compelling state interest. More significantly, in some instances it usurps a young woman's control over her own body by giving either a parent or a court the power effectively to veto her decision to have an abortion. . . .

[I omitted]

II

I strongly disagree with the Court's conclusion that the State may constitutionally force a minor woman either to notify both parents (or in some cases only one parent) and then wait 48 hours before proceeding with an abortion, or disclose her intimate affairs to a judge and ask that he grant her permission to have an abortion. First, the parental notification and delay requirements significantly restrict a young woman's right to reproductive choice. I base my conclusion not on my intuition about the needs and attitudes of young women, but on a sizable and impressive collection of empirical data documenting the effects of parental notification statutes and of delaying an abortion. Second, the burdensome restrictions are not narrowly tailored to serve any compelling state interest. Finally . . . the judicial bypass procedure does not save the notice and delay requirements.

JUSTICE SCALIA, concurring in the judgment in part and dissenting in part.

As I understand the various opinions today: One Justice holds that two-parent notification is unconstitutional (as least in the present circumstances) without judicial bypass, but constitutional with bypass; four Justices would hold that two-parent notification is unconstitutional with or without bypass, though the four apply two different standards; six Justices hold that one-parent notification with bypass is constitutional, though for two different sets of reasons; and three Justices would hold that one-parent notification with bypass is unconstitutional. One will search in vain the document we are supposed to be construing for text that provides the basis for the argument over these distinctions; and will find in our society's tradition regarding abortion no hint that the distinctions are constitutionally relevant, much less any indication how a constitutional argument about them ought to be resolved. The random and unpredictable results of our consequently unchanneled individual views make it increasingly evident, Term after Term, that the tools for this job are not to be found in the lawyer's—and hence not in the judge's—workbox. I continue to dissent from this enterprise of devising an Abortion Code, and from the illusion that we have authority to do so.

JUSTICE KENNEDY, with whom THE CHIEF JUSTICE, JUSTICE WHITE, and JUSTICE SCALIA join, concurring in the judgment in part and dissenting in part.

. . . Today, the Court holds that a statute requiring a minor to notify both parents that she plans to have an abortion is not a permissible means of furthering the interest described with such specificity in *Bellotti II* [1979]. This conclusion, which no doubt will come as a surprise to most parents, is incompatible with our constitutional tradition and any acceptable notion of judicial review of legislative enactments. I dissent from the portion of the Court's judgment affirming the Court of Appeals conclusion that Minnesota [*sic*] two-parent notice statute is unconstitutional. . . .

[I omitted]

II

The State identifies two interests served by the law. The first is the State's interest in the welfare of pregnant minors. The second is the State's interest in acknowledging and promoting the role of parents in the care and upbringing of their children. JUSTICE STEVENS, writing for two Members of the Court, acknowledges the legitimacy of the first interest, but decides that the second interest is somehow illegitimate, at least as to whichever parent a minor chooses not to notify. I cannot agree that the Constitution prevents a State from keeping both parents informed of the medical condition or medical treatment of their child under the terms and conditions of this statute. . . .

Protection of the right of each parent to participate in the upbringing of her or his own children is a further discrete interest that the State recognizes by the statute. The common law historically has given recognition to the right of parents, not merely to be notified of their children's actions, but to speak and act on their behalf. . . .

A State pursues a legitimate end under the Constitution when it attempts to foster and preserve the parent-child relation by giving all parents the opportunity to participate in the care and nurture of their children. We have held that parents have a liberty interest, protected by the Constitution, in having a reasonable opportunity to develop close relations with their children. We have recognized, of course, that there are limits to the constitutional right of parents to have custody of or to participate in decisions affecting their children. If a parent has relinquished the opportunity to develop a relation with the child, and his or her only link to the child is biological, the Constitution does not require a State to allow parental participation. But the fact that the Constitution does not protect the parent-child relationship in all circumstances does not mean that the State cannot attempt to foster parental participation where the Constitution does not demand that it do so. . . .

Minnesota has done no more than act upon the common-sense proposition that, in assisting their daughter in deciding whether to have an abortion, parents can best fulfill their roles if they have the same information about their own child's medical condition and medical choices as the child's doctor does; and that to deny parents this knowledge is to risk, or perpetuate, estrangement or alienation from the child when she is in the greatest need of parental guidance and support. The Court does the State, and our constitutional tradition, sad disservice by impugning the legitimacy of these elemental objectives. . . .

□□□

No. 88-805

Ohio, Appellant v. Akron Center for Reproductive Health et al.

On appeal from the United States Court of Appeals
for the Sixth Circuit

[June 25, 1990]

JUSTICE KENNEDY announced the judgment of the Court and delivered the opinion of the Court with respect to Parts I, II, III, and IV, and an opinion with respect to Part V, in which THE CHIEF JUSTICE, and JUSTICE WHITE, and JUSTICE SCALIA join.

The Court of Appeals held invalid an Ohio statute that, with certain exceptions, prohibits any person from performing an abortion on an unmarried, unemancipated, minor woman absent notice to one of the woman's parents or a court order of approval. We reverse, for we determine that the statute accords with our precedents on parental notice and consent in the abortion context and does not violate the Fourteenth Amendment.

I

A

The Ohio Legislature, in November 1985, enacted Amended Substitute House Bill 319 (H.B. 319).... Section 2919.12(B), the cornerstone of this legislation, makes it a criminal offense, except in four specified circumstances, for a physician or other person to perform an abortion on an unmarried and unemancipated woman under eighteen years of age....

The first and second circumstances in which a physician may perform an abortion relate to parental notice and consent. First, a physician may perform an abortion if he provides "at least twenty-four hours actual notice, in person or by telephone," to one of the women's [*sic*] parents (or her guardian or custodian) of his intention to perform the abortion. The physician, as an alternative, may notify a minor's adult brother, sister, stepparent, or grandparent, if the minor and the other relative each file an affidavit in the juvenile court stating that the minor fears physical, sexual, or severe emotional abuse from one of her parents. If the physician cannot give the notice "after a reasonable effort," he may perform the abortion after "at least forty-eight hours constructive notice" by both ordinary and certified mail. Second, a physician may perform an abortion on the minor if one of her parents (or her guardian or custodian) has consented to the abortion in writing.

The third and fourth circumstances depend on a judicial procedure that allows a minor to bypass the notice and consent provisions just described. The statute allows a physician to perform an abortion without notifying one of the minor's parents or receiving the parent's consent if a juvenile court issues an order authorizing the minor to consent, or if a juvenile court or court of appeals, by its inaction, provides constructive authorization for the minor to consent.

The bypass procedure requires the minor to file a complaint in the juvenile court, stating (1) that she is pregnant; (2) that she is unmarried, under 18 years of age, and unemancipated; (3) that she desires to have an abortion without notifying one of her parents; (4) that she has sufficient maturity and information to make an intelligent decision whether to have an abortion without such notice, *or* that one of her parents has engaged in a pattern of physical, sexual, or emotional abuse against her, *or* that notice is not in her best interests; and (5) that she has or has not retained an attorney. . . .

The juvenile court must hold a hearing at the earliest possible time, but not later than the fifth business day after the minor files the complaint. The court must render its decision immediately after the conclusion of the hearing. Failure to hold the hearing within this time results in constructive authorization for the minor to consent to the abortion. At the hearing the court must appoint a guardian ad litem and an attorney to represent the minor if she has not retained her own counsel. The minor must prove her allegation of maturity, pattern of abuse, or best interests by clear and convincing evidence, and the juvenile court must conduct the hearing to preserve the anonymity of the complainant, keeping all papers confidential.

The minor has the right to expedited review. The statute provides that, within four days after the minor files a notice of appeal, the clerk of the juvenile court shall deliver the notice of appeal and record to the state court of appeals. The clerk of the court of appeals dockets the appeal upon receipt of these items. The minor must file her brief within four days after the docketing. If she desires an oral argument, the court of appeals must hold one within five days after the docketing and must issue a decision immediately after oral argument. If she waives the right to an oral argument, the court of appeals must issue a decision within five days after the docketing. If the court of appeals does not comply with these time limits, a constructive order results authorizing the minor to consent to the abortion.

B

Appellees in this action include the Akron Center for Reproductive Health, a facility that provides abortions; Max Pierre Gaujean, M.D., a physician who performs abortions at the Akron Center; and Rachel Roe, an unmarried, unemancipated minor woman, who sought an abortion at the facility. In March 1986, days before the effective date of H.B. 319, appellees and others brought a facial challenge to the constitutionality of the statute in the United State District Court for the Northern District of Ohio. The District Court, after various proceedings, issued a preliminary injunction and later a permanent injunction preventing the State of Ohio from enforcing the statute.

The Court of Appeals for the Sixth Circuit affirmed, concluding that H.B. 319 had six constitutional defects. These points, discussed below, related to the sufficiency of the expedited procedures, the guarantee of anonymity, the constructive authorization provisions, the clear and convincing evidence standard, the pleading requirements, and the physician's personal obligation to give notice to one of the minor's parents. The State of Ohio challenges the Court of Appeals' decision in its entirety. Appellees seek affirmance on the grounds adopted by the Court of Appeals and on other grounds as well.

II

We have decided five cases addressing the constitutionality of parental notice or parental consent statutes in the abortion context. See *Planned Parenthood of Central Missouri v. Danforth* (1976); *Bellotti v. Baird* (1979); *H. L. v. Matheson* (1981); *Planned Parenthood Assn. of Kansas City, Mo., Inc. v. Ashcroft* (1983); *Akron v. Akron Center for Reproductive Health, Inc.* (1983). We do not need to determine whether a statute that does not accord with these cases would violate the Constitution, for we conclude that H.B. 319 is consistent with them.

A

This dispute turns, to a large extent, on the adequacy of H.B. 319's judicial bypass procedure. In analyzing this aspect of the dispute, we note that, although our cases have required bypass procedures for parental consent statutes, we have not decided whether parental notice statutes must contain such procedures. We leave the question open, because, whether or not the Fourteenth Amendment requires notice statutes to contain bypass procedures, H.B. 319's bypass procedure meets the requirements identified for parental consent statutes in *Danforth, Bellotti, Ashcroft,* and *Akron. Danforth* established that, in order to prevent another person from having an absolute veto power over a minor's decision to have an abortion, a State must provide some sort of bypass procedure if it elects to require parental consent. . . .

The plurality opinion in *Bellotti* stated four criteria that a bypass procedure in a consent statute must satisfy. Appellees contend that the bypass procedure does not satisfy these criteria. We disagree. First, the *Bellotti* plurality indicated that the procedure must allow the minor to show that she possesses the maturity and information to make her abortion decision, in consultation with her physician, without regard to her parents' wishes.... In the case now before us, we have no difficulty concluding that H.B. 319 allows a minor to show maturity in conformity with the plurality opinion in *Bellotti*....

Second, the *Bellotti* plurality indicated that the procedure must allow the minor to show that, even if she cannot make the abortion decision by herself, "the desired abortion would be in her best interests." We believe that H.B. 319 satisfies the *Bellotti* language as quoted. The statute requires the juvenile court to authorize the minor's consent where the court determines that the abortion is in the minor's best interest and in cases where the minor has shown a pattern of physical, sexual, or emotional abuse.

Third, the *Bellotti* plurality indicated that the procedure must insure the minor's anonymity. Section 2151.85(D) provides that "[t]he [juvenile] court shall not notify the parents, guardian, or custodian of the complainant that she is pregnant or that she wants to have an abortion." Section 2151.85(F) further states:

> "Each hearing under this section shall be conducted in a manner that will preserve the anonymity of the complainant. The complaint and all other papers and records that pertain to an action commenced under this section shall be kept confidential and are not public records."

Section 2505.073(B), in a similar fashion, requires the court of appeals to preserve the minor's anonymity and confidentiality of all papers on appeal. The State, in addition, makes it a criminal offense for an employee to disclose documents not designated as public records....

Fourth, the *Bellotti* plurality indicated that courts must conduct a bypass procedure with expedition to allow the minor an effective opportunity to obtain the abortion. H.B. 319 ... requires the trial court to make its decision within five "business day[s]" after the minor files her complaint, § 2151.85(B)(1); requires the court of appeals to docket an appeal within four "days" after the minor files a notice of appeal, § 2505.073(A); and requires the court of appeals to render a decision within five "days" after docketing the appeal.

The District Court and the Court of Appeals assumed that all of the references to days ... meant business days as opposed to calendar days. They calculated, as a result, that the procedure could take up to 22 calendar days because the minor could file at a time during the year in which the 14 business days needed for the bypass procedure would encompass three Saturdays, three Sundays, and two legal holidays.... Interpreting the term "days" in § 2505.073(A) to mean business days instead of calendar days seems inappropriate and unnecessary because of the express and contrasting use of "business day[s]" in § 2151.85(B)(1). . . . The Court of Appeals should not have invalidated the Ohio statute on a facial challenge based upon a worst-case analysis that may never occur. . . . Moreover, under our precedents, the mere possibility that the procedure may require up to twenty-two days in a rare case is plainly insufficient to invalidate the statute on its face. *Ashcroft,* for example, upheld a Missouri statute that contained a bypass procedure that could require 17 calendar days plus a sufficient time for deliberation and decisionmaking at both the trial and appellate levels. . . .

B

Appellees . . . challenge the constructive authorization provisions in H.B. 319, which enable a minor to obtain an abortion without notifying one of her parents if either the juvenile court or the court of appeals fails to act within the prescribed time limits. They speculate that the absence of an affirmative order when a court fails to process the minor's complaint will deter the physician from acting.

We discern no constitutional defect in the statute. Absent a demonstrated pattern of abuse or defiance, a State may expect that its judges will follow mandated procedural requirements. There is no showing that the time limitations imposed by H.B. 319 will be ignored. . . .

III

Appellees contend our inquiry does not end even if we decide that H.B. 319 conforms to *Danforth, Bellotti, Matheson, Ashcroft,* and *Akron.* They maintain that H.B. 319 gives a minor a state law substantive right "to avoid unnecessary or hostile parental involvement" if she can demonstrate that her maturity or best interests favor abortion without notifying one of her parents. They argue that H.B. 319 deprives the minor of this right without due process because the pleading requirements, the alleged lack of expedition and anonymity, and the clear and convincing evidence standard make the bypass procedure unfair. See *Mathews v. Eldridge* (1976). We find no merit in this argument.

The confidentiality provisions, the expedited procedures, and the pleading form requirements, on their face, satisfy the dictates of minimal due process. We see little risk of erroneous deprivation under these provisions and no need to require additional procedural safeguards. The clear and convincing evidence standard, for reasons we have described, does not place an unconstitutional burden on the types of proof to be does not place an unconstitutional burden on the types of proof to be presented. The minor is assisted by an attorney and a guardian ad litem and the proceeding is *ex parte.* The standard ensures that the judge will take special care in deciding whether the minor's consent to an abortion should proceed without parental notification. . . .

IV

Appellees, as a final matter, contend that we should invalidate H.B. 319 in its entirety because the statute requires the parental notice to be given by the physician who is to perform the abortion. In *Akron,* the court found unconstitutional a requirement that the attending physician provide the information and counseling relevant to informed consent. Although the Court did not disapprove of informing a woman of the health risks of an abortion, it explained that "[t]he State's interest is in ensuring that the woman's consent is informed and unpressured; the critical factor is whether she obtains the necessary information and counseling from a qualified person, not the identity of the person from whom she obtains it." Appellees maintain, in a similar fashion, that Ohio has no reason for requiring the minor's physician, rather than some other qualified person, to notify one of the minor's parents.

Appellees, however, have failed to consider our precedent on this matter. We upheld, in *Matheson,* a statute that required a physician to notify the minor's parents. The distinction between notifying a minor's parents and informing a woman of the routine risks of an abortion has ample justification. . . . We continue to believe that a State may require the physician himself or herself to take reasonable steps to notify a minor's parent because the parent often will provide important medical data to the physician. . . .

V

The Ohio statute, in sum, does not impose an undue, or otherwise unconstitutional, burden on a minor seeking an abortion. We believe, in addition, that the legislature acted in a rational matter in enacting H.B. 319. . . . It is both rational and fair for the State to conclude that, in most instances, the family will strive to give a lonely or even terrified minor advice that is both compassionate and mature. The statute in issue here is a rational way to further those ends. It would deny all dignity to the family to say that the State cannot take this reasonable step in regulating its health professions to ensure that, in most cases, a young woman will receive guidance and understanding from a parent. We uphold H.B. 319 on its face and reverse the Court of Appeals.

It is so ordered.

JUSTICE SCALIA, concurring.

I join the opinion of the Court, because I agree that the Ohio statute neither deprives minors of procedural due process nor contradicts our holdings regarding the constitutional right to abortion. I continue to believe, however, as I said in my separate concurrence last Term in *Webster v. Reproductive Health Services* (1989), that the Constitution contains no right to abortion. It is not to be found in the longstanding traditions of our society, nor can it be logically deduced from the text of the Constitution—not, that is, without volunteering a judicial answer to the nonjusticible question of when human life begins. Leaving this matter to the political process is not only legally correct, it is pragmatically so. That alone—and not lawyerly dissection of federal judicial precedents— can produce compromises satisfying a sufficient mass of the electorate that this deeply felt issue will cease distorting the remainder of our democratic process. The Court should end its disruptive intrusion into this field as soon as possible.

JUSTICE STEVENS, concurring in part and concurring in the judgment.

As the Court emphasizes, appellees have challenged the Ohio statute only on its face. The State may presume that, in most of its applications, the statute will reasonably further its legitimate interest in protecting the welfare of its minor citizens. In some of its applications, however, the one-parent notice requirement will not reasonably further that interest. There will be exceptional situations in which notice will cause a realistic risk of physical harm to the pregnant woman, will cause trauma to an ill parent, or will enable the parent to prevent the abortion for reasons that are unrelated to the best interests of the minor. The Ohio statute recognizes that possibility by providing a judicial bypass. The question in this case is whether that statutory protection for the exceptional case is so obviously inadequate that the entire statute should be invalidated. I am not willing to reach that conclusion before the statute has been implemented and the significance of its restrictions evaluated in the light of its administration. I therefore agree that the Court of Appeals' judgment must be reversed and I join Parts I-IV of the Court's opinion. . . .

JUSTICE BLACKMUN, with whom JUSTICE BRENNAN and JUSTICE MARSHALL join, dissenting.

I

. . . "Any independent interest the parent may have in the termination of the minor daughter's pregnancy is no more weighty than the right of privacy of the competent minor mature enough to have become pregnant." [*Planned Parenthood of Central Mo. v. Danforth* (1976)]

"The abortion decision differs in important ways from other decisions that may be made during minority. The need to protect the constitutional right and the unique nature of the abortion decision, especially when made by a minor, require a State to act with *particular sensitivity* when it legislates to foster parental involvement in this matter ... because "there are few situations in which denying a minor the right to make an important decision will have consequences so grave and indelible." [*Bellotti v. Baird* (1979) *(Bellotti II)*]. . . .

The State of Ohio has acted with particular *in*sensitivity in enacting the statute the Court today upholds. Rather than create a judicial-bypass system that reflects the sensitivity necessary when dealing with a minor making this deeply intimate decision, Ohio has created a tortuous maze. Moreover, the State has failed utterly to show that it has any significant state interest in deliberately placing its pattern of obstacles in the path of the pregnant minor seeking to exercise her constitutional right to terminate a pregnancy. The challenged provisions of the Ohio statute are merely "poorly disguised elements of discouragement for the abortion decision." *Thornburgh v. American College of Obstetricians and Gynecologists* (1986).

III

. . . The language of the Ohio statute purports to follow the standards for a bypass procedure that are set forth in *Bellotti II,* but at each stage along the way, the statute deliberately places "substantial state-created obstacles in the pregnant [minor's] path to an abortion," in the legislative hope that she will stumble, perhaps fall, and at least ensuring that she "conquer a multi-faceted obstacle course" before she is able to exercise her constitutional right to an abortion. . . .

A

The obstacle course begins when the minor first enters the courthouse to fill out the complaint forms. The "pleasing trap," as it appropriately was described by the Court of Appeals, requires the minor to choose among three forms. The first alleges *only* maturity; the second alleges *only* that the abortion is in her best interest. Only if the minor chooses the third form, which alleges both, may the minor attempt to prove both maturity *and* best interest as is her right under *Bellotti II.* The majority makes light of what it acknowledges might be "some initial confusion" of the unsophisticated minor who is trying to deal with an unfamiliar and mystifying court system on an intensely intimate matter. . . .

The majority fails to elucidate *any* state interest in setting up this barricade for the young pregnant woman—a barricade that will "serve only to confuse . . . her and to heighten her anxiety." The justification the State put forward before the Court of Appeals was the "absurd contention that '[a]ny minor claiming to be mature and well enough informed to independently make such an important decision as an abortion should also be mature enough to file her complaint under [the appropriate subsection].' " This proffered "justification" is even more harsh than the Court of Appeals noted. . . . Surely, the goal of the court proceeding is to assist, not to entrap, the young pregnant woman. . . .

B

As the pregnant minor attempts to find her way through the labyrinth set up by the State of Ohio, she encounters yet another obstruction. . . . Far from keeping the identity of the minor anonymous, the statute requires the minor to sign her full name and the name of one of her parents on the complaint form. . . . Acknowledging that "[c]onfidentiality differs from anonymity," the majority simply asserts that "complete anonymity" is not "critical." That easy conclusion is irreconcilable with *Bellotti*'s anonymity requirement. . . .

As the District Court pointed out, there are no indications of how a clerk's office, large or small, is to ensure that the records of abortion cases will be distinguished from the records of all other cases that are available to the public. . . . This Court is well aware that, unless special care is taken, court documents of an intimate nature will find their way to the press and public. . . .

. . . I would not permit the State of Ohio to force a minor to forgo her anonymity in order to obtain a waiver of the parental-notification requirement.

C

Because a "pregnant adolescent . . . cannot preserve for long the possibility of aborting, which effectively expires in a matter of weeks from the onset of pregnancy," this Court has required that the State "must assure" that the "resolution of the issue, and any appeals that may follow, will be completed with . . . sufficient expedition to provide an effective opportunity for an abortion to be obtained." *Bellotti II*. . . . Ohio's judicial-bypass procedure can consume up to three weeks of a young woman's pregnancy. I would join the Sixth Circuit, the District Court, and the other federal courts that have held that a time span of this length fails to guarantee a sufficiently expedited procedure. . . .

D

The Ohio statute provides that if the juvenile or appellate courts fail to act within the statutory time frame, an abortion without parental notification is "constructively" authorized. Although Ohio's Legislature may have intended this provision to expedite the bypass procedure, the confusion that will result from the constructive-authorization provision will add further delay to the judicial-bypass proceeding, and is yet one more obstruction in the path of the pregnant minor. . . .

E

If the minor is able to wend her way through the intricate course of preliminaries Ohio has set up for her and at last reaches the court proceeding, the State shackles her even more tightly with still another "extra layer and burden of regulation on the abortion decision." The minor must demonstrate by "clear and convincing evidence" either (1) her maturity; (2) or that one of her parents has engaged in a pattern of physical, sexual, or emotional abuse against her; or (3) that notice to a parent is not in her best interest.". . .

. . . By imposing such a stringent standard of proof, this Ohio statute improperly places the risk of an erroneous decision on the minor, the very person whose fundamental right is at stake. . . . Even if the judge is satisfied that the minor is mature or that an abortion is in her best interest, the court may not authorize the procedure unless it additionally finds that the evidence meets a "clear and convincing" standard of proof. . . .

Although I think the provision is constitutionally infirm for all minors, I am particularly concerned about the effect it will have on sexually or physically abused minors. I agree that parental interest in the welfare of their children is "particularly strong where a *normal* family relationship exists." . . .

Sadly, not all children in our country are fortunate enough to be members of loving families. For too many young pregnant women, parental involvement in this most intimate decision threatens harm, rather than promises comfort. . . .

[III omitted]

IV

. . . The underlying nature of the Ohio statute is proclaimed by its strident and offensively restrictive provisions. It is as though the Legislature said: "If the courts of the United States insist on upholding a limited right to an abortion, let us make that abortion as difficult as possible to obtain" because, basically, whether on professed moral or religious grounds or whatever, "we believe that is the way it must be." This often may be the way legislation is enacted, but few are the instances where the injustice is so evident and the impediments so gross as those inflicted by the Ohio Legislature on these vulnerable and powerless young women.

□□□

Nos. 89-453 and 89-700

Metro Broadcasting, Inc., Petitioner v. Federal Communications Commission et al.
Astroline Communications Company Limited Partnership, Petitioner v. Shurberg Broadcasting of Hartford, Inc., et al.

On writs of certiorari to the United States Court of Appeals for the District of Columbia Circuit

[June 27, 1990]

JUSTICE BRENNAN delivered the opinion of the Court.

The issue in these cases, consolidated for decision today, is whether certain minority preference policies of the Federal Communications Commission violate the equal protection component of the Fifth Amendment. The policies in question are (1) a program awarding an enhancement for minority ownership in comparative proceedings for new licenses, and (2) the minority "distress sale" program, which permits a limited category of existing radio and television broadcast stations to be transferred only to minority-controlled firms. We hold that these policies do not violate equal protection principles.

I

A

The policies before us today can best be understood by reference to the history of federal efforts to promote minority participation in the broadcasting industry. In the Communications Act of 1934, as amended, Congress assigned to the Federal Communications Commission (FCC or Commission) exclusive authority to grant licenses, based on "public convenience, interest, or necessity," to persons wishing to construct and operate radio and television broadcast stations in the United States. Although for the past two decades minorities have constituted at least one-fifth of the United States population, during this time relatively few members of minority groups have held broadcast licenses. In 1971, minorities owned only 10 of the approximately 7,500 radio stations in the country and none of the more than 1,000 television stations; in 1978, minorities owned less than 1 percent of the Nation's radio and television stations; and in 1986, they owned just 2.1 percent of the more than 11,000 radio and television stations in the United States. Moreover, these statistics fail to reflect the fact that, as late entrants who often have been able to obtain only the less valuable stations, many minority broadcasters serve geographically limited markets with relatively small audiences.

The Commission has recognized that the viewing and listening public suffers when minorities are underrepresented among owners of television and radio stations ... [and] has therefore worked to encourage minority participation in the broadcast industry....

... [T]he FCC adopted in May 1978 its *Statement of Policy on Minority Ownership of Broadcasting Facilities.* After recounting its past efforts to expand broadcast diversity, the FCC concluded:

> "[W]e are compelled to observe that the views of racial minorities continue to be inadequately represented in the broadcast media. This situation is detrimental not only to the minority audience but to all of the viewing and listening public. Adequate representation of minority viewpoints in programming serves not only the needs and interests of the minority community but also enriches and educates the non-minority audience. It enhances the diversified programming which is a key objective not only of the Communications Act of 1934 but also of the First Amendment."

Describing its actions as only "first steps," the FCC outlined two elements of a minority ownership policy.

First, the Commission pledged to consider minority ownership as one factor in comparative proceedings for new licenses....

Second, the FCC outlined a plan to increase minority opportunities to receive reassigned and transferred licenses through the so-called "distress sale" policy. As a general rule, a licensee whose qualifications to hold a broadcast license come into question may not assign or transfer that license until the FCC has resolved its doubts in a noncomparative hearing. The distress sale policy is an exception to that practice, allowing a broadcaster whose license has been designated for a revocation hearing, or whose renewal application has been designated for hearing, to assign the license to an FCC-approved minority enterprise....

B

1

In No. 89-453, petitioner Metro Broadcasting, Inc. (Metro) challenges the Commission's policy awarding preferences to minority owners in comparative licensing proceedings. Several applicants, including Metro and Rainbow Broadcasting (Rainbow), were involved in a comparative proceeding to select among three mutually exclusive proposals to construct and operate a new UHF television station in the Orlando, Florida, metropolitan area. After an evidentiary hearing, an Administrative Law Judge (ALJ) granted Metro's application. The ALJ disqualified Rainbow from consideration because of "misrepresentations" in its application. On review of the ALJ's decision, however, the Commission's Review Board disagreed with the ALJ's finding regarding Rainbow's candor and concluded that Rainbow was qualified. The Board proceeded to consider Rainbow's comparative showing and found it superior to Metro's. In so doing, the Review Board awarded Rainbow a substantial enhancement on the ground that it was 90 percent Hispanic-owned, whereas Metro had only one minority partner who owned 19.8 percent of the enterprise. The Review Board found that Rainbow's minority credit outweighed Metro's local residence and civic participation advantage. The Commission denied review of the Board's decision largely without discussion, stating merely that it "agree[d] with the Board's resolution of this case."

Metro sought review of the Commission's order in the United States Court of Appeals for the District of Columbia Circuit, but the appeal's disposition was delayed; at the Commission's request, the court granted a remand of the record for further consideration in light of a separate ongoing inquiry at the Commission regarding the validity of its minority and female ownership policies, including the minority enhancement credit. The Commission determined that the outcome in the licensing proceeding between Rainbow and Metro might depend on whatever the Commission concluded in its general evaluation of minority ownership policies, and accordingly it held the licensing proceeding in abeyance. . . .

Prior to the Commission's completion of its . . . inquiry, however, Congress enacted and the President signed into law the FCC appropriations legislation for fiscal year 1988. The measure prohibited the Commission from spending any appropriated funds to examine or change its minority ownership policies. Complying with this directive, the Commission closed its . . . inquiry. The FCC also reaffirmed its grant of the license in this case to Rainbow Broadcasting.

The case returned to the Court of Appeals, and a divided panel affirmed the Commission's order awarding the license to Rainbow. The court concluded that its decision was controlled by prior circuit precedent and noted that the Commission's action was supported by " 'highly relevant congressional action that showed clear recognition of the extreme underrepresentation of minorities and their perspectives in the broadcast mass media.' " . . .

2

The dispute in No. 89-700 emerged from a series of attempts by Faith Center, Inc., the licensee of a Hartford, Connecticut, television station, to execute a minority distress sale. In December 1980, the FCC designated for a hearing Faith Center's application for renewal of its license. In February 1981, Faith Center filed with the FCC a petition for special relief seeking permission to transfer its license under the distress sale policy. The Commission granted the request, but the proposed sale was not completed, apparently due to the purchaser's inability to obtain adequate financing. In September 1983, the Commission granted a second request by Faith Center to pursue a distress sale to another minority-controlled buyer. The FCC rejected objections to the distress sale raised by Alan Shurberg, who at that time was acting in his individual capacity. This second distress sale also was not consummated, apparently because of similar financial difficulties on the buyer's part.

In December 1983, respondent Shurberg Broadcasting of Hartford, Inc. (Shurberg) applied to the Commission for a permit to build a television station in Hartford. The application was mutually exclusive with Faith Center's renewal application, then still pending. In June 1984, Faith Center again sought the FCC's approval for a distress sale, requesting permission to sell the station to Astroline Communications Company, Limited Partnership (Astroline), a minority applicant. Shurberg opposed the sale to Astroline on a number of grounds, including that the FCC's distress sale program violated Shurberg's right to equal protection.... In December 1984, the FCC approved Faith Center's petition for permission to assign its broadcast license to Astroline ... [and] rejected Shurberg's equal protection challenge to the policy as "without merit."

Shurberg appealed the Commission's order to the United States Court of Appeals for the District of Columbia Circuit, but disposition of the appeal was delayed pending completion of the Commission's ... inquiry into the minority ownership policies. After Congress enacted and the President signed into law the appropriations legislation ... the Commission reaffirmed its order granting Faith Center's request to assign its Hartford license to Astroline pursuant to the minority distress sale policy.

A divided Court of Appeals invalidated the Commission's minority distress sale policy. *Shurberg Broadcasting of Hartford, Inc. v. FCC* (1989). In a *per curiam* opinion, the panel majority held that the policy "unconstitutionally deprives Alan Shurberg and Shurberg Broadcasting of their equal protection rights under the Fifth Amendment because the program is not narrowly tailored to remedy past discrimination or to promote programming diversity" and that "the program unduly burdens

Shurberg, an innocent nonminority, and is not reasonably related to the interests it seeks to vindicate.". . .

II

It is of overriding significance in these cases that the FCC's minority ownership programs have been specifically approved—indeed, mandated—by Congress. In *Fullilove v. Klutznick* (1980), Chief Justice Burger, writing for himself and two other Justices, observed that although "[a] program that employs racial or ethnic criteria . . . calls for close examination," when a program employing a benign racial classification is adopted by an administrative agency at the explicit direction of Congress, we are "bound to approach our task with appropriate deference to the Congress. . . . We explained that deference was appropriate in light of Congress' institutional competence as the national legislature.

A majority of the Court in *Fullilove* did not apply strict scrutiny to the race-based classification at issue. Three Members inquired "whether the *objectives* of th[e] legislation are within the power of Congress" and "whether the limited use of racial and ethnic criteria . . . is a constitutionally permissible *means* for achieving the congressional objectives." Three other Members would have upheld benign racial classifications that "serve important governmental objectives and are substantially related to achievement of those objectives." We apply that standard today. We hold that benign race-conscious measures mandated by Congress—even if those measures are not "remedial" in the sense of being designed to compensate victims of past governmental or societal discrimination—are constitutionally permissible to the extent that they serve important governmental objectives within the power of Congress and are substantially related to achievement of those objectives. . . .

We hold that the FCC minority ownership policies pass muster under the test we announce today. First, we find that they serve the important governmental objective of broadcast diversity. Second, we conclude that they are substantially related to the achievement of that objective.

A

Congress found that the "effects of past inequities stemming from racial and ethnic discrimination have resulted in a severe underrepresentation of minorities in the media of mass communications." Congress and the Commission do not justify the minority ownership policies strictly as remedies for victims of this discrimination, however. Rather, Congress and the FCC have selected the minority ownership policies primarily to promote programming diversity, and they urge that such diversity is an important governmental objective that can serve as a constitutional basis for the preference policies. We agree.*

We have long recognized that "[b]ecause of the scarcity of [electromagnetic] frequencies, the Government is permitted to put restraints on licensees in favor of others whose views should be expressed on this unique medium." *Red Lion Broadcasting v. FCC* (1969). The Government's role in distributing the limited number of broadcast licenses . . . may be regulated in light of the rights of the viewing and listening audience and that "the widest possible dissemination of information from diverse and antagonistic sources is essential to the welfare of the public." *Associated Press v. United States* (1945). Safeguarding the public's right to receive a diversity of views and information over the airwaves is therefore an integral component of the FCC's mission. . . .

Against this background, we conclude that the interest in enhancing broadcast diversity is, at the very least, an important governmental objective and is therefore a sufficient basis for the Commission's minority ownership policies. . . .

B

We also find that the minority ownership policies are substantially related to the achievement of the Government's interest. One component of this inquiry concerns the relationship between expanded minority ownership and greater broadcast diversity; both the FCC and Congress have determined that such a relationship exists. . . .

C

The judgment that there is a link between expanded minority ownership and broadcast diversity does not rest on impermissible stereotyping. Congressional policy does not assume that in every case minority ownership and management will lead to more minority-oriented programming or to the expression of a discrete "minority viewpoint" on the airwaves. Neither does it pretend that all programming that appeals to minority audiences can be labeled "minority programming" or that programming that might be described as "minority" does not appeal to nonminorities. Rather, both Congress and the FCC maintain simply that expanded minority ownership of broadcast outlets will, in the aggregate, result in greater broadcast diversity. A broadcasting industry with representative minority participation will produce more variation and diversity than will one whose ownership is drawn from a single racially and ethnically homogeneous group. . . .

Our cases demonstrate that the reasoning employed by the Commission and Congress is permissible. We have recognized, for example, that the fair cross-section requirement of the Sixth Amendment forbids the exclusion of groups on the basis of such characteristics as race and gender from a jury venire because "[w]ithout that requirement, the State could draw up jury lists in such manner as to produce a pool of prospective jurors disproportionately ill disposed towards one or all classes of defendants, and thus more likely to yield petit juries with similar disposition." *Holland v. Illinois* (1990). It is a small step from this logic to the conclusion that including minorities in the electromagnetic spectrum will be more likely to produce a "fair cross section" of diverse content. In addition, many of our voting rights cases operate on the assumption that minorities have particular viewpoints and interests worthy of protection. . . .

D

. . . [T]he Commission established minority ownership preferences only after long experience demonstrated that race-neutral means could not produce adequate broadcasting diversity. The FCC did not act precipitately in devising the programs we uphold today; to the contrary, the Commission undertook thorough evaluations of its policies *three* times—in 1960, 1971, and 1978—before adopting the minority ownership programs. In endorsing the minority ownership preferences, Congress agreed with the Commission's assessment that race-neutral alternatives had failed to achieve the necessary programming diversity.

Moreover, the considered nature of the Commission's judgment in selecting the particular minority ownership policies at issue today is illustrated by the fact that the Commission has rejected other types of minority preferences. For example, the Commission has studied but refused to implement the more expansive alternative of setting aside certain frequencies for minority broadcasters. . . .

The minority ownership policies, furthermore, are aimed directly at the barriers that minorities face in entering the broadcasting industry. The Commission's Task Force identified as key factors hampering the growth of minority ownership a lack of adequate financing, paucity of information regarding license availability, and broadcast inexperience. The Commission assigned a preference to minority status in the comparative licensing proceeding, reasoning that such an enhancement might help to compensate for a dearth of broadcasting experience. Most license acquisitions, however, are by necessity purchases of existing stations, because only a limited number of new stations are available, and those are often in less desirable markets or on less profitable portions of spectrum, such as the UHF band. Congress and the FCC therefore found a need for the minority distress sale policy, which helps to overcome the problem of inadequate access to capital by lowering the sale price and the problem of lack of information by providing existing licensees with an incentive to seek out minority buyers. The Commission's choice of minority ownership policies thus addressed the very factors it had isolated as being responsible for minority underrepresentation in the broadcast industry....

... Furthermore, there is provision for administrative and judicial review of all Commission decisions, which guarantees both that the minority ownership policies are applied correctly in individual cases, and that there will be frequent opportunities to revisit the merits of those policies. Congress and the Commission have adopted a policy of minority ownership not as an end in itself, but rather as a means of achieving greater programming diversity. Such a goal carries its own natural limit, for there will be no need for further minority preferences once sufficient diversity has been achieved....

Finally, we do not believe that the minority ownership policies at issue impose impermissible burdens on nonminorities. Although the nonminority challengers in these cases concede that they have not suffered the loss of an already-awarded broadcast license, they claim that they have been handicapped in their ability to obtain one in the first instance. But just as we have determined that "[a]s part of this Nation's dedication to eradicating racial discrimination, innocent persons may be called upon to bear some of the burden of the remedy," *Wygant* [*v. Jackson Board of Education* (1986)], we similarly find that a congressionally mandated benign race-conscious program that is substantially related to the achievement of an important governmental interest is consistent with equal protection principles so long as it does not impose *undue* burdens on nonminorities....

III

The Commission's minority ownership policies bear the imprimatur of longstanding congressional support and direction and are substantially related to the achievement of the important governmental objective of broadcast diversity. The judgment in No. 89-453 is affirmed, the judgment in No. 89-700 is reversed, and the cases are remanded for proceedings consistent with this opinion.

It is so ordered.

JUSTICE STEVENS, concurring.

Today the Court squarely rejects the proposition that a governmental decision that rests on a racial classification is never permissible except as a remedy for a past wrong. I endorse this focus on the future benefit, rather than the remedial justification, of such decisions.

I remain convinced, of course, that racial or ethnic characteristics provide a relevant basis for disparate treatment only in extremely rare situations and that it is therefore "especially important that the reasons for any such classification be clearly identified and unquestionably legitimate." *Fullilove v. Klutznick* (1980) (dissenting opinion). The Court's opinion explains how both elements of that standard are satisfied. . . .

Therefore, I join both the opinion and the judgment of the Court.

JUSTICE O'CONNOR, with whom THE CHIEF JUSTICE, JUSTICE SCALIA, and JUSTICE KENNEDY join, dissenting.

At the heart of the Constitution's guarantee of equal protection lies the simple command that the Government must treat citizens "as *individuals,* not 'as simply components of a racial, religious, sexual or national class.'" *Arizona Governing Committee v. Norris* (1983). Social scientists may debate how peoples' thoughts and behavior reflect their background, but the Constitution provides that the Government may not allocate benefits and burdens among individuals based on the assumption that race or ethnicity determines how they act or think. To uphold the challenged programs, the Court departs from these fundamental principles and from our traditional requirement that racial classifications are permissible only if necessary and narrowly tailored to achieve a compelling interest. This departure marks a renewed toleration of racial classifications and a repudiation of our recent affirmation that the Constitution's equal protection guarantees extend equally to all citizens. The Court's application of a lessened equal protection standard to congressional actions finds no support in our cases or in the Constitution. I respectfully dissent.

I

As we recognized last Term, the Constitution requires that the Court apply a strict standard of scrutiny to evaluate racial classifications such as those contained in the challenged FCC distress sale and comparative licensing policies. "Strict scrutiny" requires that, to be upheld, racial classifications must be determined to be necessary and narrowly tailored to achieve a compelling state interest. The Court abandons this traditional safeguard against discrimination for a lower standard of review, and in practice applies a standard like that applicable to routine legislation. Yet the Government's different treatment of citizens according to race is no routine concern. . . .

In both the challenged policies, the FCC provides benefits to some members of our society and denies benefits to others based on race or ethnicity. Except in the narrowest of circumstances, the Constitution bars such racial classifications as a denial to particular individuals, of any race or ethnicity, of "the equal protection of the laws." . . . Racial classifications, whether providing benefits to or burdening particular racial or ethnic groups, may stigmatize those groups singled out for different treatment and may create considerable tension with the Nation's widely shared commitment to evaluating individuals upon their individual merit. . . .

The Constitution's guarantee of equal protection binds the Federal Government as it does the States, and no lower level of scrutiny applies to the Federal Government's use of race classifications. In *Bolling v. Sharpe* [1954], the companion case to *Brown v. Board of Education* (1954), the Court held that equal protection principles embedded in the Fifth Amendment's Due Process Clause prohibited the Federal Government from maintaining racially segregated schools in the District of Columbia: "[I]t would be unthinkable that the same Constitution would impose a lesser duty on the Federal Government." Consistent with this view, the Court has repeatedly indicated that "the reach of the equal protection guarantee of the Fifth Amendment is coextensive with that of the Fourteenth." *United States v. Paradise* (1987) (plurality opinion).

Nor does the congressional role in prolonging the FCC's policies justify any lower level of scrutiny. As with all instances of judicial review of federal legislation, the Court does not lightly set aside the considered judgment of a coordinate branch. Nonetheless, the respect due a coordinate branch yields neither less vigilance in defense of equal protection principles nor any corresponding diminution of the standard of review. . . .

The Court's reliance on "benign racial classifications" is particularly troubling. " 'Benign' racial classification" is a contradiction in terms. Governmental distinctions among citizens based on race or ethnicity, even in the rare circumstances permitted by our cases, exact costs and carry with them substantial dangers. To the person denied an opportunity or right based on race, the classification is hardly benign. The right to equal protection of the laws is a personal right, securing to *each* individual an immunity from treatment predicated simply on membership in a particular racial or ethnic group. The Court's emphasis on "benign racial classifications" suggests confidence in its ability to distinguish good from harmful governmental uses of racial criteria. History should teach greater humility. Untethered to narrowly confined remedial notions, "benign" carries with it no independent meaning, but reflects only acceptance of the current generation's conclusion that a politically acceptable burden, imposed on particular citizens on the basis of race, is reasonable. The Court provides no basis for determining when a racial classification fails to be "benevolent." By expressly distinguishing "benign" from remedial race-conscious measures, the Court leaves the distinct possibility that any racial measure found to be substantially related to an important governmental objective is also, by definition, "benign."....

II

Our history reveals that the most blatant forms of discrimination have been visited upon some members of the racial and ethnic groups identified in the challenged programs. Many have lacked the opportunity to share in the Nation's wealth and to participate in its commercial enterprises. It is undisputed that minority participation in the broadcasting industry falls markedly below the demographic representation of those groups ... and this shortfall may be traced in part to the discrimination and the patterns of exclusion that have widely affected our society. As a Nation we aspire to create a society untouched by that history of exclusion, and to ensure that equality defines all citizens' daily experience and opportunities as well as the protection afforded to them under law.

For these reasons, and despite the harms that may attend the Government's use of racial classifications, we have repeatedly recognized that the Government possesses a compelling interest in remedying the effects of identified race discrimination. We subject even racial classifications claimed to be remedial to strict scrutiny, however, to ensure that the Government in fact employs any race-conscious measures to further this remedial interest and employs them only when, and no more broadly than, the interest demands. The FCC or Congress may yet conclude after suitable examination that narrowly tailored race-conscious measures are required to remedy discrimination that may be identified in the allocation of broadcasting licenses. Such measures are clearly within the Government's power.

Yet it is equally clear that the policies challenged in these cases were not designed as remedial measures and are in no sense narrowly tailored to remedy identified discrimination. The FCC appropriately concedes that its policies embodied no remedial purpose and has disclaimed the possibility that discrimination infected the allocation of licenses. The congressional action at most simply endorsed a policy designed to further the interest in achieving diverse programming. ... The Court refers to the bare suggestion, contained in a report addressing different legislation passed in 1982, that "past inequities" have led to "underrepresentation of minorities in the media of mass communications, as it has adversely affected their participation in other sectors of the economy as well." This statement ... identifies no discrimination in the broadcasting industry. ... I agree that the racial classifications cannot be upheld as remedial measures.

III

Under the appropriate standard, strict scrutiny, only a compelling interest may support the Government's use of racial classifications. Modern equal protection doctrine has recognized only one such interest: remedying the effects of racial discrimination. The interest in increasing the diversity of broadcast viewpoints is clearly not a compelling interest. It is simply too amorphous, too insubstantial, and too unrelated to any legitimate basis for employing racial classifications....

... The Court has recognized an interest in obtaining diverse broadcasting viewpoints as a legitimate basis for the FCC, acting pursuant to its "public interest" statutory mandate, to adopt limited measures to increase the number of competing licensees and to encourage licensees to present varied views on issues of public concern. We have also concluded that these measures do not run afoul of the First Amendment's usual prohibition of Government regulation of the marketplace of ideas, in part because First Amendment concerns support limited but inevitable Government regulation of the peculiarly constrained broadcasting spectrum. But the conclusion that measures adopted to further the interest in diversity of broadcasting viewpoints are neither beyond the FCC's statutory authority nor contrary to the First Amendment hardly establishes the interest as important for equal protection purposes.

The FCC's extension of the asserted interest in diversity of views in this case presents, at the very least, an unsettled First Amendment issue. The FCC has concluded that the American broadcasting public receives the incorrect mix of ideas and claims to have adopted the challenged policies to supplement programming content with a particular set of views. Although we have approved limited measures designed to increase information and views generally, the Court has never upheld a broadcasting measure designed to amplify a distinct set of views or the views of a particular class of speakers. Indeed, the Court has suggested that the First Amendment prohibits allocating licenses to further such ends.... Even if an interest is determined to be legitimate in one context, it does not suddenly become important enough to justify distinctions based on race.

IV

Our traditional equal protection doctrine requires, in addition to a compelling state interest, that the Government's chosen means be necessary to accomplish and narrowly tailored to further the asserted interest.... The Court instead finds the racial classifications to be "substantially related" to achieving the Government's interest, a far less rigorous fit requirement. The FCC's policies fail even this requirement.

1

... The FCC assumes a particularly strong correlation of race and behavior. The FCC justifies its conclusion that insufficiently diverse viewpoints are broadcast by reference to the percentage of minority owned stations. This assumption is correct only to the extent that minority owned stations provide the desired additional views, and that stations owned by individuals not favored by the preferences cannot, or at least do not, broadcast underrepresented programming. Additionally, the FCC's focus on ownership to improve programming assumes that preferences linked to race are so strong that they will dictate the owner's behavior in operating the station, overcoming the owner's personal inclinations and regard for the market. This strong link between race and behavior, especially when mediated by market forces, is the assumption that Justice Powell rejected in his discussion of health care service in *Bakke.* In that case, the state medical school argued that it could prefer members of minority groups because they were more likely to serve communities particularly needing medical care. Justice Powell rejected this rationale, concluding that the assumption was unsupported and that such individual choices could not be presumed from ethnicity or race.

The majority addresses this point by arguing that the equation of race with distinct views and behavior is not "impermissible" in this particular case. Apart from placing undue faith in the Government and courts' ability to distinguish "good" from "bad" stereotypes, this reasoning repudiates essential equal protection principles that prohibit racial generalizations. The Court embraces the FCC's reasoning that an applicant's race will likely indicate that the applicant possesses a distinct perspective, but notes that the correlation of race to behavior is "not a rigid assumption about how minority owners will behave in every case." The corollary to this notion is plain: individuals of unfavored racial and ethnic backgrounds are unlikely to possess the unique experiences and background that contribute to viewpoint diversity. Both the reasoning and its corollary reveal but disregard what is objectionable about a stereotype: the racial generalization inevitably does not apply to certain individuals, and those persons may legitimately claim that they have been judged according to their race rather than upon a relevant criterion....

2

... Moreover, the FCC's programs cannot survive even intermediate scrutiny because race-neutral and untried means of directly accomplishing the governmental interest are readily available. The FCC could directly advance its interest by requiring licensees to provide programming that the FCC believes would add to diversity. The interest the FCC asserts is in programming diversity, yet in adopting the challenged policies, the FCC expressly disclaimed having attempted *any* direct efforts to achieve its asserted goal. The Court suggests that administrative convenience excuses this failure, yet intermediate scrutiny bars the Government from relying upon that excuse to avoid measures that directly further the asserted interest. The FCC and the Court suggest that First Amendment interests in some manner should exempt the FCC from employing this direct, race-neutral means to achieve its asserted interest. They essentially argue that we may bend our equal protection principles to avoid more readily apparent harm to our First Amendment values. But the FCC cannot have it both ways: either the First Amendment bars the FCC from seeking to accomplish indirectly what it may not accomplish directly; or the FCC may pursue the goal, but must do so in a manner that comports with equal protection principles. And if the FCC can direct programming in any fashion, it must employ that direct means before resorting to indirect race-conscious means. . . .

[3 omitted]

4

Finally, the Government cannot employ race classifications that unduly burden individuals who are not members of the favored racial and ethnic groups. The challenged policies fail this independent requirement, as well as the other constitutional requirements. The comparative licensing and distress sale programs provide the eventual licensee with an exceptionally valuable property and with a rare and unique opportunity to serve the local community. The distress sale imposes a particularly significant burden. The FCC has at base created a specialized market reserved exclusively for minority controlled applicants. There is no more rigid quota than a 100 % set-aside. This fact is not altered by the observation that the FCC and seller have some discretion over whether stations may be sold through the distress program. For the would-be purchaser or person who seeks to compete for the station, that opportunity depends entirely upon race or ethnicity. The Court's argument that the distress sale allocates only a small percentage of all license sales also misses the mark. This argument readily supports complete preferences and avoids scrutiny of particular programs: it is no response to a person denied admission at one school, or discharged from one job, solely on the basis of race, that other schools or employers do not discriminate. . . .

In sum, the Government has not met its burden even under the Court's test that approves of racial classifications that are substantially related to an important governmental objective. Of course, the programs even more clearly fail the strict scrutiny that should be applied. The Court has determined, in essence, that Congress and all federal agencies are exempted, to some ill-defined but significant degree, from the Constitution's equal protection requirements. This break with our precedents, greatly undermines equal protection guarantees, and permits distinctions among citizens based on race and ethnicity which the Constitution clearly forbids. I respectfully dissent.

JUSTICE KENNEDY, with whom JUSTICE SCALIA joins, dissenting.

Almost 100 years ago in *Plessy v. Ferguson* (1896), this Court upheld a government-sponsored race-conscious measure, a Louisiana law that required "equal but separate accommodations" for "white" and "colored" railroad passengers. The Court asked whether the measures were "reasonable," and it stated that "[i]n determining the question of reasonableness, [the legislature] is at liberty to act with reference to the established usages, customs and traditions of the people, and with a view to the promotion of their comfort." The *Plessy* Court concluded that the "race-conscious measures" it reviewed were reasonable because they served the governmental interest of increasing the riding pleasure of railroad passengers. The fundamental errors in *Plessy,* its standard of review and its validation of rank racial insult by the State, distorted the law for six decades before the Court announced its apparent demise in *Brown v. Board of Education* (1954). *Plessy*'s standard of review and its explication have disturbing parallels to today's majority opinion that should warn us something is amiss here. . . .

Once the Government takes the step, which itself should be forbidden, of enacting into law the stereotypical assumption that the race of owners is linked to broadcast content, it follows a path that becomes even more tortuous. It must decide which races to favor. While the Court repeatedly refers to the preferences as favoring "minorities," and purports to evaluate the burdens imposed on "nonminorities," it must be emphasized that the discriminatory policies upheld today operate to exclude the many racial and ethnic *minorities* that have not made the Commission's list. The enumeration of the races to be protected is borrowed from a remedial statute, but since the remedial rationale must be disavowed in order to sustain the policy, the race classifications bear scant relation to the asserted governmental interest. The Court's reasoning provides little justification for welcoming the return of racial classifications to our Nation's laws.

I cannot agree with the Court that the Constitution permits the Government to discriminate among its citizens on the basis of race in order to serve interests so trivial as "broadcast diversity.". . . .

. . . Perhaps the Court can succeed in its assumed role of case-by-case arbiter of when it is desirable and benign for the Government to disfavor some citizens and favor others based on the color of their skin. Perhaps the tolerance and decency to which our people aspire will let the disfavored rise above hostility and the favored escape condescension. But history suggests much peril in this enterprise, and so the Constitution forbids us to undertake it. I regret that after a century of judicial opinions, we interpret the Constitution to do no more than move us from "separate but equal" to "unequal but benign."

□□□

6 | *How the Court Works*

The Constitution makes the Supreme Court the final arbiter in "cases" and "controversies" arising under the Constitution or the laws of the United States. As the interpreter of the law, the Court often is viewed as the least mutable and most tradition-bound of the three branches of the federal government.

But the Court has undergone innumerable changes in its history, some of which have been mandated by law. Almost all of the changes, however, were made because the justices thought they would provide a more efficient or a more equitable way of dealing with the Court's responsibilities. Some of the changes are embodied in Court rules; others are informal adaptations to needs and circumstances.

The Schedule of the Term

The Court's annual schedule reflects both continuity and change. During its formal annual sessions, certain times are set aside for oral argument, for conferences, for the writing of opinions, and for the announcement of decisions. Given the number of cases they face each year, the justices are confronted with a tremendous—some say excessive—amount of work during the regular term, which now lasts nine months.

Their work does not end when the session is finished, however. During the summer recess, the justices receive new cases to consider. About a fourth of the applications for review filed during the term are read by the justices and their law clerks during the summer interim.

Annual Terms

By law, the Supreme Court begins its regular annual term on the first Monday in October and may hold a special term whenever necessary. The regular session, known as the October term, lasts nine months. The summer recess, which is not determined by statute or Court rules, generally begins in late June or early July of the following year, when the Court has taken action on the last case argued before it during the term.

In the past the Court actually adjourned its session when the summer recess began. The chief justice would announce in open court, "All cases submitted and all business before the Court at this term in readiness for disposition having been disposed of, it is ordered by this Court that all cases on the docket be, and they are hereby, continued to the next term." Since 1979, however, the Court has been in continuous session throughout the year, marked by periodic recesses. This system makes it unnecessary to convene a special term to deal with matters arising in the summer.

Opening Day

Opening day ceremonies of the new term have changed considerably since the Court first met on February 1, 1790. Chief Justice John Jay was forced to postpone the first formal session for a day because some of the justices were unable to reach New York City—at that time the nation's capital and home of the Court. It began proceedings the next day in a crowded courtroom and with an empty docket.

Beginning in 1917 and until 1975, the opening day and week were spent in conference. The justices discussed cases that had not been disposed of during the previous term and some of the petitions that had reached the Court during the summer recess. The decisions arrived at during this initial conference on which cases to accept for oral argument were announced on the second Monday of October.

At the beginning of the October 1975 term, this practice was changed. That year the justices reassembled for this initial conference during the last week in September. When the justices convened formally on the first Monday in October, oral arguments began.

Arguments and Conferences

At least four justices must request that a case be argued before it can be accepted. Arguments are heard on Monday, Tuesday, and Wednesday for seven two-week sessions, beginning in the first week in October and ending in the last week of April or the first week of May. There are usually two consecutive weeks of oral arguments during this period, with two-week or longer recesses during which the justices consider the cases and deal with other Court business.

The schedule for oral arguments—10:00 a.m. to noon and 1 p.m. to 3 p.m.—began during the 1969 term. Since most cases receive one hour apiece for argument, the Court can hear twelve cases a week.

The Court holds conferences each Friday during the weeks when arguments are heard, and on the Friday just before the two-week oral argument periods. To reduce the workload of its Friday sessions, the Court also holds Wednesday conferences during the weeks when oral arguments are scheduled.

The conferences are designed for consideration of cases heard in oral argument during the preceding week, and to resolve other business. Prior to each of the Friday conferences, the chief justice circulates a "discuss"

Visiting the Supreme Court

The Supreme Court Building comprises six levels, only two of which are accessible to the public. The basement contains a parking garage, a printing press, and offices for security guards and maintenance personnel. A public information office is on the ground floor, while the courtroom itself is on the main floor. The second floor contains the justices' offices, dining rooms and library as well as various other offices; the third floor, the Court library; and the fourth floor, the gym and storage areas.

From October to the end of April, the Court hears oral arguments Monday through Wednesday for about two weeks a month. These sessions begin at 10 a.m. and continue until 3 p.m., with a one-hour recess starting at noon. They are open to the public on a first-come, first-served basis.

Visitors may inspect the Supreme Court chamber at any time the Court is not in session. Historical exhibits and a free motion picture on how the court works also are available throughout the year. The Supreme court building is open from 9 a.m. to 4:30 p.m. Monday through Friday, except for legal holidays. When the Court is not in session, lectures are given in the courtroom every hour on the half hour between 9:30 a.m. and 3:30 p.m.

list—a list of cases deemed important enough for discussion and a vote. Appeals (of which there are now only a small number) are placed on the discuss list almost automatically, but as many as three-quarters of the petitions for certiorari are summarily denied a place on the list and simply disappear. No case is denied review during conference, however, without an initial examination by the justices and their law clerks. Any one of the justices can have a case placed on the Court's conference agenda for review. Most of the cases scheduled for the discuss list also are denied review in the end, but only after discussion by the justices during the conference.

Although the last oral arguments have been heard by late April or early May of each year, the Friday and Monday conferences of the justices continue until the end of the term to consider cases remaining on the Court's agenda.

All conferences are held in strict secrecy, with no legal assistants or other staff present. The attendance of six justices constitutes a quorum. Conferences begin with handshakes all around. In discussing a case, the chief justice speaks first, followed by each justice in order of seniority.

Decision Days

In the Court's early years, conferences were held whenever the justices decided one was necessary—sometimes in the evening or on weekends. Similarly, decisions were announced whenever they were ready. There was no formal or informal schedule for conferences or for the announcement of decisions.

The tradition of announcing decisions on Monday—"Decision Monday"—began in 1857, apparently without any formal announcement or rule to that effect. This practice continued until the Court said on April 5, 1965, that "commencing the week of April 26, 1965, it will no longer adhere to the practice of reporting its decisions only at Monday sessions and that in the future they will be reported as they become ready for decision at any session of the Court." At present, opinions are released on Tuesdays and Wednesdays only during the weeks that the Court is hearing oral arguments; during other weeks, they are released on Mondays along with the orders.

In addition to opinions, the Court also releases an "orders" list—the summary of the Court's action granting or denying review. The orders list is posted at the beginning of the Monday session. It is not orally announced, but can be obtained from the clerk and the public information officer.

When urgent or important matters arise, the Court's summary orders may be announced on a day other than Monday. And when the last oral arguments of the term have been presented, the Court may release decisions and written opinions, as well as the orders list, on Mondays.

Unlike its orders, decisions of the Court are announced orally in open Court. The justice who wrote the opinion announces the Court's decision, and justices writing concurring or dissenting opinions may state their views as well. When more than one decision is to be rendered, the justices who wrote the opinion make their announcements in reverse order of seniority. Rarely, all or a large portion of the opinion is read aloud. More often, the author will summarize the opinion or simply announce the result and state that a written opinion has been filed.

Reviewing Cases

In determining whether to accept a case for review, the Court has considerable discretion, subject only to the restraints imposed by the Constitution and Congress. Article III, Section 2, of the Constitution provides that "In all Cases affecting Ambassadors, other public Ministers and Consuls, and those in which a State shall be Party, the Supreme Court shall have original jurisdiction. In all the other Cases ... the

Supreme Court shall have appellate Jurisdiction, both as to Law and Fact, with such Exceptions, and under such Regulations as the Congress shall make."

Original jurisdiction refers to the right of the Supreme Court to hear a case before any other court does. Appellate jurisdiction is the right to review the decision of a lower court. The vast majority of cases reaching the Supreme Court are appeals from rulings of the lower courts; generally only a handful of original jurisdiction cases are filed each term.

After enactment of the Judiciary Act of 1925, the Supreme Court had broad discretion to decide for itself what cases it would hear. Since Congress in 1988 virtually eliminated the Court's mandatory jurisdiction through which it was obliged to hear most appeals, that discretion has been virtually unlimited.

Methods of Appeal

Cases come to the Supreme Court in several ways. They may come through petitions for writs of certiorari, appeals, and requests for certification.

In petitioning for a writ of certiorari, a litigant who has lost a case in a lower court sets out the reasons why the Supreme Court should review the case. If it is granted, the Court requests a certified record of the case from the lower court.

Supreme Court rules state:

> Whenever a petition for writ of certiorari to review a decision of any court is granted, the clerk shall enter an order to that effect and shall forthwith notify the court below and counsel of record. The case will then be scheduled for briefing and oral argument. If the record has not previously been filed, the Clerk of this Court shall request the clerk of the court possessed of the record to certify it and transmit it to this Court. A formal writ shall not issue unless specially directed.

The main difference between the certiorari and appeal routes is that the Court has complete discretion to grant a request for a writ of certiorari, but is under more obligation to accept and decide a case that comes to it on appeal.

Most cases reach the Supreme Court by means of the writ of certiorari. In the relatively few cases to reach the Court by means of appeal, the appellant must file a jurisdictional statement explaining why the case qualifies for review and why the Court should grant it a hearing. Often the justices dispose of these cases by deciding them summarily, without oral argument or formal opinion.

Those whose petitions for certiorari have been granted must pay the Court's standard $300 fee for docketing the case. The U.S. government does not have to pay these fees, nor do persons too poor to afford them.

The latter may file *in forma pauperis* (in the character or manner of a pauper) petitions. Another, seldom used, method of appeal is certification, the request by a lower court—usually a court of appeals—for a final answer to questions of law in a particular case. The Supreme Court, after examining the certificate, may order the case argued before it.

Process of Review

Each year the Court is asked to review some 5,000 cases. All petitions are examined by the staff of the clerk of the Court; those found to be in reasonably proper form are placed on the docket and given a number. All cases, except those falling within the Court's original jurisdiction, are placed on single docket, known simply as "the docket." Only in the numbering of the cases is a distinction made between prepaid and *in forma pauperis* cases on the docket. Beginning with the 1971 term, prepaid cases were labeled with the year and the number. The first case filed in 1990, for example, would be designated 90-1. *In forma pauperis* cases contain the year and begin with the number 5001. The second *in forma pauperis* case filed in 1990 would thus be number 90-5002.

Each justice, aided by law clerks, is responsible for reviewing all cases on the dockets. In recent years a number of justices have used a "cert pool" system in this review. Their clerks work together to examine cases, writing a pool memo on several petitions. The memo is then given to the justices who determine if more research is needed. (Other justices prefer to use a system in which they or their clerks review each petition themselves.)

Justice William O. Douglas (1939-1975) called the review of cases on the dockets "in many respects the most important and interesting of all our functions." Others, apparently, have found it time-consuming and tedious and support the cert pool as a mechanism to reduce the burden on the justices and their staffs.

Petitions on the docket vary from elegantly printed and bound documents, of which multiple copies are submitted to the Court, to single sheets of prison stationery scribbled in pencil. All are considered by the justices, however, in the process of deciding which merit review. The decisions to grant or deny review of cases are made in conferences, which are held in the conference room adjacent to the chief justice's chambers. Justices are summoned to the conference room by a buzzer, usually between 9:30 and 10:00 a.m. They shake hands with each other, take their appointed seats, and the chief justice begins the discussion.

Discuss and Orders Lists

A few days before the conference convenes, the chief justice compiles the discuss list of cases deemed important enough for discussion and a vote. As many as three-quarters of the petitions for certiorari are denied a place on the list and thus rejected without further consideration. Any justice can have a case placed on the discuss list simply by requesting that it be placed there.

Conferences are held in strict secrecy; only the justices attend, and no legal assistants or staff are present. The junior associate justice acts as doorkeeper and messenger, sending for reference material and receiving messages and data at the door. Unlike other parts of the federal government, there have been very few leaks about what transpires during the conferences.

At the start of the conference, the chief justice makes a brief statement outlining the facts of each case. Then each justice, beginning with the senior associate justice, comments on the case, usually indicating in the course of the comments how he or she intends to vote. A traditional but unwritten rule specifies that it takes four affirmative votes to have a case scheduled for oral argument.

Petitions for certiorari, appeal, and *in forma pauperis* that are approved for review or denied review during conference are placed on a certified orders list to be released the following Monday in open court, announcing which cases will be set for later argument and which have been denied a hearing.

Arguments

Once the Court announces it will hear a case, the clerk of the Court arranges the schedule for oral argument. Cases are argued roughly in the order in which they were granted review, subject to modification if more time is needed to get in all the necessary documents. Cases generally are heard not sooner than three months after the Court has agreed to review them. Under special circumstances, the date scheduled for oral argument can be advanced or postponed.

Well before oral argument takes place, the justices receive the briefs and records from counsel in the case. The measure of attention the brief receives—from a thorough and exhaustive study to a cursory glance—depends both on the nature of the case and the work habits of the justice.

As one of the two public functions of the Court, oral arguments are viewed by some as very important. Others dispute their significance, contending that by the time a case is heard most of the justices have already made up their minds. Justice William J. Brennan, Jr., (1956-1990) said, "Oral argument is the absolute indispensable ingredient of appellate advocacy. . . . Often my whole notion of what a case is about crystallizes at oral argument. This happens even though I read the briefs before oral argument."

Time Limits

The time allowed each side for oral argument is thirty minutes. Since the time allotted must accommodate any questions the justices may wish to ask, the actual time for presentation may be considerably shorter than thirty minutes. Under the current rules of the Court, effective January 1, 1990, one counsel only will be heard for each side, except by special permission.

An exception is made for an amicus curiae—a person who volunteers or is invited to take part in matters before a court but is not a party in the case. Counsel for an amicus curiae may participate in oral argument if the party supported by the amicus allows him or her to use part of its argument time or the Court grants a motion allowing argument by counsel for the "friend of the court." The motion must show, the rules state, that the amicus's argument "is thought to provide assistance to the Court not otherwise available."

Because the Court is reluctant to extend the time that each side is given for oral argument and because amicus curiae participation in oral argument would often necessitate such an extension, the Court is generally unreceptive to such motions. And counsel in a case is usually equally unreceptive to a request to give an amicus counsel any of the precious minutes allotted to argue the case.

Court rules provide advice to counsel presenting oral arguments before the Court: "Oral argument should emphasize and clarify the written arguments appearing in the briefs on the merits." That same rule warns—with italicized emphasis—that the Court "looks with disfavor on oral argument read from a prepared text." Most attorneys appearing before the Court use an outline or notes to make sure they cover the important points.

Circulating the Argument

The Supreme Court has tape-recorded oral arguments since 1955. In 1968 the Court, in addition to its own recording, began contracting with private firms to tape and transcribe all oral arguments. The contract stipulates that the transcript "shall include everything spoken in argument, by Court, counsel, or others, and nothing shall be omitted from the transcript unless the Chief Justice or Presiding Justice so directs." But "the names of Justices asking questions shall not be recorded or transcribed; questions shall be indicated by the letter 'Q.' "

The marshal of the Court keeps the Court's tape during the term when oral arguments are presented. During that time use of these tapes usually is limited to the justices and their law clerks. At the end of the term, the tapes are sent to the National Archives. Persons wishing to listen to the tape or buy a copy of the transcript can apply to the Archives for permission to do so.

Transcripts made by the private firm can be acquired more quickly. These transcripts usually are available a week after arguments are heard. Those who purchase the transcripts from the firm must agree that they will not be photographically reproduced. Transcripts usually run from forty to fifty pages for one hour of oral argument.

Proposals have been made to tape arguments for television and radio use. To date, the Court has shown little enthusiasm for these proposals.

Use of Briefs

Supreme Court Rule 28 states, "Counsel should assume that all Justices of the Court have read the briefs in advance of oral argument." Nonetheless, justices vary considerably in the attention they personally give to an attorney's briefs. If the brief has been thoroughly digested by the justices, the attorney can use his or her arguments to highlight certain elements. But if it has merely been scanned—and perhaps largely forgotten—in the interval between the reading and the oral argument, the attorney will want to go into considerable detail about the nature of the case and the facts involved. Most lawyers therefore prepare their argument on the assumption that the justices know relatively little about their particular case but are well-acquainted with the general principles of relevant law.

The brief of the petitioner or appellant must be filed within forty-five days of the Court's announced decision to hear the case. Except for *in forma pauperis* cases, forty copies of the brief must be filed with the Court. For *in forma pauperis* proceedings, the Court requires only that documents be legible. The opposing brief from the respondent or appellee is to be filed within thirty days of receipt of the brief of the petitioner or appellant. Either party may appeal to the clerk for an extension of time in filing the brief.

Court Rules 24 sets forth the elements that a brief should contain. These are: the questions presented for review; a list of all parties to the proceeding; a table of contents and table of authorities; citations of the opinions and judgments delivered in the courts below; "a concise statement of the grounds on which the jurisdiction of this Court is invoked"; constitutional provisions, treaties, statutes, ordinances, and regulations involved; "a concise statement of the case containing all that is material to the consideration of the questions presented"; a summary of argument; the argument, which exhibits "clearly the points of fact and of law being presented and citing the authorities and statutes relied upon"; and a conclusion "specifying with particularity the relief which the party seeks."

The form and organization of the brief are covered by rules 33 and

34 of the Court. The rules limit the number of pages in various types of briefs. The rules also set out a color code for the covers of different kinds of briefs. Petitions are white; motions opposing them are orange. Petitioner's briefs on the merits are light blue, while those of respondents are to be light red. Reply briefs are yellow; amicus curiae, green; and documents filed by the United States, gray.

Questioning

During oral argument the justices may interrupt with questions or remarks as often as they wish. On the average, questions are likely to consume about a third of counsel's allotted half-hour of argument. Unless counsel has been granted special permission extending the thirty-minute limit, he or she can continue talking after the time has expired only to complete a sentence.

The frequency of questioning, as well as the manner in which questions are asked, depends on the style of the justices and their interest in a particular case. Chief Justice Warren E. Burger (1969-1986) asked very few questions. Justice Antonin Scalia has from his first day on the bench peppered attorneys with questions, sparking more active interrogation from a number of his colleagues.

Questions from the justices may upset and unnerve counsel by interrupting a well-rehearsed argument and introducing an unexpected element. Nevertheless, questioning has several advantages. It serves to alert counsel about what aspects of the case need further elaboration or more information. For the Court, questions can bring out weak points in an argument—and sometimes strengthen it.

Conferences

Cases for which oral arguments have been heard are then discussed in conference. During the Wednesday afternoon conference, the four cases that were argued the previous Monday are discussed and decided. At the all-day Friday conference, the eight cases argued on the preceding Tuesday and Wednesday are discussed and decided. These conferences also consider new motions, appeals, and petitions.

Conferences are conducted in complete secrecy. No secretaries, clerks, stenographers, or messengers are allowed into the room. This practice began many years ago when the justices became convinced that there was a leak, a premature report of a decision.

The justices meet in an oak-paneled, book-lined conference room adjacent to the chief justice's suite. Nine chairs surround the large rectangular table, each chair bearing the nameplate of the justice who sits there. The chief justice sits at the east end of the table, and the senior associate justice at the west end. The other justices take their places in order of seniority. The junior justice is charged with sending for and receiving documents or other information the Court needs.

On entering the conference room the justices shake hands with each other, a symbol of harmony that began in the 1880s. The chief justice begins the conference by calling the first case to be decided and discussing it. When the chief justice is finished, the senior associate justice speaks, followed by the other justices in order of seniority.

The justices can speak for as long as they wish, but they practice restraint because of the amount of business to be discussed. By custom each justice speaks without interruption. Other than these procedural arrangements, little is known about what actually transpires in conference. Although discussions generally are said to be polite and orderly, occasionally they can be acrimonious. Likewise, consideration of the issues in a particular case may be full and probing, or perfunctory, leaving the real debate on the question to go on in the written drafts of opinions circulating up and down the Court's corridors between chambers.

Generally, it is clear—and often explicit—in the discussion of the case how a justice plans to vote on it. It takes a majority vote to decide a case—five votes if all nine justices are participating.

Opinions

After the justices have voted on a case, the writing of the opinion or opinions begins. An opinion is a reasoned argument explaining the legal issues in the case and the precedents on which the opinion is based. Soon after a case is decided in conference, the task of writing the majority opinion is assigned. When in the majority, the chief justice designates the writer. In cases in which the chief justice was in the minority, the senior associate justice voting with the majority assigns the job of writing the majority opinion.

Any justice may decide to write a separate opinion. If in agreement with the Court's decision but not with some of the reasoning in the majority opinion, the justice may write a concurring opinion giving his or her reasoning. If in disagreement with the majority, the justice may write a dissenting opinion or simply go on record as a dissenter without an opinion. More than one justice can sign a concurring or a dissenting opinion.

Writing opinions is a highly important process. The way a majority opinion is written can have an influence beyond the actual decision. How it is written and the extent of support of or dissent from the opinion by the other justices all have impact.

The amount of time consumed between the vote on a case and the announcement of the decision varies from case to case. In simple cases where few points of law are at issue, the opinion sometimes can be written and cleared by the other justices in a week or less. In more complex cases, especially those with several dissenting or concurring opinions, the process can take six months or more. Some cases may have to be reargued or the initial decision reversed after the drafts of opinions have been circulated.

The assigning justice may consider the points made by majority justices during the conference discussion, the workload of the other justices, the need to avoid the more extreme opinions within the majority, and expertise in the particular area of law involved in a case. For example, most of the Court's major rulings on abortion have been explained through majority opinions written by Justice Harry A. Blackmun, who developed his expertise in medical law during his legal career, which included work with the famous Mayo Clinic in Minnesota, his home state.

The style of writing a Court opinion—a majority opinion or a concurring or dissenting opinion—depends primarily on the individual justice. In some cases, the justice may prefer to write a restricted and limited opinion; in others, a broader approach to the subject. The decision is likely to be influenced by the need to satisfy the other justices in the majority.

The time spent to prepare an opinion varies from justice to justice. Justices use their law clerks to obtain and sift through the material needed to write an opinion. There has been speculation that some clerks actually ghostwrite a justice's opinion—or at least that justices sometimes tell a clerk what they want in an opinion and allow the clerk to write the first draft. The traditional secrecy that surrounds each justice's office and work habits makes verification of such reports about the clerks' role in opinion writing very difficult.

When a justice is satisfied that the written opinion is conclusive or "unanswerable," it goes into print. In the past this process occurred at a print shop in the Court's basement, where the draft was printed under rigid security, with each copy numbered to prevent the removal of copies from the premises. In the 1980s, however, high technology arrived at the Court; draft opinions are circulated, revised, and printed on a computerized typesetting system.

The circulation of the drafts—whether computer-to-computer or on paper—provokes further discussion in many cases. Often the suggestions and criticisms require the writer to juggle opposing views. To retain a majority, the author of the draft opinion frequently feels obliged to make major emendations to oblige justices who are unhappy with the initial draft. Some opinions have to be rewritten several times before the majority is satisfied.

One reason for the secrecy surrounding the circulation of drafts is that some of the justices who voted with the majority may find the majority draft opinion so unpersuasive—or one or more of the dissenting drafts so convincing—that they may change their vote. If enough justices alter their votes, the majority may shift, so that a former dissent becomes instead the majority opinion. When a new majority emerges from this process, the task of writing, printing and circulating a new majority draft begins all over again.

Over the past few decades there has been considerable concern about the lack of unanimity in Court decisions and the frequent use of dissenting and concurring opinions. The chief argument in favor of greater unanimity is that it increases the authority of—and hence the respect for—the Court's decisions. A dissenting justice may hope that the dissent will convince a majority of the other justices that this opinion is the correct one or that a later Court will adopt the view.

Moreover, the dissenter generally has only himself or herself to please, a fact that makes many well-reasoned and well-written dissents more memorable or more enjoyable to read than the majority opinion. A concurring opinion indicates that the justice who wrote it agrees in general with the majority opinion but has reservations about the way it was written, the reasoning behind it, or specific points in it.

When the drafts of an opinion—including dissents and concurring views—have been written, circulated, discussed, and revised, if necessary, the final versions are printed. Before the opinion is produced the reporter of decisions adds a "headnote" or syllabus summarizing the decision and a "lineup" at the end showing how the justices voted.

One hundred seventy-five copies of the "bench opinion" are made. As the decision is announced in Court, the "bench opinion" is distributed to journalists and others in the public information office. Another copy, with any necessary corrections on it, is sent to the U.S. Government Printing Office, which prints 4,444 "slip" opinions, which are distributed to federal and state courts and agencies. The Court receives 400 of these, and they are available to the public free through the Public Information Office as long as supplies last. The Government Printing Office also prints the opinion for inclusion in *United States Reports,* the official record of Supreme Court opinions.

The public announcement of opinions in Court is probably the Court's most dramatic function. It also may be the most expendable. Depending on who delivers the opinion and how, announcements can take a considerable amount of the Court's time. Opinions are simultaneously given to the public information officer for distribution. Nevertheless, those who are in the courtroom to hear the announcement of a ruling are participating in a very old tradition. The actual delivery may be tedious or exciting, depending on the nature of the case and the eloquence of the opinion and the style of its oral delivery.

In this century, the Court has reduced the amount of time spent in delivering opinions. Before 1930 the Court generally read long opinions word for word; some opinions took days to announce. As the workload increased, this practice came to be regarded as a waste of the Court's time. The justice who has written the majority opinion now generally delivers only a summary, and dissenting justices often do the same with their opinions.

Appendix

Brief Biographies

William Hubbs Rehnquist

President Ronald Reagan's appointment of William H. Rehnquist as chief justice of the United States in 1986 clearly indicated that the president was hoping to shift the Court to the right. Since his early years as an associate justice in the 1970s, Rehnquist has been one of the Court's most conservative justices. An ardent advocate of judicial restraint, he thinks that the Court should simply call a halt to unconstitutional policies—and stop at that. Innovation in public policy, he believes, is the prerogative of elective officials, not appointed judges.

Rehnquist, the fourth associate justice to become chief, is the only justice completely comfortable with the argument that the original intent of the framers of the Constitution and the Bill of Rights is the proper standard for interpreting those documents today. He also takes a literal approach to individual rights. These beliefs have led him to dissent from the Court's rulings protecting a woman's privacy-based right to abortion, to argue that there is no constitutional barrier to school prayer, and to side with police and prosecutors on questions of criminal law.

Born in Milwaukee, Wisconsin, October 1, 1924, Rehnquist went west to college. At Stanford University, where he received both his undergraduate and law degrees, classmates recalled him as a brilliant student whose already well-entrenched conservative views set him apart from his more liberal classmates.

After graduating from law school in 1952, Rehnquist came to Washington, D.C., to serve as a law clerk to Supreme Court justice Robert H. Jackson. There, in 1952, he wrote a memorandum that later would come back to haunt him during his Senate confirmation hearings. In the memo, Rehnquist favored separate but equal schools for blacks and whites. Asked about those views by the Senate Judiciary Committee in 1971, Rehnquist repudiated them, declaring that they were Justice Jackson's—not his own.

Following his clerkship, Rehnquist decided to practice law in the Southwest. In 1952 he moved to Phoenix and immediately became immersed in Arizona Republican politics. From his earliest days in the state, he was associated with the party's most conservative wing. A 1957 speech denouncing the liberality of the Warren Court typified his views at the time.

During the 1964 presidential campaign, Rehnquist campaigned ardently for Barry Goldwater. It was during the campaign that Rehnquist met and worked with Richard G. Kleindienst, who later, as President Richard Nixon's deputy attorney general, would appoint Rehnquist to head the Justice Department's Office of Legal Counsel as an assistant attorney general.

In 1971 the once-obscure Phoenix lawyer was nominated by President Nixon to the Supreme Court.

Controversy surrounded Rehnquist's 1986 nomination for chief justice. He was accused of harassing voters and challenging their right to vote years earlier when he was a GOP poll watcher in Phoenix. Accusations also were raised against him for racial bias. His views on civil rights were questioned and he was found to have accepted anti-Semitic restrictions in a property deed to a Vermont home. In addition, his medical records were reviewed over concern about a chronic low-back problem.

More votes were cast against Rehnquist for chief justice (thirty-three nays to sixty-five ayes) than against any other successful Supreme Court nominee in the twentieth century. In 1971 he had tied for the second-highest number of negative votes (twenty-six nays to sixty-eight ayes) when he was confirmed as an associate justice.

Rehnquist has been married since 1953 to Natalie Cornell. They have two daughters and a son.

Born October 1, 1924, Milwaukee, Wisconsin; Stanford University B.A. (1948); Phi Beta Kappa; LL.B. (1952); Harvard University M.A. (1949); law clerk to Justice Robert H. Jackson, U.S. Supreme Court 1952-1953; married 1953; two daughters, one son; practiced law 1953-1969; assistant U.S. attorney general, Office of Legal Counsel 1969-1971; nominated as associate justice of the U.S. Supreme Court by President Nixon October 21, 1971; confirmed December 10, 1971; nominated as chief justice of the United States, by President Reagan June 17, 1986; confirmed September 17, 1986.

Byron Raymond White

Byron R. White is noted for his quick and precise legal mind and his incisive questioning during oral argument.

White was born June 8, 1917, in Fort Collins, Colorado, and grew up in Wellington, a small town in a sugar beet growing area of the state.

Ranking first in his high school class, White won a scholarship to the University of Colorado, which he entered in 1934.

At the university White earned his reputation as an outstnding scholar-athlete. He was first in his class, a member of Phi Beta Kappa, and the winner of three varsity letters in football, four in basketball, and three in baseball. By the end of his college career in 1938 he had been nicknamed "Whizzer" for his outstanding performance as a football player, a performance that earned him not only a national reputation but also a one-year contract with the Pittsburgh Pirates (now the Steelers). White already had accepted a coveted Rhodes Scholarship for study at Oxford but decided to postpone his year in England.

Despite his success as a professional football player, at the end of the football season White sailed for England to attend Oxford. When the European war broke out in September 1939, White returned to the United States and entered Yale Law School. But during 1940 and 1941 he alternated law study with playing football for the Detroit Lions.

After the United States entered the war, White served in the Navy in the South Pacific. There he renewed an old acquaintance with John F. Kennedy, whom he had met in England and who later would nominate White to the Supreme Court. After the war, White returned to Yale, earning his law degree magna cum laude in 1946. Following graduation, White served as law clerk to U.S. Chief Justice Fred M. Vinson. In 1947 he returned to his native Colorado, where for the next fourteen years he practiced law with the Denver law firm of Lewis, Grant, and Davis.

White renewed his contact with Kennedy during the 1960 presidential campaign, leading the nationwide volunteer group, Citizens for Kennedy. After the election, Kennedy named White to the post of deputy attorney general, a position he held until his Supreme Court appointment in 1962.

White has been married since 1946 to Marion Stearns. They have one son and one daughter.

Born June 8, 1917, in Fort Collins, Colorado; University of Colorado B.A. (1938); Phi Beta Kappa; Rhodes scholar, Oxford University; Yale Law School LL.B. magna cum laude (1946); married 1946; one son, one daughter; law clerk to Chief Justice Fred M. Vinson 1946-1947; practiced law, Denver, 1947-1960; U.S. deputy attorney general 1961-1962; nominated as associate justice, U.S. Supreme Court, by President Kennedy March 30, 1962; confirmed April 11, 1962.

Thurgood Marshall

Unlike jurists who undergo striking philosophical changes once elevated to the Supreme Court, Thurgood Marshall has deviated little from his earlier convictions. For more than a quarter of a century, Marshall exemplified, through his work with the National Association for the Advancement of Colored People (NAACP), the part of the civil rights movement that sought change through legal processes. Once on the Court Marshall continued to champion the rights of minorities. And as a member of the Court's minority liberal wing, Marshall has persisted in his defense of individual rights.

Thurgood Marshall was born July 2, 1908, in Baltimore, Maryland, the son of a primary school teacher and a club steward. In 1926 began studies at all-black Lincoln University in Chester, Pennsylvania, where he developed a reputation as an outstanding debater. After graduating cum

laude in 1930, Marshall decided to study law. He entered Howard University in Washington, D.C., in 1931.

During his law school years, Marshall began to develop an interest in civil rights. After graduating first in his law school class in 1933, Marshall began a long and historic involvement with the NAACP. In 1940 Marshall became the head of the newly formed NAACP Legal Defense and Educational Fund, a position he held for more than twenty years.

Over the next two and one-half decades, Marshall coordinated the fund's attack on segregation in voting, housing, public accommodations, and education. The culmination of his career as a civil rights attorney came in 1954 as chief counsel in a series of cases grouped under the title *Brown v. Board of Education*. In that historic case, which Marshall argued before the Supreme Court, civil rights advocates convinced the Court to declare that segregation in public schools was unconstitutional.

In 1961 President John F. Kennedy appointed Marshall to the U.S. Court of Appeals for the Second Circuit, but because of heated opposition from Southern Democratic senators Marshall was not confirmed until a year later.

Four years after he was named to the circuit court, Marshall was chosen by President Lyndon B. Johnson to be the nation's first black solicitor general. During his years as the government's chief advocate before the Supreme Court, Marshall scored impressive victories in the areas of civil and constitutional rights. He won Court approval of the 1965 Voting Rights Act, voluntarily informed the Court that the government had used electronic eavesdropping devices in two cases, and joined in a suit that successfully overturned a California constitutional amendment prohibiting open housing legislation.

On June 13, 1967, Marshall became the first black appointed to be a justice of the Supreme Court, chosen by President Johnson.

Marshall was married in 1955 to Cecelia A. Suyat. He has two sons by his first wife, Vivian Burey, who died in 1955.

Born July 2, 1908, in Baltimore, Maryland; Lincoln University B.A. (1930); Howard University LL.B. (1933); practiced law 1933-1937; assistant special counsel NAACP 1936-1938; special counsel 1938-1950; married 1929, two sons; married 1955; director-counsel, NAACP Legal Defense and Educational Fund 1940-1961; judge, U.S. Court of Appeals for the Second Circuit 1961-1965; U.S. solicitor general 1965-1967; nominated as associate justice, U.S. Supreme Court, by President Johnson June 13, 1967; confirmed August 30, 1967.

Harry Andrew Blackmun

During his first years on the Court, Harry A. Blackmun frequently was described as one of the "Minnesota Twins" along with the Court's other Minnesota native, Chief Justice Warren E. Burger. Blackmun and Burger, who retired in 1986, are lifelong friends who initially voted together on important decisions.

However, Blackmun, who originally impressed observers as a modest, even meek, addition to the Court's conservative bloc, has written some of the Court's most controversial decisions, among them its 1973 ruling upholding a woman's right to an abortion.

Blackmun was born in Nashville, Illinois, November 12, 1908, but spent most of his early years in Minneapolis-St. Paul, where his father was an official of the Twin Cities Savings and Loan Company. His lifelong friendship with Burger began in grade school.

"A whiz at math," according to people close to him, Blackmun went East after high school to attend Harvard College on a scholarship. At Harvard, Blackmun majored in mathematics and toyed briefly with the idea of becoming a physician.

But he chose the law instead. After graduating from Harvard in 1929, Phi Beta Kappa, Blackmun entered Harvard Law School, from which he graduated in 1932. During his law school years Blackmun supported himself with a variety of odd jobs, including tutoring in math and driving the launch for the college crew team.

Following law school Blackmun returned to St. Paul, where he served for a year and a half as a law clerk to United States Circuit Court judge John B. Sanborn, whom Blackmun succeeded twenty years later. He left the clerkship at the end of 1933 and joined the Minneapolis law firm of Dorsey, Colman, Barker, Scott, and Barber. At the same time he taught for a year at William Mitchell College of Law in St. Paul, the alma mater of former chief justice Burger. In addition to his practice,

 Blackmun also taught for two years during the 1940s at the University of Minnesota Law School.

In 1950 he accepted a post as "house counsel" for the world-famous Mayo Clinic in Rochester, Minnesota. Among his colleagues at the clinic, Blackmun quickly developed a reputation as a serious man, totally engrossed in his profession. The reputation followed him to the bench of the U.S. Court of Appeals for the Eighth Circuit, to which Blackmun was appointed by President Dwight D. Eisenhower in 1959. As a judge, he was known for his scholarly and thorough opinions.

Blackmun's total devotion to the law leaves little time for outside activities. He is an avid reader, delving primarily into judicial tomes. Over the years he has also been active in Methodist church affairs. Before he developed knee problems, Blackmun was a proficient squash and tennis player. It was on the tennis court that Blackmun met his future wife, Dorothy E. Clark. They were married in 1941 and have three daughters.

Born November 12, 1908, in Nashville, Illinois; Harvard College B.A. (1929); Phi Beta Kappa; Harvard Law School LL.B. (1932); clerk, John Sanborn, U.S. Court of Appeals for the Eighth Circuit, St. Paul 1932-1933; practiced law, Minneapolis, 1934-1950; married 1941; three daughters; resident counsel, Mayo Clinic, Rochester, Minnesota, 1950-1959; judge, U.S. Court of Appeals for the Eighth Circuit 1959-1970; nominated as associate justice, U.S. Supreme Court, by President Richard Nixon April 14, 1970; confirmed May 12, 1970.

John Paul Stevens

When President Gerald R. Ford nominated federal appeals court judge John Paul Stevens to the Supreme Court seat vacated by veteran liberal William O. Douglas in 1975, Court watchers and other observers struggled to pin an ideological label on the new nominee. The consensus that finally emerged was that Stevens was neither a doctrinaire liberal nor conservative, but a judicial centrist, whose scholarly opinions made him a "judge's judge." His subsequent opinions bear out this description, although in recent years he has leaned more toward the liberal side.

A soft-spoken, mild-mannered man who occasionally sports a bow tie under his judicial robes, Stevens had a long record of excellence in scholarship. A member of a prominent Chicago family, Stevens graduated Phi Beta Kappa from the University of Chicago in 1941. After a wartime stint in the Navy, during which he earned the Bronze Star, he returned to Chicago to enter Northwestern University Law School, from which he graduated magna cum laude in 1947. From there, Stevens left for Washington, where he served as a law clerk to Supreme Court justice Wiley Rutledge. He returned to Chicago to join the prominent law firm of Poppenhusen, Johnston, Thompson, and Raymond, which specialized in antitrust law. Stevens developed a reputation as a preeminent antitrust lawyer, and after three years with Poppenhusen he left in 1952 to form his own firm, Rothschild, Stevens, Barry, and Myers. He remained there, engaging in private practice and teaching part time at Northwestern and the University of Chicago law schools, until his appointment by President Richard Nixon in 1970 to the U.S. Court of Appeals for the Seventh Circuit.

Stevens developed a reputation as a political moderate during his undergraduate days at the University of Chicago, then an overwhelmingly liberal campus. But although he is a registered Republican he has never been active in partisan politics. Nevertheless, Stevens did serve as Republican counsel in 1951 to the House Judiciary Subcommittee on the Study of Monopoly Power. He also served from 1953 to 1955, during the Eisenhower administration, as a member of the Attorney General's National Committee to Study the Antitrust Laws.

An enthusiastic pilot, Stevens flies his own small plane. According to friends, he is also a creditable bridge player and golfer. He gave up playing squash following open heart surgery, from which he is said to have recovered fully. In 1942 Stevens married Elizabeth Jane Sheeren. They have four children. They were divorced in 1979. Stevens subsequently married Maryan Mulholland Simon, a longtime neighbor in Chicago.

Born April 20, 1920, Chicago, Illinois; University of Chicago B.A. (1941); Phi Beta Kappa; Northwestern University School of Law J.D. (1947); magna cum laude; married Elizabeth Jane Sheeren 1942; three daughters, one son; divorced 1979; married Maryan Mulholland Simon

1980; law clerk to Justice Wiley Rutledge, U.S. Supreme Court, 1947-1948; practiced law, Chicago, 1949-1970; judge, U.S. Court of Appeals for the Seventh Circuit 1970-1975; nominated an associate justice, U.S. Supreme Court, by President Ford November 28, 1975; confirmed December 17, 1975.

Sandra Day O'Connor

Pioneering came naturally to Sandra Day O'Connor. Her grandfather left Kansas in 1880 to take up ranching in the desert land that would eventually become the state of Arizona. O'Connor, born in El Paso where her mother's parents lived, was raised on the Lazy B Ranch, the 162,000-acre spread that her grandfather had founded in southeastern Arizona near Duncan. She spent her school years in El Paso, living with her grandmother and attending the schools there. She graduated from high school at age sixteen and then entered Stanford University.

Six years later, in 1952, Sandra Day had won degrees, with great distinction, both from the university, in economics, and from Stanford Law School. There she met John J. O'Connor III, her future husband, and William H. Rehnquist, a future colleague on the Supreme Court. During her law school years, Sandra Day was an editor of the *Stanford Law Review* and a member of Order of the Coif, both reflecting her academic leadership.

But despite her outstanding law school record, she found it difficult to secure a job as an attorney in 1952 when relatively few women were practicing law. She applied, among other places, to the firm in which William French Smith—first attorney general in the Reagan administration—was a partner, only to be offered a job as a secretary.

After she completed a short stint as deputy county attorney for San Mateo County (California) while her new husband completed law school at Stanford, the O'Connors moved with the U.S. Army to Frankfurt, Germany. There Sandra O'Connor worked as a civilian attorney for the Army, while John O'Connor served his tour of duty.

In 1957 they returned to Phoenix to live. In the next eight years their three sons were born, and O'Connor's life was a mix of mothering, homemaking, volunteer work, and some "miscellaneous legal tasks" on the side.

In 1965 she resumed her legal career full time, taking a job as an assistant attorney general for Arizona. After four years in that post she was appointed to fill a vacancy in the state Senate, where she served on the judiciary committee. In 1970 she was elected to the same body and two years later was chosen its majority leader, the first woman in the nation to hold such a post.

O'Connor was active in Republican party politics and was co-chairman of the Arizona Committee for the Re-election of the President in 1972.

In 1974 she was elected to the Superior Court for Maricopa County, where she served for five years. Then in 1979 Gov. Bruce Babbitt— acting, some said, to remove a potential rival for the governorship— appointed O'Connor to the Arizona Court of Appeals. It was from that seat that President Ronald Reagan chose her as his first nominee to the Supreme Court, succeeding Potter Stewart, who had retired. Reagan described her as "a person for all seasons."

By a vote of 99-0 the Senate confirmed O'Connor September 21, 1981, as the first woman associate justice of the U.S. Supreme Court.

Born March 26, 1930, in El Paso, Texas; Stanford University, B.A. (1950); magna cum laude; Stanford University Law School, LL.B. (1952); with high honors; deputy county attorney, San Mateo, California, 1952-1953; assistant attorney general, Arizona, 1965-1969; Arizona state senator, 1969-1975, Senate majority leader, 1972-1975; judge, Maricopa County Superior Court, 1974-1979; judge, Arizona Court of Appeals, 1979-1981; married John J. O'Connor III, December 20, 1952; three sons; nominated associate justice, U.S. Supreme Court, by President Reagan August 19, 1981; confirmed September 21, 1981.

Antonin Scalia

When Warren E. Burger resigned and the president named William H. Rehnquist to be the new chief justice, it was not surprising that he would appoint Antonin Scalia to the Supreme Court. On issues dear to Ronald Reagan, it was clear that Scalia met the president's tests for conservatism. Scalia, whom Reagan had named to the U.S. Court of Appeals for the District of Columbia in 1982, became the first Supreme Court justice of Italian ancestry. A Roman Catholic, he has nine children and opposes abortion. He also has expressed opposition to "affirmative action" preferences for minorities.

Deregulation, which Reagan pushed as president, was a subject of considerable interest to Scalia, a specialist in administrative law. From 1977 to 1982 he was editor of the magazine *Regulation,* published by the American Enterprise Institute for Public Policy Research.

In sharp contrast to the hours of floor debate over Rehnquist's nomination to succeed Burger as chief justice, only a few moments of speeches were given in opposition to the equally conservative Scalia before he was confirmed, 98-0.

Born in Trenton, New Jersey, March 11, 1936, Scalia grew up in Queens, New York. He graduated from Georgetown University in 1957 and from Harvard Law School in 1960. He worked for six years for the

firm of Jones, Day in Cleveland and then taught contract, commercial, and comparative law at the University of Virginia Law School.

Scalia served as general counsel of the White House Office of Telecommunications Policy from 1971 to 1972. He then headed the Administrative Conference of the United States, a group that advises the government on questions of administrative law and procedure. From 1974 through the Ford administration he headed the Justice Department's Office of Legal Counsel, a post Rehnquist had held three years earlier. Scalia then returned to academia, to teach at the University of Chicago Law School.

Scalia showed himself to be a hard worker, an aggressive interrogator, and an articulate advocate. On the appeals court he was impatient with what he saw as regulatory or judicial overreaching. In 1983 he dissented from a ruling requiring the Food and Drug Administration to consider whether drugs used for legal injections met FDA standards as safe and effective. The Supreme Court agreed, reversing the appeals court in 1985.

Scalia was thought to be the principal author of an unsigned decision in 1986 that declared major portions of the Gramm-Rudman-Hollings budget-balancing act unconstitutional. The Supreme Court upheld the decision later in the year.

Born March 11, 1936, Trenton, New Jersey; Georgetown University A.B. (1957); Harvard University LL.B. (1960); practiced law in Cleveland, 1960-1967; married Maureen McCarthy, 1960; nine children; taught at the University of Virginia 1967-1971; general counsel, White House Office of Telecommunications Policy 1971-1972; chairman Administrative Conference of the United States 1972-1974; head, Office of Legal Counsel 1974-1977; taught at the University of Chicago Law School 1977-1982; judge, U.S. Court of Appeals, District of Columbia, 1982-1986; nominated by President Reagan as associate justice, U.S. Supreme Court, June 17, 1986; confirmed September 17, 1986.

Anthony McLeod Kennedy

When the appointment of Anthony M. Kennedy to the Supreme Court was announced in November 1987, the Senate was cautiously prepared to cooperate with President Ronald Reagan and confirm the nomination.

The Senate and the country had agonized through Reagan's two unsuccessful attempts to replace retired justice Lewis F. Powell, Jr., with either Robert H. Bork or Douglas H. Ginsburg. The Senate had rejected Bork's nomination after contentious hearings, and Ginsburg had withdrawn his name amid controversy about his qualifications and admitted past use of marijuana.

Now there was a quiet sense of relief that Reagan had finally selected a nominee who could be confirmed without another wrenching confrontation. Kennedy, fifty-one, was viewed as a moderate conservative who stood a good chance of confirmation.

Kennedy had spent twelve years as a judge on the U.S. Court of Appeals for the Ninth Circuit. But unlike Bork, who had written and spoken extensively for twenty years, Kennedy's record was confined mostly to his approximately 500 judicial opinions.

His views thus were based in large part on issues that had been distilled at the trial level and further refined by legal and oral arguments. Furthermore, according to legal specialists, Kennedy sought to decide issues narrowly rather than use his decisions as a testing ground for constitutional theories.

The American Bar Association, which had split 10-5 in giving Bork it highest rating, "well-qualified," was unanimous in giving Kennedy the same rating for the Supreme Court.

In three days of Senate hearings, Kennedy ratified important past constitutional precedents but gave no guarantees about future opinions. In the process he demonstrated a breadth of experience and a consummate skill in articulating the legal issues that confronted the nation.

Kennedy was questioned most closely about civil rights. As an appeals court judge, he had written four decisions, in particular, that raised concerns among Hispanics, women, and blacks. But Kennedy's answers seemed to allay most senators' concerns. "We simply do not have any real freedom if we have discrimination based on race, sex, religion, or national origin, and I share that commitment," he said.

Confirmed by the Senate 97-0 February 3, 1988, Kennedy was sworn in February 18.

A native Californian, Kennedy attended Stanford University from 1954 to 1957 and the London School of Economics, 1957-1958. He received his B.A. from Stanford in 1958 and LL.B. from Harvard Law School in 1961. Admitted to the California bar in 1962, he was in private law practice until 1975 when President Gerald R. Ford appointed him to the appeals court. From 1965 to 1988 he taught constitutional law at McGeorge School of Law, University of the Pacific.

He and his wife, Mary Davis, have three children: Justin Anthony, Gregory Davis, and Kristin Marie.

Born: July 23, 1936, Sacramento, California; Stanford University, A.B. (1958); Harvard Law School, LL.B. (1961); Phi Beta Kappa; California Army National Guard, January-June 1961; married Mary Davis June 29, 1963; two sons, one daughter; Roman Catholic; associate, Thelen, Marrin, John & Bridges, San Francisco, 1961-1963; sole practitioner, Sacramento, 1963-1967; partner, Evans, Jackson & Kennedy, Sacramento, 1967-1975; professor of constitutional law, McGeorge School of Law, University of the Pacific, 1965-1988; U.S. Court of Appeals for the Ninth Circuit, Sacramento, 1975-1988; nominated as associate justice, U.S. Supreme Court, by President Reagan November 11, 1987; confirmed February 3, 1988.

David Hackett Souter

At first, the media and the senators, who would decide whether David H. Souter would be confirmed, did not know what to make of the cerebral, button-down nominee. He was little known outside of his home state of New Hampshire, where he had been attorney general (1976-1978); a trial judge (1978-1983); and a state supreme court justice (1983-1990).

Unlike Antonin Scalia and Anthony Kennedy, his immediate predecessors on the Court, Souter had virtually no scholarly writings to dissect and little federal court experience to scrutinize. Only three months earlier Bush had appointed him to the U.S. Court of Appeals for the First Circuit. Souter had yet to write a legal opinion on that court.

But Souter was impressive in confirmation hearings. The Harvard graduate and former Rhodes scholar demonstrated intellectual rigor and a masterly approach to constitutional law. Souter was able to recognize where a particular questioner was headed and to deflect most tough inquiries. He took refuge in the history of legal principles.

His earlier work as state attorney general and as a New Hampshire Supreme Court justice had a conservative bent, but Souter came across as more moderate in the hearings, winning over both Democrats and Republicans with his knowledge of judicial precedent. Although still regarded as a conservative, Souter was expected to be a swing vote.

Souter was approved by the Senate 90-9; dissenting senators cited his reluctance to take a stand on abortion. During his confirmation hearings, Souter had refused to say how he would vote if the question of overruling *Roe v. Wade* arose. In his first months on the bench, Souter was a tenacious questioner but did not tip his hand further on his philosophical viewpoint.

Souter is known for his intensely private, ascetic life. He was born September 17, 1939, in Melrose, Massachusetts. An only child, he moved with his parents to Weare, New Hampshire, at age eleven. Except for college, he had lived in Weare since.

Souter graduated from Harvard College in 1961. He attended Oxford University on a Rhodes Scholarship from 1961 to 1963, then returned to Cambridge for Harvard Law School. Graduating in 1966, he worked for two years in a Concord law firm. In 1968 he became an assistant attorney general, rose to deputy attorney general in 1971, and in 1976 was appointed attorney general, succeeding Rudman who had held the post since 1970. Under conservative governor Meldrim Thomson, Jr., Attorney General Souter defended a number of controversial orders, including the lowering of state flags to half-staff on Good Friday to observe the death of Jesus. He prosecuted Jehovah's Witnesses who had obscured the state motto "Live Free or Die" on their license plates.

Souter remained in the post until 1978, when he was named to the state's trial court. Five years later, Gov. John H. Sununu appointed Souter to the state Supreme Court. Sununu was Bush's chief of staff when Souter was named to the U.S. Supreme Court.

Souter, a bachelor, is a nature enthusiast and avid hiker.

Born September 17, 1939, in Melrose, Massachusetts; Harvard College B.A. (1961); Oxford University, Rhodes scholar, 1961-1963; Harvard University Law School LL.B. (1966); private law practice, Concord, New Hampshire, 1966-1968; assistant attorney general, 1968-1971; deputy attorney general, 1971-1976; attorney general of New Hampshire, 1976-1978; associate justice, Superior Court, 1978-1983; associate justice, New Hampshire Supreme Court, 1983-1990; U.S. Court of Appeals for the First Circuit, April 1990-present; nominated by President Bush as associate justice, U.S. Supreme Court, July 23, 1990; confirmed October 2, 1990.

William Joseph Brennan, Jr. (Retired)

On the activist Warren Court, William J. Brennan, Jr. became known as an articulate judicial scholar who framed some of the Court's key decisions. On the more conservative Burger and Rehnquist Courts, however, Brennan confined himself largely to writing dissents. But while relegated to a minority voice, Brennan continued to rise in the esteem of legal scholars, some of whom characterized him as the Court's most eminent jurist.

Brennan was born April 25, 1906, in Newark, N.J., the second of eight children of Irish immigrant parents. Brennan displayed impressive academic abilities early in life. He was an outstanding student in high school, an honors student at the University of Pennsylvania's Wharton School of Finance, and he graduated in the top 10 percent of his Harvard Law School class in 1931.

Following law school, Brennan returned to Newark, where he joined the law firm of Pitney, Hardin and Skinner and specialized in labor law. Brennan served in the Army during World War II, after which he returned to his old law firm. But as his practice swelled, Brennan, a dedicated family man, began to resent the demands it placed on his time.

A desire to temper the pace of his work was one of the reasons Brennan accepted an appointment to the newly created New Jersey Superior Court in 1949. Brennan was moved first in 1950 to the appellate division of the Superior Court and then in 1952 to the state Supreme Court. He officially joined the U.S. Supreme Court in 1957.

Brennan is a football fan and a walker. Brennan was married in 1928 to Marjorie Leonard and has three children. After his wife's death in 1982, he married Mary Fowler in March 1983.

Born April 25, 1906, in Newark, N.J.; University of Pennsylvania B.S. (1928); Harvard Law School LL.B. (1931); married 1928; two sons, one daughter; practiced law Newark 1931-1949; N.J. Superior Court judge 1949; appellate division 1951-1952; associate justice N.J. Supreme Court 1952-1956; received recess appointment as associate justice, U.S. Supreme Court, from President Eisenhower October 16, 1956; nominated as associate justice by President Eisenhower January 14, 1957; confirmed March 19, 1957; retired July 20, 1990.

Glossary of Legal Terms

Accessory. In criminal law, a person not present at the commission of an offense who commands, advises, instigates, or conceals the offense.

Acquittal. Discharge of a person from a charge of guilt. A person is acquitted when a jury returns a verdict of not guilty. A person also may be acquitted when a judge determines that there is insufficient evidence to convict him or that a violation of due process precludes a fair trial.

Adjudicate. To determine finally by the exercise of judicial authority, to decide a case.

Affidavit. A voluntary written statement of facts or charges affirmed under oath.

A fortiori. With stronger force, with more reason.

Amicus curiae. A friend of the court, a person, not a party to litigation, who volunteers or is invited by the court to give his or her views on a case.

Appeal. To take a case to a higher court for review. Generally, a party losing in a trial court may appeal once to an appellate court as a matter of right. If the party loses in the appellate court, appeal to a higher court is within the discretion of the higher court. Most appeals to the U.S. Supreme Court are within its discretion.

However, when the highest court in a state rules that a U.S. statute is unconstitutional or upholds a state statute against the claim that it is unconstitutional, appeal to the Supreme Court is a matter of right.

Appellant. The party who appeals a lower court decision to a higher court.

Appellee. One who has an interest in upholding the decision of a lower court and is compelled to respond when the case is appealed to a higher court by the appellant.

Arraignment. The formal process of charging a person with a crime, reading that person the charge, asking whether he or she pleads guilty or not guilty, and entering the plea.

Attainder, Bill of. A legislative act pronouncing a particular individual guilty of a crime without trial or conviction and imposing a sentence.

Bail. The security, usually money, given as assurance of a prisoner's due appearance at a designated time and place (as in court) in order to procure in the interim the prisoner's release from jail.

Bailiff. A minor officer of a court usually serving as an usher or a messenger.

Brief. A document prepared by counsel to serve as the basis for an argument in court, setting out the facts of and the legal arguments in support of the case.

Burden of proof. The need or duty of affirmatively providing a fact or facts which are disputed.

Case law. The law as defined by previously decided cases, distinct from statutes and other sources of law.

Cause. A case, suit, litigation, or action, civil or criminal.

Certiorari, Writ of. A writ issued from the Supreme Court, at its discretion, to order a lower court to prepare the record of a case and send it to the Supreme Court for review.

Civil law. Body of law dealing with the private rights of individuals, as distinguished from criminal law.

Class action. A lawsuit brought by one person or group on behalf of all persons similarly situated.

Code. A collection of laws, arranged systematically.

Comity. Courtesy, respect; usually used in the legal sense to refer to the proper relationship between state and federal courts.

Common law. Collection of principles and rules of action, particularly from unwritten English law, which derive their authority from long-standing usage and custom or from courts recognizing and enforcing these customs. Sometimes used synonymously with case law.

Consent decree. A court-sanctioned agreement settling a legal dispute and entered into by the consent of the parties.

Contempt (civil and criminal). Civil contempt consists in the failure to do something that the party is ordered by the court to do for the benefit of another party. Criminal contempt occurs when a person willfully exhibits disrespect for the court or obstructs the administration of justice.

Conviction. Final judgment or sentence that the defendant is guilty as charged.

Criminal law. The branch of law that deals with the enforcement of laws and the punishment of persons who, by breaking laws, commit crimes.

Declaratory judgment. A court pronouncement declaring a legal right or interpretation but not ordering a specific action.

De facto. In fact, in reality.

Defendant. In a civil action, the party denying or defending itself against charges brought by a plaintiff. In a criminal action, the person indicted for commission of an offense.

De jure. As a result of law, as a result of official action.

De novo. Anew; afresh; a second time.

Deposition. Oral testimony from a witness taken out of court in response to written or oral questions, committed to writing, and intended to be used in the preparation of a case.

Dicta. *See* Obiter dictum.

Dismissal. Order disposing of a case without a trial.

Docket. *See* Trial docket.

Due process. Fair and regular procedure. The Fifth and Fourteenth Amendments guarantee persons that they will not be deprived of life, liberty, or property by the government until fair and usual procedures have been followed.

Error, Writ of. A writ issued from an appeals court to a lower court requiring it to send to the appeals court the record of a case in which it has entered a final judgment and which the appeals court will now review for error.

Ex parte. Only from, or on, one side. Application to a court for some ruling or action on behalf of only one party.

Ex post facto. After the fact; an *ex post facto* law makes an action a crime after it has already been committed, or otherwise changes the legal consequences of some past action.

Ex rel. Upon information from; usually used to describe legal proceedings begun by an official in the name of the state, but at the instigation of, and with information from, a private individual interested in the matter.

Grand jury. Group of twelve to twenty-three persons impanelled to hear, in private, evidence presented by the state against persons accused of crime and to issue indictments when a majority of the jurors find probable cause to believe that the accused has committed a crime. Called a "grand" jury because it comprises a greater number of persons than a "petit" jury.

Grand jury report. A public report, often called "presentments," released by a grand jury after an investigation into activities of public officials that fall short of criminal actions.

Guilty. A word used by a defendant in entering a plea or by a jury in returning a verdict, indicating that the defendant is legally responsible as charged for a crime or other wrongdoing.

Habeas corpus. Literally, "you have the body"; a writ issued to inquire whether a person is lawfully imprisoned or detained. The writ demands that the persons holding the prisoner justify the detention or release the prisoner.

Immunity. A grant of exemption from prosecution in return for evidence or testimony.

In camera. In chambers. Refers to court hearings in private without spectators.

In forma pauperis. In the manner of a pauper, without liability for court costs.

In personam. Done or directed against a particular person.

In re. In the affair of, concerning. Frequent title of judicial proceedings in which there are no adversaries, but rather where the matter itself—as a bankrupt's estate—requires judicial action.

In rem. Done or directed against the thing, not the person.

Indictment. A formal written statement based on evidence presented by the prosecutor from a grand jury decided by a majority vote, charging one or more persons with specified offenses.

Information. A written set of accusations, similar to an indictment, but filed directly by a prosecutor.

Injunction. A court order prohibiting the person to whom it is directed from performing a particular act.

Interlocutory decree. A provisional decision of the court before completion of a legal action which temporarily settles an intervening matter.

Judgment. Official decision of a court based on the rights and claims of the parties to a case which was submitted for determination.

Jurisdiction. The power of a court to hear a case in question, which exists when the proper parties are present, and when the point to be decided is within the issues authorized to be handled by the particular court.

Juries. *See* Grand jury; Petit jury.

Magistrate. A judicial officer having jurisdiction to try minor criminal cases and conduct preliminary examinations of persons charged with serious crimes.

Mandamus. "We command." An order issued from a superior court directing a lower court or other authority to perform a particular act.

Moot. Unsettled, undecided. A moot question is also one that is no longer material; a moot case is one that has become hypothetical.

Motion. Written or oral application to a court or a judge to obtain a rule or an order.

Nolo contendere. "I will not contest it." A plea entered by a defendant at the discretion of the judge with the same legal effect as a plea of guilty, but it may not be cited in other proceedings as an admission of guilt.

Obiter dictum. Statements by a judge or justice expressing an opinion and included with, but not essential to, an opinion resolving a case before the court. Dicta are not necessarily binding in future cases.

Parole. A conditional release from imprisonment under conditions that if the prisoner abides by the law and other restrictions that may be placed upon him or her, the prisoner will not have to serve the remainder of the sentence.

Per curiam. "By the court." An unsigned opinion of the court, or an opinion written by the whole court.

Petit jury. A trial jury, originally a panel of twelve persons who tried to reach a unanimous verdict on questions of fact in criminal and civil proceedings. Since 1970 the Supreme Court has upheld the legality of state juries with fewer than twelve persons. Because it comprises fewer persons than a "grand" jury, it is called a "petit" jury.

Petitioner. One who files a petition with a court seeking action or relief, including a plaintiff or an appellant. But a petitioner is also a person who files for other court action where charges are not necessarily made; for example, a party may petition the court for an order requiring another person or party to produce documents. The opposite party is called the respondent.

When a writ of certiorari is granted by the Supreme Court, the parties to the case are called petitioner and respondent in contrast to the appellant and appellee terms used in an appeal.

Plaintiff. A party who brings a civil action or sues to obtain a remedy for injury to his or her rights. The party against whom action is brought is termed the defendant.

Plea bargaining. Negotiations between prosecutors and the defendant aimed at exchanging a plea of guilty from the defendant for concessions by the prosecutors, such as reduction of charges or a request for leniency.

Pleas. *See* Guilty; Nolo contendere.

Presentment. *See* Grand jury report.

Prima facie. At first sight; referring to a fact or other evidence presumably sufficient to establish a defense or a claim unless otherwise contradicted.

Probation. Process under which a person convicted of an offense, usually a first offense, receives a suspended sentence and is given his freedom, usually under the guardianship of a probation officer.

Quash. To overthrow, annul, or vacate; as to quash a subpoena.

Recognizance. An obligation entered into before a court or magistrate requiring the performance of a specified act—usually to appear in court at a later date. It is an alternative to bail for pretrial release.

Remand. To send back. In the event of a decision being remanded, it is sent back by a higher court to the court from which it came for further action.

Respondent. One who is compelled to answer the claims or questions posed in court by a petitioner. A defendant and an appellee may be called respondents, but the term also includes those parties who answer in court during actions where charges are not necessarily brought or where the Supreme Court has granted a writ of certiorari.

Seriatim. Separately, individually, one by one.

Stare decisis. "Let the decision stand." The principle of adherence to settled cases, the doctrine that principles of law established in earlier judicial decisions should be accepted as authoritative in similar subsequent cases.

Statute. A written law enacted by a legislature. A collection of statutes for a particular governmental division is called a code.

Stay. To halt or suspend further judicial proceedings.

Subpoena. An order to present oneself before a grand jury, court, or legislative hearing.

Subpoena duces tecum. An order to produce specified documents or papers.

Tort. An injury or wrong to the person or property of another.

Transactional immunity. Protects a witness from prosecution for any offense mentioned in or related to his or her testimony, regardless of independent evidence against the witness.

Trial docket. A calendar prepared by the clerks of the court listing the cases set to be tried.

Use immunity. Protects a witness against the use of his or her testimony against the witness in prosecution.

Vacate. To make void, annul, or rescind.

Writ. A written court order commanding the designated recipient to perform or not perform acts specified in the order.

Constitution of the United States

We the People of the United States, in Order to form a more perfect Union, establish Justice, insure domestic Tranquility, provide for the common defence, promote the general Welfare, and secure the Blessings of Liberty to ourselves and our Posterity, do ordain and establish this Constitution for the United States of America.

Article I

Section 1. All legislative Powers herein granted shall be vested in a Congress of the United States, which shall consist of a Senate and House of Representatives.

Section 2. The House of Representatives shall be composed of Members chosen every second Year by the People of the several States, and the Electors in each State shall have the Qualifications requisite for Electors of the most numerous Branch of the State Legislature.

No Person shall be a Representative who shall not have attained to the age of twenty five Years, and been seven Years a Citizen of the United States, and who shall not, when elected, be an Inhabitant of that State in which he shall be chosen.

[Representatives and direct Taxes shall be apportioned among the several States which may be included within this Union, according to their respective Numbers, which shall be determined by adding to the whole Number of free Persons, including those bound to Service for a Term of Years, and excluding Indians not taxed, three fifths of all other Persons.][1] The actual Enumeration shall be made within three Years after the first Meeting of the Congress of the United States, and within every subsequent Term of ten Years, in such Manner as they shall by Law direct. The Number of Representatives shall not exceed one for every thirty Thousand, but each State shall have at Least one Representative; and until such enumeration shall be made, the State of New Hampshire shall be entitled to chuse three, Massachusetts eight, Rhode-Island and Providence Plantations one, Connecticut five, New-York six, New Jersey four, Pennsylvania eight, Delaware one, Maryland six, Virginia ten, North Carolina five, South Carolina five, and Georgia three.

When vacancies happen in the Representation from any State, the Executive Authority thereof shall issue Writs of Election to fill such Vacancies.

The House of Representatives shall chuse their Speaker and other Officers; and shall have the sole Power of Impeachment.

Section 3. The Senate of the United States shall be composed of two Senators from each State, [chosen by the Legislature thereof,]² for six Years; and each Senator shall have one Vote.

Immediately after they shall be assembled in Consequence of the first Election, they shall be divided as equally as may be into three Classes. The Seats of the Senators of the first Class shall be vacated at the Expiration of the second Year, of the second Class at the Expiration of the fourth Year, and of the third Class at the Expiration of the sixth Year, so that one third may be chosen every second Year; [and if Vacancies happen by Resignation, or otherwise, during the Recess of the Legislature of any State, the Executive thereof may make temporary Appointments until the next Meeting of the Legislature, which shall then fill such Vacancies.]³

No Person shall be a Senator who shall not have attained to the Age of thirty Years, and been nine Years a Citizen of the United States, and who shall not, when elected, be an Inhabitant of that State for which he shall be chosen.

The Vice President of the United States shall be President of the Senate, but shall have no Vote, unless they be equally divided.

The Senate shall chuse their other Officers, and also a President pro tempore, in the Absence of the Vice President, or when he shall exercise the Office of President of the United States.

The Senate shall have the sole Power to try all Impeachments. When sitting for that Purpose, they shall be on Oath or Affirmation. When the President of the United States is tried the Chief Justice shall preside: And no Person shall be convicted without the Concurrence of two thirds of the Members present.

Judgment in Cases of Impeachment shall not extend further than to removal from Office, and disqualification to hold and enjoy any Office of honor, Trust or Profit under the United States: but the Party convicted shall nevertheless be liable and subject to Indictment, Trial, Judgment and Punishment, according to Law.

Section 4. The Times, Places and Manner of holding Elections for Senators and Representatives, shall be prescribed in each State by the Legislature thereof; but the Congress may at any time by Law make or alter such Regulations, except as to the Places of chusing Senators.

The Congress shall assemble at least once in every Year, and such Meeting shall [be on the first Monday in December],⁴ unless they shall by Law appoint a different Day.

Section 5. Each House shall be the Judge of the Elections, Returns and Qualifications of its own Members, and a Majority of each shall constitute a Quorum to do Business; but a smaller Number may adjourn from day to day, and may be authorized to compel the Attendance of absent Members, in such Manner, and under such Penalties as each House may provide.

Each House may determine the Rules of its Proceedings, punish its Members for disorderly Behaviour, and, with the Concurrence of two thirds, expel a Member.

Each House shall keep a Journal of its Proceedings, and from time to time publish the same, excepting such Parts as may in their Judgment require Secrecy; and the Yeas and Nays of the Members of either House on any question shall, at the Desire of one fifth of those Present, be entered on the Journal.

Neither House, during the Session of Congress, shall, without the Consent of the other, adjourn for more than three days, nor to any other Place than that in which the two Houses shall be sitting.

Section 6. The Senators and Representatives shall receive a Compensation for their Services, to be ascertained by Law, and paid out of the Treasury of the United States. They shall in all Cases, except Treason, Felony and Breach of the Peace, be privileged from Arrest during their Attendance at the Session of their respective Houses, and in going to and returning from the same; and for any Speech or Debate in either House, they shall not be questioned in any other Place.

No Senator or Representative shall, during the Time for which he was elected, be appointed to any civil Office under the Authority of the United States, which shall have been created, or the Emoluments whereof shall have been encreased during such time; and no Person holding any Office under the United States, shall be a Member of either House during his Continuance in Office.

Section 7. All Bills for raising Revenue shall originate in the House of Representatives; but the Senate may propose or concur with amendments as on other Bills.

Every Bill which shall have passed the House of Representatives and the Senate, shall, before it become a Law, be presented to the President of the United States; If he approve he shall sign it, but if not he shall return it, with his Objections to that House in which it shall have originated, who shall enter the Objections at large on their Journal, and proceed to reconsider it. If after such Reconsideration two thirds of that House shall agree to pass the Bill, it shall be sent, together with the Objections, to the other House, by which it shall likewise be reconsidered, and if approved by two thirds of that House, it shall become a Law. But in all such Cases the Votes of both Houses shall be determined by yeas and Nays, and the Names of the Persons voting for and against the Bill shall be entered on the Journal of each House respectively. If any Bill shall not be returned by the President within ten Days (Sundays excepted) after it shall have been presented to him, the Same shall be a Law, in like Manner as if he had signed it, unless the Congress by their Adjournment prevent its Return, in which Case it shall not be a Law.

Every Order, Resolution, or Vote to which the Concurrence of the Senate and House of Representatives may be necessary (except on a question of Adjournment) shall be presented to the President of the United States; and before the Same shall take Effect, shall be approved by him, or being disapproved by him, shall be repassed by two thirds of the Senate and House of Representatives, according to the Rules and Limitations prescribed in the Case of a Bill.

Section 8. The Congress shall have Power To lay and collect Taxes, Duties, Imposts and Excises, to pay the Debts and provide for the common Defence and general Welfare of the United States; but all Duties, Imposts and Excises shall be uniform throughout the United States;

To borrow Money on the credit of the United States;

To regulate Commerce with foreign Nations, and among the several States, and with the Indian Tribes;

To establish an uniform Rule of Naturalization, and uniform Laws on the subject of Bankruptcies throughout the United States;

To coin Money, regulate the Value thereof, and of foreign Coin, and fix the Standard of Weights and Measures;

To provide for the Punishment of counterfeiting the Securities and current Coin of the United States;

To establish Post Offices and post Roads;

To promote the Progress of Science and useful Arts, by securing for limited Times to Authors and Inventors the exclusive Right to their respective Writings and Discoveries;

To constitute Tribunals inferior to the supreme Court;

To define and punish Piracies and Felonies commited on the high Seas, and Offences against the Law of Nations;

To declare War, grant Letters of Marque and Reprisal, and make Rules concerning Captures on Land and Water;

To raise and support Armies, but no Appropriation of Money to that Use shall be for a longer Term than two Years;

To provide and maintain a Navy;

To make Rules for the Government and Regulation of the land and naval Forces;

To provide for calling forth the Militia to execute the Laws of the Union, suppress Insurrections and repel Invasions;

To provide for organizing, arming, and disciplining, the Militia, and for governing such Part of them as may be employed in the Service of the United States, reserving to the States respectively, the Appointment of the Officers, and the Authority of training the Militia according to the discipline prescribed by Congress;

To exercise exclusive Legislation in all Cases whatsoever, over such District (not exceeding ten Miles square) as may, by Cession of Particular States, and the Acceptance of Congress, become the Seat of the Government of the United States, and to exercise like Authority over all Places purchased by the Consent of the Legislature of the State in which the Same shall be, for the Erection of Forts, Magazines, Arsenals, dock-Yards, and other needful Buildings; —And

To make all Laws which shall be necessary and proper for carrying into Execution the foregoing Powers, and all other Powers vested by this Constitution in the Government of the United States, or in any Department or Officer thereof.

Section 9. The Migration or Importation of such Persons as any of the States now existing shall think proper to admit, shall not be prohibited by the Congress prior to the Year one thousand eight hundred and eight, but a Tax or duty may be imposed on such Importation, not exceeding ten dollars for each Person.

The Privilege of the Writ of Habeas Corpus shall not be suspended, unless when in Cases of Rebellion or Invasion the public Safety may require it.

No Bill of Attainder or ex post facto Law shall be passed.

No capitation, or other direct, Tax shall be laid, unless in Proportion to the Census of Enumeration herein before directed to be taken.[5]

No Tax or Duty shall be laid on Articles exported from any State.

No Preference shall be given by any Regulation of Commerce or Revenue to the Ports of one State over those of another; nor shall Vessels bound to, or from, one State, be obliged to enter, clear or pay Duties in another.

No Money shall be drawn from the Treasury, but, in Consequence of Appropriations made by Law; and a regular Statement and Account of the Receipts and Expenditures of all public Money shall be published from time to time.

No Title of Nobility shall be granted by the United States: And no Person holding any Office of Profit or Trust under them, shall, without the Consent of the Congress, accept of any present, Emolument, Office, or Title, of any kind whatever, from any King, Prince or foreign State.

Section 10. No State shall enter into any Treaty, Alliance, or Confederation; grant Letters of Marque and Reprisal; coin Money; emit Bills of Credit; make any Thing but gold and silver Coin a Tender in Payment of Debts; pass any Bill of Attainder, ex post facto Law, or Law impairing the Obligation of Contracts, or grant any Title of Nobility.

No State shall, without the Consent of the Congress, lay any Imposts or Duties on Imports or Exports, except what may be absolutely necessary for executing it's inspection Laws: and the net Produce of all Duties and Imposts, laid by any State on Imports or Exports, shall be for the Use of the Treasury of the United States; and all such Laws shall be subject to the Revision and Controul of the Congress.

No State shall, without the Consent of Congress, lay any Duty of Tonnage, keep Troops, or Ships of War in time of Peace, enter into any Agreement or Compact with another State, or with a foreign Power, or engage in War, unless actually invaded, or in such imminent Danger as will not admit of delay.

Article II

Section 1. The executive Power shall be vested in a President of the United States of America. He shall hold his Office during the Term of four Years, and, together with the Vice President, chosen for the same Term, be elected, as follows.

Each State shall appoint, in such Manner as the Legislature thereof may direct, a Number of Electors, equal to the whole Number of Senators and Representatives to which the State may be entitled in the Congress: but no Senator or Representative, or Person holding an Office of Trust or Profit under the United States, shall be appointed an Elector.

[The Electors shall meet in their respective States, and vote by Ballot for two Persons, of whom one at least shall not be an Inhabitant of the same State with themselves. And they shall make a List of all the Persons voted for, and of the Number of Votes for each; which List they shall sign and certify, and transmit sealed to the Seat of the Government of the United States, directed to the President of the Senate. The President of the Senate shall, in the Presence of the Senate and House of Representatives, open all the Certificates, and the Votes shall then be counted. The Person having the greatest Number of Votes shall be the President, if such Number be a Majority of the whole Number of Electors appointed; and if there be more than one who have such Majority, and have an equal Number of Votes, then the House of Representatives shall immediately chuse by Ballot one of them for President; and if no Person have a Majority, then from the five highest on the list the said House shall in like Manner chuse the President. But in chusing the President, the Votes shall be taken by States, the Representation from each State having one Vote; a quorum for this Purpose shall consist of a Member or Members from two thirds of the States, and a Majority of all the States shall be necessary to a Choice. In every Case, after the Choice of the President, the Person having the greatest Number of Votes of the Electors shall be the Vice President. But if there should remain two or more who have equal Votes, the Senate shall chuse from them by Ballot the Vice President.][6]

The Congress may determine the Time of chusing the Electors, and the Day on which they shall give their Votes; which Day shall be the same throughout the United States.

No Person except a natural born Citizen, or a Citizen of the United States, at the time of the Adoption of this Constitution, shall be eligible to the Office of President; neither shall any Person be eligible to that Office who shall not have attained to the Age of thirty five Years, and been fourteen Years a Resident within the United States.

In Case of the Removal of the President from Office, or of his Death, Resignation, or Inability to discharge the Powers and Duties of the said Office,[7] the Same shall devolve on the Vice President, and the Congress may by Law provide for the Case of Removal, Death, Resignation or Inability, both of the President and Vice President, declaring what Officer shall then act as President, and such Officer shall act accordingly, until the Disability be removed, or a President shall be elected.

The President shall, at stated Times, receive for his Services, a Compensation, which shall neither be encreased nor diminished during the Period for which he shall have been elected, and he shall not receive within that Period any other Emolument from the United States, or any of them.

Before he enter on the Execution of his Office, he shall take the following Oath or Affirmation: —"I do solemnly swear (or affirm) that I will faithfully execute the Office of President of the United States, and will to the best of my Ability, preserve, protect and defend the Constitution of the United States."

Section 2. The President shall be Commander in Chief of the Army and Navy of the United States, and of the Militia of the several States, when called into the actual Service of the United States; he may require the Opinion, in writing, of the principal Officer in each of the executive Departments, upon any Subject relating to the Duties of their respective Offices, and he shall have Power to grant Reprieves and Pardons for Offenses against the United States, except in Cases of Impeachment.

He shall have Power, by and with the Advice and Consent of the Senate, to make Treaties, provided two thirds of the Senators present concur; and he shall nominate, and by and with the Advice and Consent of the Senate, shall appoint Ambassadors, other public Ministers and Consuls, Judges of the supreme Court, and all other Officers of the

United States, whose Appointments are not herein otherwise provided for, and which shall be established by Law: but the Congress may by Law vest the Appointment of such inferior Officers, as they think proper, in the President alone, in the Courts of Law, or in the Heads of Departments.

The President shall have Power to fill up all Vacancies that may happen during the Recess of the Senate, by granting Commissions which shall expire at the End of their next Session.

Section 3. He shall from time to time give to the Congress Information of the State of the Union, and recommend to their Consideration such Measures as he shall judge necessary and expedient; he may, on extraordinary Occasions, convene both Houses, or either of them, and in Case of Disagreement between them, with Respect to the Time of Adjournment, he may adjourn them to such Time as he shall think proper; he shall receive Ambassadors and other public Ministers; he shall take Care that the Laws be faithfully executed, and shall Commission all the Officers of the United States.

Section 4. The President, Vice President and all Civil Officers of the United States, shall be removed from office on Impeachment for, and Conviction of, Treason, Bribery, or other high Crimes and Misdemeanors.

Article III

Section 1. The judicial Power of the United States, shall be vested in one supreme Court, and in such inferior Courts as the Congress may from time to time ordain and establish. The Judges, both of the supreme and inferior Courts, shall hold their Offices during good Behaviour, and shall, at stated Times, receive for their Services, a Compensation, which shall not be diminished during their Continuance in Office.

Section 2. The judicial Power shall extend to all Cases, in Law and Equity, arising under this Constitution, the Laws of the United States, and Treaties made, or which shall be made, under their Authority; —to all Cases affecting Ambassadors, other public Ministers and Consuls; —to all Cases of admiralty and maritime Jurisdiction; —to Controversies to which the United States shall be a Party; —to Controversies between two or more States; —between a State and Citizens of another State;[8] — between Citizens of different States; —between Citizens of the same State claiming Lands under Grants of different States, and between a State, or the Citizens thereof, and foreign States, Citizens or Subjects.[8]

In all Cases affecting Ambassadors, other public Ministers and Consuls, and those in which a State shall be Party, the supreme Court shall have original Jurisdiction. In all the other Cases before mentioned, the supreme Court shall have appellate Jurisdiction, both as to Law and Fact, with such Exceptions, and under such Regulations as the Congress shall make.

The Trial of all Crimes, except in cases of Impeachment, shall be by Jury; and such Trial shall be held in the State where the said Crimes shall have been committed; but when not committed within any State, the Trial shall be at such Place or Places as the Congress may by Law have directed.

Section 3. Treason against the United States, shall consist only in levying War against them, or in adhering to their Enemies, giving them Aid and Comfort. No Person shall be convicted of Treason unless on the Testimony of two Witnesses to the same overt Act, or on Confession in open Court.

The Congress shall have Power to declare the Punishment of Treason, but no Attainder of Treason shall work Corruption of Blood, or Forfeiture except during the Life of the Person attainted.

Article IV

Section 1. Full Faith and Credit shall be given in each State to the public Acts, Records, and judicial Proceedings of every other State. And the Congress may by general Laws prescribe the Manner in which such Acts, Records and Proceedings shall be proved, and the Effect thereof.

Section 2. The Citizens of each State shall be entitled to all Privileges and Immunities of Citizens in the several States.

A Person charged in any State with Treason, Felony, or other Crime, who shall flee from Justice, and be found in another State, shall on Demand of the executive Authority of the State from which he fled, be delivered up, to be removed to the State having Jurisdiction of the Crime.

[No Person held to Service or Labour in one State, under the Laws thereof, escaping into another, shall, in Consequence of any Law or Regulation therein, be discharged from such Service or Labour, but shall be delivered up on Claim of the Party to whom such Service or Labour may be due.][9]

Section 3. New States may be admitted by the Congress into this Union; but no new State shall be formed or erected within the Jurisdiction of any other State; nor any State be formed by the Junction of two or more States, or Parts of States, without the Consent of the Legislatures of the States concerned as well as of the Congress.

The Congress shall have Power to dispose of and make all needful Rules and Regulations respecting the Territory or other Property belonging to the United States; and nothing in this Constitution shall be so construed as to Prejudice any Claims of the United States, or of any particular State.

Section 4. The United States shall guarantee to every State in this Union a Republican Form of Government, and shall protect each of them against Invasion; and on Application of the Legislature, or of the Executive (when the Legislature cannot be convened) against domestic Violence.

Article V

The Congress, whenever two thirds of both Houses shall deem it necessary, shall propose Amendments to this Constitution, or, on the Application of the Legislatures of two thirds of the several States, shall call a Convention for proposing Amendments, which, in either Case, shall be valid to all Intents and Purposes, as Part of this Constitution, when ratified by the Legislatures of three fourths of the several States, or by Conventions in three fourths thereof, as the one or the other Mode of Ratification may be proposed by the Congress; Provided [that no Amendment which may be made prior to the Year One thousand eight hundred and eight shall in any Manner affect the first and fourth Clauses in the Ninth Section of the first Article; and][10] that no State, without its Consent, shall be deprived of its equal Suffrage in the Senate.

Article VI

All Debts contracted and Engagements entered into, before the Adoption of this Constitution, shall be as valid against the United States under this Constitution, as under the Confederation.

This Constitution, and the Laws of the United States which shall be made in Pursuance thereof; and all Treaties made, or which shall be made, under the Authority of the United States, shall be the supreme Law of the Land; and the Judges in every State shall be bound thereby, any Thing in the Constitution or Laws of any State to the Contrary notwithstanding.

The Senators and Representatives before mentioned, and the Members of the several State Legislatures, and all executive and judicial Officers, both of the United States and of the several States, shall be bound by Oath or Affirmation, to support this Constitution; but no religious Test shall ever be required as a Qualification to any Office or public Trust under the United States.

Article VII

The Ratification of the Conventions of nine States, shall be sufficient for the Establishment of this Constitution between the States so ratifying the Same. Done in Convention by the Unanimous Consent of the States present the Seventeenth Day of September in the Year of our Lord one thousand seven hundred and Eighty seven and of the Independence of the United States of America the Twelfth. In witness whereof We have hereunto subscribed our Names, George Washington, President and deputy from Virginia.

New Hampshire:	John Langdon, Nicholas Gilman.
Massachusetts:	Nathaniel Gorham, Rufus King.
Connecticut:	William Samuel Johnson, Roger Sherman.
New York:	Alexander Hamilton.
New Jersey:	William Livingston, David Brearley, William Paterson, Jonathan Dayton.
Pennsylvania:	Benjamin Franklin, Thomas Mifflin, Robert Morris, George Clymer, Thomas FitzSimons, Jared Ingersoll, James Wilson, Gouverneur Morris.
Delaware:	George Read, Gunning Bedford Jr., John Dickinson, Richard Bassett, Jacob Broom.
Maryland:	James McHenry, Daniel of St. Thomas Jenifer, Daniel Carroll.
Virginia:	John Blair, James Madison Jr.
North Carolina:	William Blount, Richard Dobbs Spaight, Hugh Williamson.

South Carolina:　　　John Rutledge,
　　　　　　　　　　　　Charles Cotesworth Pinckney,
　　　　　　　　　　　　Charles Pinckney,
　　　　　　　　　　　　Pierce Butler.

Georgia:　　　　　　William Few,
　　　　　　　　　　　　Abraham Baldwin.

[The language of the original Constitution, not including the Amendments, was adopted by a convention of the states on Sept. 17, 1787, and was subsequently ratified by the states on the following dates: Delaware, Dec. 7, 1787; Pennsylvania, Dec. 12, 1787; New Jersey, Dec. 18, 1787; Georgia, Jan. 2, 1788; Connecticut, Jan. 9, 1788; Massachusetts, Feb. 6, 1788; Maryland, April 28, 1788; South Carolina, May 23, 1788; New Hampshire, June 21, 1788.

Ratification was completed on June 21, 1788.

The Constitution subsequently was ratified by Virginia, June 25, 1788; New York, July 26, 1788; North Carolina, Nov. 21, 1789; Rhode Island, May 29, 1790; and Vermont, Jan. 10, 1791.]

Amendments

Amendment I

(First ten amendments ratified December 15, 1791.)

Congress shall make no law respecting an establishment of religion, or prohibiting the free exercise thereof; or abridging the freedom of speech, or of the press; or the right of the people peaceably to assemble, and to petition the Government for a redress of grievances.

Amendment II

A well regulated Militia, being necessary to the security of a free State, the right of the people to keep and bear Arms, shall not be infringed.

Amendment III

No Soldier shall, in time of peace be quartered in any house, without the consent of the Owner, nor in time of war, but in a manner to be prescribed by law.

Amendment IV

The right of the people to be secure in their persons, houses, papers, and effects, against unreasonable searches and seizures, shall not be violated, and no Warrants shall issue, but upon probable cause, supported by Oath or affirmation, and particularly describing the place to be searched, and the persons or things to be seized.

Amendment V

No person shall be held to answer for a capital, or otherwise infamous crime, unless on a presentment or indictment of a Grand Jury, except in cases arising in the land or naval forces, or in the Militia, when in actual service in time of War or public danger; nor shall any person be subject for the same offence to be twice put in jeopardy of life or limb; nor shall be compelled in any criminal case to be a witness against himself, nor be deprived of life, liberty, or property, without due process of law; nor shall private property be taken for public use, without just compensation.

Amendment VI

In all criminal prosecutions, the accused shall enjoy the right to a speedy and public trial, by an impartial jury of the State and district wherein the crime shall have been committed, which district shall have been previously ascertained by law, and to be informed of the nature and cause of the accusation; to be confronted with the witnesses against him; to have compulsory process for obtaining witnesses in his favor, and to have the Assistance of Counsel for his defence.

Amendment VII

In Suits at common law, where the value in controversy shall exceed twenty dollars, the right of trial by jury shall be preserved, and no fact tried by a jury, shall be otherwise re-examined in any Court of the United States, than according to the rules of the common law.

Amendment VIII

Excessive bail shall not be required, nor excessive fines imposed, nor cruel and unusual punishments inflicted.

Amendment IX

The enumeration in the Constitution, of certain rights, shall not be construed to deny or disparage others retained by the people.

Amendment X

The powers not delegated to the United States by the Constitution, nor prohibited by it to the States, are reserved to the States respectively, or to the people.

Amendment XI

(Ratified February 7, 1795)

The Judicial power of the United States shall not be construed to extend to any suit in law or equity, commenced or prosecuted against one of the United States by Citizens of another State, or by Citizens or Subjects of any Foreign State.

Amendment XII

(Ratified June 15, 1804)

The Electors shall meet in their respective states and vote by ballot for President and Vice-President, one of whom, at least, shall not be an inhabitant of the same state with themselves; they shall name in their ballots the person voted for as President, and in distinct ballots the person voted for as Vice-President, and they shall make distinct lists of all persons voted for as President, and of all persons voted for as Vice-President, and of the number of votes for each, which lists they shall sign and certify, and transmit sealed to the seat of the government of the United States, directed to the President of the Senate; —The President of the Senate shall, in the presence of the Senate and House of Representatives, open all the certificates and the votes shall then be counted; — The person having the greatest number of votes for President, shall be the President, if such number be a majority of the whole number of Electors appointed; and if no person have such majority, then from the persons having the highest numbers not exceeding three on the list of those voted for as President, the House of Representatives shall choose immediately, by ballot, the President. But in choosing the President, the votes shall be taken by states, the representation from each state having one vote; a quorum for this purpose shall consist of a member or members from two-thirds of the states, and a majority of all the states shall be necessary to a choice. [And if the House of Representatives shall not choose a President whenever the right of choice shall devolve upon them, before the fourth day of March next following, then the Vice-President shall act as President, as in the case of the death or other constitutional disability of the President—][11] The person having the greatest number of votes as Vice-President, shall be the Vice-President, if such number be a majority of the whole number of Electors appointed, and if no person have a majority, then from the two highest numbers on the list, the Senate shall choose the Vice-President; a quorum for the purpose shall consist of two-thirds of the whole number of Senators, and a majority of the whole number shall be necessary to a choice. But no person constitutionally ineligible to the office of President shall be eligible to that of Vice-President of the United States.

Amendment XIII

(Ratified December 6, 1865)

Section 1. Neither slavery nor involuntary servitude, except as a punishment for crime whereof the party shall have been duly convicted, shall exist within the United States, or any place subject to their jurisdiction.

Section 2. Congress shall have power to enforce this article by appropriate legislation.

Amendment XIV

(Ratified July 9, 1868)
Section 1. All persons born or naturalized in the United States and subject to the jurisdiction thereof, are citizens of the United States and of the State wherein they reside. No State shall make or enforce any law which shall abridge the privileges or immunities of citizens of the United States; nor shall any State deprive any person of life, liberty, or property, without due process of law; nor deny to any person within its jurisdiction the equal protection of the laws.

Section 2. Representatives shall be apportioned among the several States according to their respective numbers, counting the whole number of persons in each State, excluding Indians not taxed. But when the right to vote at any election for the choice of electors for President and Vice President of the United States, Representatives in Congress, the Executive and Judicial officers of a State, or the members of the Legislature thereof, is denied to any of the male inhabitants of such State, being twenty-one years of age,[12] and citizens of the United States, or in any way abridged, except for participation in rebellion, or other crime, the basis of representation therein shall be reduced in the proportion which the number of such male citizens shall bear to the whole number of male citizens twenty-one years of age in such State.

Section 3. No person shall be a Senator or Representative in Congress, or elector of President and Vice President, or hold any office, civil or military, under the United States, or under any State, who, having previously taken an oath, as a member of Congress, or as an officer of the United States, or as a member of any State legislature, or as an executive or judicial officer of any State, to support the Constitution of the United States, shall have engaged in insurrection or rebellion against the same, or given aid or comfort to the enemies thereof. But Congress may by a vote of two-thirds of each House, remove such disability.

Section 4. The validity of the public debt of the United States, authorized by law, including debts incurred for payment of pensions and bounties for services in suppressing insurrection or rebellion, shall not be questioned. But neither the United States nor any State shall assume or pay any debt or obligation incurred in aid of insurrection or rebellion against the United States, or any claim for the loss or emancipation of any slave; but all such debts, obligations and claims shall be held illegal and void.

Section 5. The Congress shall have power to enforce, by appropriate legislation, the provisions of this article.

Amendment XV

(Ratified February 3, 1870)

Section 1. The right of citizens of the United States to vote shall not be denied or abridged by the United States or by any State on account of race, color, or previous condition of servitude.

Section 2. The Congress shall have power to enforce this article by appropriate legislation.

Amendment XVI

(Ratified February 3, 1913)

The Congress shall have power to lay and collect taxes on incomes, from whatever source derived, without apportionment among the several States, and without regard to any census or enumeration.

Amendment XVII

(Ratified April 8, 1913)

The Senate of the United States shall be composed of two Senators from each State, elected by the people thereof, for six years; and each

Senator shall have one vote. The electors in each State shall have the qualifications requisite for electors of the most numerous branch of the State legislatures.

When vacancies happen in the representation of any State in the Senate, the executive authority of such State shall issue writs of election to fill such vacancies: *Provided,* That the legislature of any State may empower the executive thereof to make temporary appointments until the people fill the vacancies by election as the legislature may direct.

This amendment shall not be so construed as to affect the election or term of any Senator chosen before it becomes valid as part of the Constitution.

Amendment XVIII

(Ratified January 16, 1919)

Section 1. After one year from the ratification of this article the manufacture, sale, or transportation of intoxicating liquors within, the importation thereof into, or the exportation thereof from the United States and all territory subject to the jurisdiction thereof for beverage purposes is hereby prohibited.

Section 2. The Congress and the several States shall have concurrent power to enforce this article by appropriate legislation.

Section 3. This article shall be inoperative unless it shall have been ratified as an amendment to the Constitution by the legislatures of the several States, as provided in the Constitution, within seven years from the date of the submission hereof to the States by the Congress.[13]

Amendment XIX

(Ratified August 18, 1920)

The right of citizens of the United States to vote shall not be denied or abridged by the United States or by any State on account of sex.

Congress shall have power to enforce this article by appropriate legislation.

Amendment XX

(Ratified January 23, 1933)

Section 1. The terms of the President and Vice President shall end at noon on the 20th day of January, and the terms of Senators and Representatives at noon on the 3d day of January, of the years in which such terms would have ended if this article had not been ratified; and the terms of their successors shall then begin.

Section 2. The Congress shall assemble at least once in every year, and such meeting shall begin at noon on the 3d day of January, unless they shall by law appoint a different day.

Section 3.[14] If, at the time fixed for the beginning of the term of the President, the President elect shall have died, the Vice President elect shall become President. If a President shall not have been chosen before the time fixed for the beginning of his term, or if the President elect shall have failed to qualify, then the Vice President elect shall act as President until a President shall have qualified; and the Congress may by law provide for the case wherein neither a President elect nor a Vice President elect shall have qualified, declaring who shall then act as President, or the manner in which one who is to act shall be selected, and such person shall act accordingly until a President or Vice President shall have qualified.

Section 4. The Congress may by law provide for the case of the death of any of the persons from whom the House of Representatives may choose a President whenever the right of choice shall have devolved upon them, and for the case of the death of any of the persons from whom the Senate may choose a Vice President whenever the right of choice shall have devolved upon them.

Section 5. Sections 1 and 2 shall take effect on the 15th day of October following the ratification of this article.

Section 6. This article shall be inoperative unless it shall have been ratified as an amendment to the Constitution by the legislatures of three-fourths of the several States within seven years from the date of its submission.

Amendment XXI

(Ratified December 5, 1933)

Section 1. The eighteenth article of amendment to the Constitution of the United States is hereby repealed.

Section 2. The transportation or importation into any State, Territory or possession of the United States for delivery or use therein of intoxicating liquors, in violation of the laws thereof, is hereby prohibited.

Section 3. This article shall be inoperative unless it shall have been ratified as an amendment to the Constitution by conventions in the several States, as provided in the Constitution, within seven years from the date of the submission hereof to the States by the Congress.

Amendment XXII

(Ratified February 27, 1951)

Section 1. No person shall be elected to the office of the President more than twice, and no person who has held the office of President, or acted as President, for more than two years of a term to which some other person was elected President shall be elected to the office of the President more than once. But this Article shall not apply to any person holding the office of President when this Article was proposed by the Congress, and shall not prevent any person who may be holding the office of President, or acting as President, during the term within which this Article becomes operative from holding the office of President or acting as President during the remainder of such term.

Section 2. This Article shall be inoperative unless it shall have been ratified as an amendment to the Constitution by the legislatures of three-fourths of the several States within seven years from the date of its submission to the States by the Congress.

Amendment XXIII

(Ratified March 29, 1961)

Section 1. The District constituting the seat of Government of the United States shall appoint in such manner as the Congress may direct:

A number of electors of President and Vice President equal to the whole number of Senators and Representatives in Congress to which the District would be entitled if it were a State, but in no event more than the least populous State; they shall be in addition to those appointed by the States, but they shall be considered, for the purposes of the election of President and Vice President, to be electors appointed by a State; and they shall meet in the District and perform such duties as provided by the twelfth article of amendment.

Section 2. The Congress shall have power to enforce this article by appropriate legislation.

Amendment XXIV

(Ratified January 23, 1964)

Section 1. The right of citizens of the United States to vote in any primary or other election for President or Vice President, for electors for President or Vice President, or for Senator or Representative in Congress, shall not be denied or abridged by the United States or any State by reason of failure to pay any poll tax or other tax.

Section 2. The Congress shall have power to enforce this article by appropriate legislation.

Amendment XXV

(Ratified February 10, 1967)

Section 1. In case of the removal of the President from office or of his death or resignation, the Vice President shall become President.

Section 2. Whenever there is a vacancy in the office of the Vice President, the President shall nominate a Vice President who shall take office upon confirmation by a majority vote of both Houses of Congress.

Section 3. Whenever the President transmits to the President pro tempore of the Senate and the Speaker of the House of Representatives his written declaration that he is unable to discharge the powers and duties of his office, and until he transmits to them a written declaration to the contrary, such powers and duties shall be discharged by the Vice President as Acting President.

Section 4. Whenever the Vice President and a majority of either the principal officers of the executive departments or of such other body as Congress may by law provide, transmit to the President pro tempore of the Senate and the Speaker of the House of Representatives their written declaration that the President is unable to discharge the powers and duties of his office, the Vice President shall immediately assume the powers and duties of the office as Acting President.

Thereafter, when the President transmits to the President pro tempore of the Senate and the Speaker of the House of Representatives his written declaration that no inability exists, he shall resume the powers and duties of his office unless the Vice President and a majority of either the principal officers of the executive department or of such other body as Congress may by law provide, transmit within four days to the President pro tempore of the Senate and the Speaker of the House of Representatives their written declaration that the President is unable to discharge the powers and duties of his office. Thereupon Congress shall decide the issue, assembling within forty-eight hours for that purpose if not in session. If the Congress, within twenty-one days after receipt of the latter written declaration, or, if Congress is not in session, within twenty-one days after Congress is required to assemble, determines by two-thirds vote of both houses that the President is unable to discharge the powers and duties of his office, the Vice President shall continue to discharge the same as Acting President; otherwise, the President shall resume the powers and duties of his office.

Amendment XXVI

(Ratified July 1, 1971)

Section 1. The right of citizens of the United States, who are eighteen years of age or older, to vote shall not be denied or abridged by the United States or by any State on account of age.

Section 2. The Congress shall have power to enforce this article by appropriate legislation.

Notes

1. The part in brackets was changed by section 2 of the Fourteenth Amendment.
2. The part in brackets was changed by section 1 of the Seventeenth Amendment.
3. The part in brackets was changed by the second paragraph of the Seventeenth Amendment.
4. The part in brackets was changed by section 2 of the Twentieth Amendment.
5. The Sixteenth Amendment gave Congress the power to tax incomes.
6. The material in brackets has been superseded by the Twelfth Amendment.
7. This provision has been affected by the Twenty-fifth Amendment.
8. These clauses were affected by the Eleventh Amendment.
9. This paragraph has been superseded by the Thirteenth Amendment.
10. Obsolete.
11. The part in brackets has been superseded by section 3 of the Twentieth Amendment.
12. See the Twenty-sixth Amendment.
13. This Amendment was repealed by section 1 of the Twenty-first Amendment.
14. See the Twenty-fifth Amendment.

Source: U.S. House of Representatives, Committee on the Judiciary, *The Constitution of the United States of America, As Amended Through July 1971,* H. Doc. 93-215, 93d Cong., 2d sess., 1974.

Index